PSYCHOANALYSIS
AND EDUCATION

PSYCHOANALYSIS AND EDUCATION

Minding a Gap

Edited by

Alan Bainbridge and Linden West

KARNAC

First published in 2012 by
Karnac Books Ltd
118 Finchley Road, London NW3 5HT

British Library Cataloguing in Publication Data

A C.I.P. for this book is available from the British Library

  ISBN 978 1 78049 045 8

Edited, designed and produced by The Studio Publishing Services Ltd
www.publishingservicesuk.co.uk
e-mail: studio@publishingservicesuk.co.uk

Printed in Great Britain

www.karnacbooks.com

CONTENTS

CHAPTER THIRTEEN

CHAPTER FOURTEEN

CHAPTER FIFTEEN

CHAPTER SIXTEEN

Editors

Alan Bainbridge is a doctor of clinical science and previously taught in secondary schools for almost twenty years before moving into higher education, where he is a senior lecturer in education. In recent years, he has become more convinced of the value of using psychoanalytic ideas and language to explore educational settings. His interests are in the application of psychoanalytic thought and practices to education in its widest sense. Alan's research has focused on early intervention mental health programmes and the career pathways of education professionals. He has written chapters on children's learning and development, and contributed to general psychology texts. Together with Linden West, he has edited and contributed to *Cliopsy*, 6 (2011), an electronic journal published by Paris Ouest Nanterre University, France, on psychoanalysis and education. He is a UKCP registered psychoanalytic psychotherapist and has a small private practice. Alan and Linden West have organised conferences on psychoanalysis and education at Canterbury Christ Church University in 2009 and 2012.

Linden West, PhD, FRSA, is a professor and Director of Research Development in the Faculty of Education at Canterbury Christ Church University, Kent, UK, and Visiting Professor at the Paris Ouest Nanterre University, France. His books include the highly acclaimed *Beyond Fragments* (published by Taylor & Francis); *Doctors on the Edge* (Free Association Books); *Using Life History and Biographical Approaches in the Study of Adult and Lifelong Learning* (published by Peter Lang). He is co-author of *Using Biographical Methods in Social Research* (recently published by Sage). He has been co-editor of the journal *Cliopsy*, and is author of diverse articles and chapters on themes such as managing change and transitions, on learning in families, communities, and professional contexts, and on psychosocial perspectives and how these can inform understanding of the construction and experience of selfhood. He has written widely on the use of auto/biographical methods in research. His writing is translated into many languages, including French, Italian, Spanish, Chinese, and Polish. Linden co-ordinates a European Life History and Biographical Research Network, and is also a qualified psychoanalytical psychotherapist.

Contributors

Lene Auestad is Research Fellow in Philosophy, University of Oslo, affiliated with the Centre for Studies of the Holocaust and Religious Minorities, Oslo. She moved to the UK to pursue her long-standing interest in British psychoanalysis. She is a co-ordinator of the conference series, "Psychoanalysis and politics". Working at the interface of psychoanalytic thinking and ethics/political theory, her writing has focused on the themes of emotions, prejudice, and minority rights. Some publications include: "The pariah's story: the moral significance of Arendt's storytelling, as seen in Rahel Varnhagen", in Audun Øfstied; *The Public Sphere. Essays in Honour of Karl-Otto Apel* (Oslo: Res Publica, 2008); *Handling, frihet, humanitet. Møter med Hannah Arendt* (Action, Freedom, Humanity. Encounters with Hannah Arendt) co-edited with Helgard Mahrdt (Trondheim: Tapir Academic Publishers, 2011); "Splitting, attachment and instrumental rationality. A re-view of Menzies Lyth's 'Social Criticism'", in *Psychoanalysis, Culture & Society*, 16(4), 2011. Her forthcoming book is *Psychoanalysis and Politics: Exclusion and the Politics of Representation* (London: Karnac, 2012).

Anne Bastin began teaching as a French tutor in an American college. At present, she teaches in primary schools and is involved in training as a part-time lecturer at the universities of Paris Ouest and Paris 8. In preparing her PhD, she questions the links between the teacher's personal and professional identities from a psychoanalytical perspective.

Claudine Blanchard-Laville is Emeritus Professor in Educational Sciences (Paris Ouest Nanterre University, France). Her main work is concerned with observing the practice of teaching from the viewpoint of clinical psychoanalysis, and also facilitating a clinical group approach to understanding professional practice in the fields of education and training. She is a co-founder and the editorial director of the on-line educational sciences review *Cliopsy*: www.revue.cliopsy.fr

Valentina Boursier is a psychoanalyst for children, adolescents, and parents (*SIPsIA*), researcher in clinical psychology, and assistant professor in Developmental Clinical Psychology at University of Naples "Federico II". She is an associate member of Séminaire Inter-Universitaire Européen d'Einsegnement et de Recherche de la Psychanalyse et de la Psychopathologie (SIUEERPP). Her clinical and research interests are clinical psychology and development psychoanalysis, gender studies, children's psychopathology prevention, and support to parents and families. She is also interested in observation and its applications for clinical research and for prevention and therapy in clinical and socially marginalised family contexts, and in gender identity development, specifically in gender identity disorders and intersex disorders in children and adolescents.

Tony Brown is a Doctor in mathematics education and has a Masters degree in Psychoanalytic Studies. He taught extensively in primary and secondary schools, before becoming a curriculum adviser for Cornwall and subsequently working in teacher education in Cardiff, Winchester, and Plymouth. He later became Head of the Centre for Learning Development at the University of Hull, and, subsequently, Director of ESCalate, the UK Higher Education Subject Centre at the University of Bristol. He remains a visiting fellow at Bristol and is an associate lecturer at the University of Plymouth. He is joint author of *The Really Useful Maths Book*, published by Routledge, and has authored articles and book chapters on the application of psychoanalytic theory to higher education pedagogy.

Jacki Cartlidge is a senior lecturer at Canterbury Christ Church University. She has thirty years experience of teaching non-traditional and older learners at all levels and she has been active in the development and delivery of a range of programmes. Her research interest is combining psychoanalytical perspectives and narrative theory in an educational context.

Laure Castelnau is a teacher specialising in pupils who encounter learning problems, and is preparing a Doctorate in Educational Sciences at Paris Ouest Nanterre University, France. She is interested in psychic transmission in the class.

Philippe Chaussecourte is a Full Professor of Education Sciences at Paris Ouest Nanterre University. He is also an Agrégé de mathématiques and a clinical psychologist. He has conducted an observation of an infant, following the Esther Bick method, and leads "analysis of practice" groups. He directs the "Clinical Approach of the Rapport to Knowledge" research team and a professional Master's programme called Formation à l'intervention et à l'analyse de pratiques. He is interested in unconscious phenomena as they affect the education and continuing education fields, and is a specialist in observation following psychoanalytical principles.

Alessandra Delli Veneri has a PhD in Gender Studies and is psychologist and psychotherapist. She obtained a Master's degree in Psychology and Psychotraumatology of Emergency, and currently holds a research grant in the University "Federico II" of Naples, Italy. Her interests range from clinical psychology to learning process fostered by new technologies.

Anastasios Gaitanidis (PhD) has been teaching in various psychotherapy and counselling courses for the past thirteen years. He is currently a senior lecturer in counselling psychology, psychotherapy, and counselling at Roehampton University. He is also an associate lecturer in Cultural Studies at the Open University and a psychoanalytic counsellor/psychotherapist in private practice with almost fourteen years of post-qualifying clinical experience. He has published a number of papers on the relation between psychoanalysis, philosophy, and education in several peer-reviewed journals and he is the editor of *Narcissism: A Critical Reader* (2007), and *The Male in Analysis: Psychoanalytic and Cultural Perspectives* (2011). He is currently co-editing the book *Authoring the Sublime: Psychoanalysis and Aesthetics* with Dr Tessa Adams.

Larry Green has been a psychotherapist in private practice in Vancouver, Canada for forty years. Initially he specialised in panic disorder syndrome and performance anxiety. Later, he began to work with patients experiencing existential and mid-life crises. This interest evolved into a study of transformative learning. His latest presentations include "Crisis, trauma, and transformative learning" presented to the 9th Transformative Learning Conference in Athens (2011). More recently, he was a member of a panel discussing "The (im)possibility of immortal conversations" at the Ohio Valley's Philosophy of Education's annual conference in September 2011. Finally, he was a panel member in the Simon Fraser University's presentation on the topic of "Psychoanalysis and the politics of fear" in October 2011. In addition to his psychotherapeutic work, Green is an artist whose sculptural pieces and digital imagery makes visible the phenomenology of experience.

Celia Hunt is Emeritus Reader in Continuing Education (Creative Writing) at the University of Sussex, and Visiting Research Fellow at Canterbury Christ Church University. She is interested in the developmental and therapeutic effects of writing fictional autobiography, which is the subject of *Therapeutic Dimensions of Autobiography in Creative Writing* (2000). Her latest book, *Creative Life Writing as a Tool for Transformative Learning*, is due for publication by Routledge in 2012. She was awarded a National Teaching Fellowship by the Higher Education Academy in 2004.

Mark Murphy is a lecturer in higher education, King's Learning Institute, King's College London. He gained his Doctorate in Education from Northern Illinois University, his dissertation focusing on European Union education policy. He has published widely, with numerous articles in journals such as the *Journal of Education Policy*, *Journal of European Public Policy*, *European Journal of Education*, and the *British Journal of Sociology of Education*. Recent and forthcoming books include (with T. Fleming), *Habermas, Critical Theory and Education*

(Routledge, 2010) and *Social Theory and Educational Research* (Routledge, forthcoming). His current research interests include educational sociology, critical theory, accountability in higher education, and public sector reform.

Adele Nunziante Cesàro is Full Professor of Clinical Psychology at Università degli Studi di Napoli Federico II; she has been head of the Department of Scienze Relazionali "G. Iacono" (2005–2010). From 2002 to 2010, she has been Co-ordinator of the Doctoral Programme in Gender Studies at the Doctoral School in Psychological and Pedagogical Sciences, where she has taught courses on gender and psychoanalysis, feminism, parenthood, and gender identity troubles. Adele is currently a Member of the Senato Accademico of the Università degli Studi di Napoli Federico II, of the Regional Association of Psychologists (Campania) of the SIUEERPP (Paris), and member of many journals' Scientific Boards. She is also Director of the counselling service to prevent mobbing at the Università degli Studi di Napoli Federico II. Her research interests have always focused on many issues related to gender and sexuality from a psychoanalytic perspective, including the problems of sterility, parenthood, and the prevention of psychosocial risk in children; indeed, she has been Scientific Supervisor for the Project "Adozione sociale" in co-operation with Comune di Napoli, Regione Campania, and Asl Na1 Centro. Currently, she is Scientific Supervisor for the Project Hermes-Linking network to fight sexual and gender stigma, co-financed by EU within the Daphne III Programme and promoted by the Dipartimento TEOMESUS, Università degli Studi di Napoli Federico II.

Olivia Sagan (PhD) is Programme Director of the UCL MSc in Psychoanalytic Developmental Psychology, based at the Anna Freud Centre, London. She continues to undertake narrative research in the area of mental health and its interface with learning and creativity. Olivia is currently looking at strategies and resilience in the narratives of mentally ill artists, and exploring these through a lens that reflects, challengingly, both positive psychology and psychoanalysis.

Alper Sahin is Assistant Professor at Maltepe University Istanbul. His main academic focus is pedagogy and psychoanalysis, specifically teacher–student relationships. He has carried out academic work at

Harvard, Nijmegen, Jyvaskyla, and Lyon II universities. He is a member of the Istanbul Psychoanalytic Association Turkish Study Group and, after a seventeen-year career as a psychologist, he is now psychotherapist and psychoanalyst in training, with a private practice. Sahin is one of the organisers of National Conferences on Psychoanalysis and School, Psychoanalysis, and Music. He has written on human rights at schools as well as many articles on pedagogy and psychoanalysis. He works as a consultant for schools and as a teacher trainer. He campaigns for women rights and is writing on psychoanalysis, cinema, and classical Turkish music.

Anna Zurolo (PhD) earned her Doctoral degree in Gender Studies from Università degli Studi di Napoli Federico II, Naples. During her doctoral course, she constantly increased her interests in gender matters, familial violence, violence against women and children. She is a psychologist and psychotherapist in training at ICLeS (Naples). She is a member of the Scuola Romana Rorschach (Italy) and Membre Affilié of the Séminaire Inter-Universitaire Européen d'enseignement et de Recherche de la Psychanalyse et de la Psychopathologie (SIUEERPP), France. She has taught courses on clinical psychology, dynamic psychology, and clinical working at Università degli Studi di Napoli Federico II. Anna had various experiences of teaching in the field of gender studies, as attested by participation in projects financed by the Ministero delle Pari Opportunità (Ministry of Equal Opportunities), in co-operation with FORMEZ. She has published articles on gender, sexuality, and psychoanalysis, violence against women, psychoanalysis and transsexualism, training and teaching in a psychoanalytic perspective. She is currently a post-doctoral researcher and Project Manager for the Project "Hermes-Linking network to fight sexual and gender stigma", co-financed by EU within the Daphne III Programme and promoted by the Dipartimento TEOMESUS—Università degli Studi di Napoli Federico II.

EDITORS' NOTES AND ACKNOWLEDGEMENTS

This book derives from an intense collaboration among colleagues from various countries as well as a dialogue between the two of us about the current state of education—and for that matter the State and education—and a sense of deep dissatisfaction that seems to pervade discussions around these issues. We have needed to understand more of each other's perspectives too, given our different biographies and, to an extent, preoccupations. Alan has worked, in the main in schools and with children and young people—although adults too in professional education programmes—while Linden's background has been largely in adult and higher education. However, we are also, both, psychoanalytic psychotherapists, which has been important in developing our dialogue as well as in engaging with our collaborators. Fundamentally, our view of the psychoanalytic project, like education, is that it is a lifetime's work, in which early and subsequent experience are constantly intertwined, for better if also worse. And that both, ideally, have to do with getting beneath the surface of things and understanding the complex dynamics of conscious and unconscious processes, present and past, old and new ways of knowing, self and other, the social, cultural and symbolic order.

There are a number of people we would like to thank in helping us with the project and the 'challenging' process of editing: not least Helen Reynolds who has been a tower of strength in working through, with us, various draft chapters and sensitively and carefully negotiating with particular authors around questions of meaning and English usage. Her name might well have appeared on the cover of the book—as one of the editors—but in characteristic modesty she resisted this. Then there is Anne Haynes, who helped with the formatting as well as wider work to do with bridging the gap between educational and psychoanalytic worlds, alongside Sarah Roberts and Emma Miles. We would also like to thank Poppy Reay for the front cover art work. We are grateful to them all.

Please note that important aspects of Chapter Ten were originally produced as an article in *Studies in the Education of Adults*, and we thank the editors and the National Institute for Adult and Continuing Education (NIACE) for permission to use this material, although some of the content and ideas have been developed further. Chapter Two, "To think or not to think", was originally published in *The Journal of Social & Psychological Sciences*, Volume 3, Issue 2, 2010. It appears here as a shorter piece with the permission of the editors. Chapters Three, Five to Seven, Ten, Eleven to Thirteen and Fifteen have been developed from shorter articles originally published in *Cliopsy, Revue électronique*, Volume 6, and have been re-presented with the permission of the editors.

Alan Bainbridge and Linden West
Canterbury Christ Church University

CHAPTER ONE

Introduction: minding a gap

Alan Bainbridge and Linden West

Starting points

In December 2009, diverse educators, psychotherapists, and others from the UK, Scandinavia, France, Italy, Turkey, South America, and Australia met at a conference held in Canterbury Christ Church University. The focus was to engage in discussing the applications of psychoanalysis, broadly defined, to education, in its widest sense, including adult and lifelong learning and higher education as well as schooling. This book originates from what, in retrospect, can be seen as a significant conference, and seeks to capture the complex, often messy, and yet potentially liberating world of education. Such a project, to connect these two worlds, was not novel, yet it should be noted that recent academic texts related to this broad area can be counted in tens rather than hundreds (e.g., Appel, 1999; Bibby, 2011; Britzman, 2009; Salzberger-Wittenberg, Williams, & Osborne, 1983; Youell, 2006). It is also clear, from a UK perspective at least, perhaps more widely, that psychoanalytic thought has had relatively minimal impact, especially in recent years, on education and the wider education-focused academy. Indeed, this book will present evidence of increasing hostility from many educators and academics towards its claims, aspirations, and ways of knowing.

Such tendencies can be considered as part of a wider cultural marginalisation of psychoanalysis, at least in its classical guise: some 150 years after Freud's birth, it is often seen as fair game for criticism, with questions constantly asked of its early basic assumptions, most famously drive theory or penis envy. Today's *zeitgeist* seems to be moving in a different direction, away from any such intense personal preoccupation with the past, as the critical theorist Honneth (2009) has noted, towards managing the unpredictability of the present. Moreover, psychoanalysis is often framed by its critics as if its core interpretative repertoire has remained fixed since the time of Freud. In fact, modern psychoanalytic theory can bear little relation to what is most often criticised (such as its alleged neglect of the socio-cultural in processes of becoming human), but this does not seem to inhibit detractors (Hunt & West, 2006).

The situation in other European countries, such as France, in regard to psychoanalysis and education, might be marginally better: a number of faculties of educational science in universities provide psychoanalytically informed "clinical" workshops, in "a Balint style", which focus on the experience of professionals, including the role of unconscious processes (like the transference and countertransference) in locations such as the classroom. This clinical tradition of intense focus on such processes has generated a body of associated research, using, for instance, in-depth observational methods, derived from the work of Esther Bick as well as intensive group discussion and writing (Chaussecourte, 2009). There is an interest in what is termed the psychic qualities of relationships between teachers and students, but also in the relationships of everyone to academic subjects themselves. This includes how subjects, such as maths, are taught, and how this has changed, bringing, for some teachers, feelings of loss, even trauma, as their ways of understanding and communicating the roots of their discipline are declared anachronistic. Teachers, in turn, can act out with their pupils, in cynical and even destructive ways.

Yet, despite a body of research and writing (under the umbrella of the electronic journal *Cliopsy* (www.revue.cliopsy.fr), for instance), French academic educators such as Claudine Blanchard-Laville and Philippe Chaussecourte at Paris Ouest Nanterre University, and Bernard Pechberty at Université Paris 5, René Descartes, consider themselves to be increasingly marginal in the educational sciences. However, from our perspective in the UK, arguably at least, the connection between education and psychoanalysis, in France and some other continental European countries, remains stronger. This might be to do with the greater willingness in some continental academic traditions to engage, philosophically, with what, through Anglo-Saxon eyes, can be dismissed as highly speculative, unobservable, and empirically untestable supposition. In Germany, for instance, the German Educational Research Association, unlike its British Educational Research Association counterpart (BERA), has a psychoanalytic interest group (Section 13.1: Psychoanalysis and Education).

Notwithstanding, however, the position overall, if to varying degrees, across many countries and cultures is one in which psychoanalysis has become more marginal in educational literatures. Those institutions in the UK, such as the Tavistock Clinic in London, that offer opportunities to engage with the emotional factors in learning and teaching, from a psychoanalytic perspective, might be struggling to recruit teachers and others to their programmes, at least as reported in discussions at the Conference. This is an era where cognitive–behavioural approaches have become dominant, given, so the argument might proceed, that they take less time for people to engage with, are cheaper to provide as a therapy, and might be relatively easily applied to education (given the dominance of cognitively framed perceptions of learning). They are also more conducive to measurement, however questionable some of the research and reductive of complex psychic causalities and interior life, this might be (Leader, 2011).

Our book results from growing concern about these trends and a desire to bring education and psychoanalysis into renewed dialogue: not least because the latter, we believe, can illuminate the messiness, muddle, and ambivalence that education is always and inevitably heir to. And, crucially, it can illuminate more of what it means to be a person and a learner: not least the idea that "the human is always a divided, inwardly ruptured being", yet one "who has the ability to reduce or even overcome that rupturedness through its own reflective activity" (Honneth, 2009, p. 127). Rupture, in this view, is a product of the repression of desire consequent on our absolute dependence on the (m)other for survival, as it is an aspect of loss in processes of separation both in earliest and also subsequent experience. For Britzman (2009), how the infant negotiates this rupture, represents the fundamental process of education, one that remains with us across the lifespan.

The aspiration to build dialogue is, of course, nothing new: many early pioneers in psychoanalytic thinking considered that it offered essential perspectives for making sense of education and personhood. Anna Freud (1930) and Sigmund Freud (1925f) both wrote about education, and Anna was a teacher and educational pioneer. In 1908, Ferenczi presented a paper (later published in 1949) on the relationship between psychoanalysis and education at the 1st International Congress of Psychoanalysis. Klein (1975) explored the child's "epistemophilic instinct" in the acquisition or avoidance of knowledge. Building on this, Bion (1962) articulated a model of learning based on the qualities of interaction, what he termed reverie, between (m)other and baby in the early stages of their relationship, where a baby's capacity for thinking is a product of the mother's ability to thoughtfully process the former's confused thoughts and feelings and to feed these back in digestible ways. Being able to think and learn is, thus, rooted in early relationships and their capacity for the containment of anxiety. Eric Erikson trained as a psychoanalyst and worked with young people in educational settings (Friedman, 1999), and Aichhorn (1951) worked closely with the ideas of Anna Freud to establish centres for problem youth. It could also be argued that the essential roles of education and psychoanalysis are similar, in that each seeks to bring the individual into an understanding of their worlds and selves, to enable more thoughtful, life-enhancing decisions to be made. However, the similarities of focus notwithstanding, the two worlds have drifted apart; and the status of psychoanalytic perspectives has diminished.

We need to make clear that psychoanalysis, like education, is a broad church, as the chapters make clear. And the success of the CCCU conference might indicate a growing desire to reclaim a space in which the dynamic unconscious—which retains a central place in most theorising—can be thought about and better understood. Significantly, the conference has already been a catalyst for a number of developments, aside from the present book: this includes a major collaboration between Canterbury Christ Church University and colleagues in the Faculty of Education Sciences at Paris Ouest Nanterre University. A special edition of the French on-line journal *Cliopsy* has been produced (*Revue Electronique*, 6, October, 2011: www.revue. cliopsy.fr), as have various articles comparing research into qualities of psychic and transitional space in varied educational settings (West,

2010; see also this volume). We both serve on the scientific committee of *Cliopsy*, while Linden has been Visiting Professor at Nanterre, and there is now collaboration in doctoral student supervision and assessment.

Lifelong education

We should also make clear that our perspective on education is both lifelong and life-wide. In fact, we were worried about this in planning the conference and in preparing the book: the hegemonic language of education tends, still, to be synonymous with schools and schooling, despite the growing importance of learning as a lifelong imperative. This was partly driven, in Linden's case, by a background of research in adult learning with a focus on transitional processes in higher education, professional life, and informal learning, derived from careful chronicling and systematic understanding of learners' perspectives, using biographical narrative research methods. Such preoccupations can be marginal in mainstream educational literature, driven as this might be by the dominant agenda of schools: schooling, instruction, and assessment of formal learning (Bainbridge, 2012; Merrill & West, 2009; West, 1996, 2001, 2007). We wanted to use the book to engage with education in the broadest terms, without neglecting the central, if problematic, role of schools. We wanted to encompass learning and educational processes in families, in relationships, in social, community, and professional contexts, at work as well as in higher education. Defining education broadly, we thought, might help loosen up and energise discussion on its fundamental characteristics and purposes, not least by making reference to a psychoanalytically informed research literature on adult and lifelong learning. This can bring into sharp relief some of the damage that schools and schooling can do, but also, importantly, how reparation is possible, and why, despite the most disturbed of childhoods.

Psychoanalytic assumptions, broadly applied, push us towards addressing many difficult questions, beyond a narrowly obsessive focus on "standards", curricula, measurable outcomes, or, for that matter, childhood; not least in a "runaway" globalising world, where inherited and familial templates can become rapidly redundant and where composing a coherent and meaningful biography becomes a perpetual reflexive challenge (Giddens, 1999). We are both psycho-analytic psychotherapists, and have found that the insights of psycho-analysis have evoked new possibilities in our research and teaching. They have enabled us to appreciate the complexity of experience—for adults, young people, and children—and of selves struggling to be, and to view education as far more than a rational exercise of mind, but, rather, a deeply embodied process, alive with the play of phan-tasy, desire, and resistance, new and older ways of knowing, across lives. Psychoanalysis, broadly defined, has encouraged us to delve beneath surface appearances, and to challenge overly sanitised, emo-tionally deadened, and ultimately unsustainable accounts of learning, to build richer, deeper, whole person understandings, redolent with vulnerability, but also resilience in "keeping on keeping on", whether as a teacher, young person, or adult learner.

Minding gaps

Clearly, we have wondered about how and why a gap between psy-choanalysis and education, in its broadest sense, has become so wide and what might be done about it. The phrase "minding a gap" is borrowed from an important book by Frosh (1989), which addressed another gulf, that between mainstream psychology and psychoana-lysis. He argued that this was also to be regretted, and in analogous ways. If psychoanalysis had something to learn from mainstream psychology, in terms of clarity of ideas, acknowledging the power and complexity of cognitive processes, and methodological stringency, psychology had, Frosh insisted, more to learn from psychoanalysis.

Psychology had become, in its mainstream variants, overly con-cerned with what might be termed the "syntax" of human behaviour, establishing general rules and principles underlining this, to the neglect of "semantics" and the meaning of actions to people them-selves. One example of syntactical-level explanation is Piaget's struc-tures of knowledge, operative at various developmental stages from the sensorimotor to preoperational, concrete operational and formal operational intelligence, as a person develops from infancy to adult-hood. Piaget, however, is interested here in understanding how certain cognitive abilities arise, and "the histories which he provides are histories of concepts rather than people" (Frosh, 1989, p. 87). In fact, within psychology, at one extreme, under the current seductive influence of neuropsychology, there can be a view that "no mental level needs to be considered: it is the physiological processes of the brain that are the real causal entities. Psychology, at least in principle, reduces to neuroanatomy and brain chemistry" (ibid., p. 22). We lose completely any notion here of the experiencing individual, or any imperative to engage with the world of meaning and subjectivity.

Yet, advances made in generating models of mental functioning, from observations of brain activities, as Frosh notes in some detail, need not be done at the expense of chronicling and understanding subjectivity and of the meanings of personhood, including reflexive struggles to break free of historic and compulsive constraints. Such models, if not, leave important epistemological gaps. Frosh poses a question as to why a particular Jack might have hit a specific Jill to make this point: such an action cannot be reduced to neurones firing in particular ways, provoking movement in an arm. We need rather more by way of explanation, a point we return to in our final chapter. Suffice it to say, for now, that psychoanalysis asks relevant "semantic" questions: of the meaning of actions, of their subjective significance and intention, and of the position they hold in and across a person's life. We create a different level and quality of understanding as to Jack and his actions. Mainstream psychology has striven to establish rules, the validity of which are judged by directly observable and measurable evidence and the ability to generalise, while psychoanalysis has been more preoccupied with meaning, and with chronicling and understanding the particularities of experience. Mainstream psychology has sometimes, in fact, eschewed any scientific interest in the workings of the internal world, which, as Frosh argues, might have diminished potentially rich dialogue within the discipline.

Like mainstream psychology, education might just be losing more than psychoanalysis, from any gap between them. The conception of learning in education—shaped by psychologically orientated social and cognitive learning theories, in the main—has been more focused on the acquisition and development of cognitive structures, rather than on relationships, emotionality, experiences, and meanings of selfhood. Any consideration of the emotions, let alone the unconscious, has been more marginal (Greenhalgh, 1994; Illeris, 2007). It is interesting, in this context, to note how models such as Bloom's taxonomies (Krathwohl, Bloom, & Masia, 1964) are widely used by practitioners and academics in discussions of teaching and learning. However, it is significant that the usage is almost exclusively focused on Bloom's work in the cognitive domain: little attention is paid to his two other domains of learning: the affective and the psychomotor, which he identified as equally crucial.

The historical dominance of an isolated, even disembodied, cognition might have been strengthened by heated debates within the psychoanalytic community itself (see Britzman's (2003) discussion), where, historically, different schools have existed, sometimes in open hostility to one another. For whatever reason, the loss of influence, in contemporary educational discourse, of a dynamic, person-centred, subjectivist understanding of education is to be regretted. Not least, in helping teachers and learners to understand more of why education can be so troubling. Freud (1925f) was aware that education was not easy to experience, because it continuously threatened the coherence of self. Selves might feel unstable, at times, when caught between the known and unknown, comfort and discomfort, new and old conceptual frames. For Freud and Britzman, education is difficult and knowledge troublesome, and retreat from engaging with it always a temptation. The ego can be threatened by new knowledge, anxiety can be intense, and resistances thus evoked. Freud also thought teaching was an "impossible profession", where the outcome of one's actions can never be certain, and the response of the learner to new ways of knowing can be confused and even hostile, or simply conformist and lacking depth.

Therapeutic education, adult learning, and psychoanalysis

There are further gaps of comprehension, and, indeed, hostility towards aspects of psychoanalysis that concern us. These include recent, strident criticism of what is called "therapeutic education", for which, at least in part, psychoanalysis is seen as responsible. The claim here is that a preoccupation with the emotions, to the neglect of cogito, fuelled, among other things, by psychoanalysis, obstructs really serious, disciplined learning. In a recent book, Ecclestone and Hayes (2009), two professors of education, argue that educators and education have lost their way in a messy swamp of "therapeutic education", in which an older idea of disciplined intellectual engagement with a subject, and an associated commitment to reason and the scientific project, has been submerged in a tsunami of emotionalism. Rational humanism and education grounded in a critical yet dispassionate engagement with knowledge are being replaced by a pernicious subjectivism and an obsession with fragile selves.

Ecclestone and Hayes critique what they see to be many examples of "therapeutic education" at all levels of education. They argue that the view of education and people implicit in this is far from progressive or benign, but, rather, derives from a diminished and fragile view of the human subject, in need of therapy from cradle to the grave. A curriculum of the self—supported by an army of peer mentors, life-coaches, counsellors, psychologists, and therapists—has replaced a curriculum derived from canons of rigorous knowledge and sustained engagement with a discipline, led by confident subject specialists. Learners, in the Ecclestone and Hayes' view, are being coached to feel better about themselves, rather than encouraged to think critically and rigorously. An obsession with circle time, or its equivalents, has replaced thinking and serious engagement with ideas. Herein lies the diminished self and the marginalised subjects, constituting what they see to be the contemporary crisis of education. And psychoanalysis, in part, is to blame.

Their argument, also supported by Furedi (2004), has received much professional and media interest. And there is sympathy towards some of their ideas in the present book (see Brown and Murphy, in Chapter Fifteen), while Hinshelwood (2009) has warned of how seductive it might be for teachers to become focused on avoiding anxiety rather than encouraging learners to contain this. As Brown and Murphy suggest, there might well be forms of therapeutic compensatory practice in education that may strip the latter of intellectual and personal challenge. Yet, the world of "therapy" Ecclestone and Hayes present is largely anecdotal and hardly recognisable to professionals who work in this environment. They seem to elide counselling, mentoring, psychotherapy, and psychoanalysis and regard the primary goal of all these as being to reduce anxiety and emotional distress, by avoiding challenging learning. What they misunderstand is how psychoanalytically informed therapies and associated educational perspectives construe and work with anxiety, and how it is seen as a necessary spur to learning, rather than something to be avoided.

Anxiety, from a psychoanalytic perspective, is an entirely normal response in education: a product of very real tensions between how an individual might wish to respond to a situation and psychological, societal, and cultural expectations. For the vast majority of people, such tension might induce no overwhelming paralysis, and, as such, the "anxiety" goes largely undetected. For a number, however, the anxiety can be sufficient to interfere with normal functioning: the capacity for an imaginative playfulness, including with the symbolic, that can be considered essential for new understanding to emerge and for experiences of selfhood to find expression, is frozen. The function of psychoanalytically informed understanding is not to protect individuals from anxiety or engagement with difficult ideas, but, rather, to understand why processes can be so difficult. Likewise, to be in "therapy" is to become aware of, confront, and understand its roots, not to be consoled or for anxiety to be repressed.

In short, what matters is for educators and learners to know more of what gets in the way of new ways of knowing and/or making connections, and of why letting go of established thinking can be so difficult. All learners, at all stages and ages, can be required to reconcile the known with new knowledge, evoked by experience. There is an inner–outer dialectic, mediated in our relationships with others, which can be deeply troubling. What might be of interest is why some people can thrive in the face of such challenges, and learn, while others might retreat, if in largely unconscious ways. We can agree with Ecclestone and Hayes about a tendency among some educators to pseudo-psychoanalyse inappropriately. Yet, babies can be thrown out with this particular bathwater. Education can shake us to the core—like a new idea, such as feminism, as Linden has chronicled in his work on women and adult education (West, 1996)—and we can be paralysed by anxiety and resistant to the implications of a new way of seeing, because it could bring into question the meaning of a life.

Adult education

The criticisms of "therapy culture" also resonate with a long-held antipathy in some of the adult education literature about applying psychoanalytic ideas to learning in adulthood. Although analytic ideas, broadly defined, have some place (for example, Dirkx, 2011;

Hunt & West, 2006, 2009, and this volume; West, 1996, 2011), the general tone in the literature can be critical. Tennant (1997), for example, is concerned that psychoanalysis is ultimately about getting people to adjust to the status quo, rather than challenging it. He cites Erik Erikson, for whom mental health emanates from successful adjustment to the demands of society, without reference to the fact that some forms of social organisation might be unhealthy and alienating. Tennant concedes that more recent psychoanalytical writing (including by feminists) has a potentially more radical, challenging, culturally questioning edge (see Sayers, 1995; Brown & Murphy, this volume), and that this brings with it a view that forms of social organisation can indeed be alienating and emotionally unhealthy while others can be liberating (Frosh, 1991).

Despite some of the negativity, there are encouraging signs for psychoanalysis. There are many challenges to overly cognitivist or reductionist narratives of education and its purpose. In recent years, for example, the influence of learning theories that recognise the importance of social interactions has grown in teacher and other professional education. Vygotsky (1978), for example, has argued that higher level cognitive functioning develops through social interactions with significant others. During these interactions, culturally important symbols, such as language, the use of artefacts, and knowledge, are mediated by and through significant others. This enables the child learner (and adult, too) to appropriate and internalise the meanings of the symbols as thought processes: this is learning that is situated, fundamentally, in a social–relational context. Furthermore, Lave and Wenger's (1991) theory of situated learning is conceptualised in terms of increased participation in meaningful communities, where knowledge and practices are in a state of continual co-construction by participants. These shifts towards a more relational, less solipsistic view of learners and learning can be welcomed: they can open space for the idea of a dynamic unconscious at work in our relationships and the quality of our participation in communities of practice.

Neglect and its consequences

Thus, the core preoccupation of our book is to understand the whole human being, the sentio as well as the cogito, the defended as well as social subject, the meaning maker or resistant soul, at the heart of educational processes. If there is a danger of pathologising learning and learners, there is a greater one of sanitising education and neglecting how it is subjectively experienced. The neglect can encompass what happens to students and also tutors in universities, including in initial education and continuing development for diverse professionals. This matters to us, working as we do in a university with large professional education programmes. The gap between the lived experiences of students, as trainee professionals, as well as their tutors, and the formal element of the curriculum, as chronicled in biographical research, can matter, dramatically. There can be little or no room for learning from experience, including from the emotional messiness of classrooms (Bainbridge, this volume; West, 2001, 2009). Even high achieving graduates can struggle, desperately, when working in difficult schools, faced, as they might be in programmes like Teach First in England, with disturbed and disturbing young people, or social pathologies, like racism, in the classroom (West, 2009).

The absence of psychoanalytic-informed discourses can mean that teachers and other professionals might be left feeling inadequate, even in distress, lacking any adequate repertoire, or space, to process such experience. Supervision, to help them give words and meaning to confused and defensive feelings, is, more often than not, absent. And the way in which their own personal biographies might be implicated in professional struggles is given short shrift. Lortie (2002), for example, provides a detailed portrait of the professional practice of (school) teachers, and refers to "the apprenticeship of observation" (p. 62). This acknowledges that professional practices are shaped by earlier, biographical encounters with education. Yet, despite recognising this fundamental psychoanalytic premise that the past influences the present and a present may evoke a past, Lortie neglects these often unconscious processes.

Gaps between languages: getting lost in translation

We have struggled, in bringing together this collection, with problems of language and translation. In the relationship between Canterbury Christ Church and Paris Nanterre, we have often worked in the two languages of French and English. There are many reasons for this, including the need to understand education and psychoanalysis through the play of another language. Post-structuralist sensibilities have taught how language is forged in cultures, but also how language constitutes as well as represents "reality". Often, we have searched for words, within different language communities, to express some core ideas, and we have struggled. Words that seem equivalent—such as agency in English, and *agence* in French—might be troubling *faux amis*. In English, the word can denote small shifts in the experiencing self, while in French the meaning is more mundane: to do with a place of business. We can fall short, persistently, to find equivalent expressions (like *pouvoir d'agir*). Managing the gaps of comprehension, and of being lost in translation, has been a major editorial preoccupation. English, for many reasons, was the chosen language, not least the pressure on certain authors outside the Anglophone world to be published in that medium. This meant giving many hours to negotiating meanings as well as to concern about what can be lost in translation. However, gaps can be bridged and the richness of the book derives as much as anything else from international collaboration. If some of the language is idiosyncratic, we felt it unimportant to respect this, as long as the ideas were meaning-full.

Psychoanalysis and research: biographical and observational studies

New forms of research are helping to bridge some of the gaps in our understanding of why education can be troubling as well as potentially transformative. There is, as will be observed, a flowering of certain kinds of research, such as biographical and observational studies, which use psychoanalytic or psychosocial ideas to illuminate the interplay of outer and inner worlds, desire and resistance, in education. Biographical narrative research methods are used by various authors (see the chapters by Hunt and West, Sagan, Bainbridge, and Cartlidge). It should be noted that biographical methods have claimed an increasing (if also marginal) place in academic research and are alive and well (if contested) in numerous academic disciplines such as literature, history, sociology, anthropology, social policy, and education, as well as feminist and minority studies (Smith, 1998). A number of sociologists (Berger & Luckmann, 1966; Honneth, 2009) have embraced psychoanalytic ideas, including object relations theory, to help explain the apparent irrationality of subjective behaviour as well as its development in a social context. Hollway and Jefferson (2000) use the label "psychosocial" to describe chronicling and theorising of people and apparently "irrational" accounts of crime and its significance. Salling Olesen (2007) and Weber (2007), in their studies of doctors and their learning as well of gender, caring, and reactions to training programmes, make use of psychoanalytic ideas, such as the dynamic unconscious understood by reference to the workings of power and dominant cultural stories that make it difficult or impossible to think and/or speak in certain ways. West (2007, 2009) notes how the idea of adult learning as a vehicle for building greater agency among marginalised peoples is well established, but a detailed focus on the interplay of outer and inner worlds, intersubjective as well as intrasubjective dynamics, in struggles to challenge negative projections, is relatively new.

We can also note the emergence of biographical narrative research methods of "a clinical style" (Bainbridge, 2012; Frosh, Phoenix, & Pattman, 2005; Hollway & Jefferson, 2000; Merrill & West, 2009). Such methods can involve an exploration of openness, contradiction, and emotionally marked material. There is greater social awareness in psychoanalytic theorising, alongside more willingness in social psychology, to engage with "meaning" in exploring how subjects, for instance, might be positioned by powerful cultural and interpretative repertoires. Yet, differing responses of individuals to their positioning requires in-depth psychological understanding, too: precisely the kind of understanding that, uniquely, psychoanalysis provides. Frosh and colleagues, for instance, argue that social discourses around being gay and of what constitutes a good father should not simply be seen as templates to be passively drawn on. Rather, there are more dynamic internal forces "constructing and policing certain modes of masculinity and inhibiting others" (Frosh, Phoenix, & Pattman, 2005, p. 53). The need to bring dynamic internal forces into the equation is more possible because of the detailed chronicling of lives and relationships in biographical research, which can include the here and now of the relationship with researchers. In fact, we suggest, at the end of the book, an interesting parallel between certain in-depth, emotionally attuned forms of enquiry and clinical processes themselves, which enable richer, more nuanced, and interdisciplinary understanding to emerge.

The structure of the book

The next two chapters take us into the territory of fundamental issues of what it means to think and of currently dominant educational trends that might serve to diminish what education can be. We then move into the comparatively well-known terrain of mainstream education, considering experiences of pupils and teachers in depth, and how particular kinds of research can engage with messy complexities in classrooms between teachers and pupils. We then progress to wider territory, of young people and adults learning in professional as well as informal settings. Finally, we consider the transformational potential of education while returning to the troubling theme of how contemporary neo-liberal influences can impoverish education.

Lene Auested, in Chapter Two, distinguishes between learning as mechanical reproduction and as creative process. She recognises how thinking can be encouraged or suppressed because of wider social influences and highlights a fundamental misconception that "thinking is easy". She straddles, as do a number of authors, philosophical and psychoanalytic boundaries, drawing on Hannah Arendt and Wilfred Bion. Arendt described how, in totalitarianism, the disappearance of a person from a neighbourhood might induce denial, a repression of memory, and communication between people. Bion noted how, in the psyche, thoughts and feelings could become a nameless dread, without the availability of the other to process and transform these as well as to offer them back in digestible forms. Freedom can die in both spaces. The following chapter, by Anastasios Gaintanidis, explores what can be meant by a liberal education, and why this is still an important goal. Yet, ultimately, he contends that the current education system in the UK provides a "pseudo-education", no less, where a cold, hard, overly distant rationalism can predominate at the expense of genuine experiential learning, rooted in relationship, and subtler, more empathic understandings of selves and the other.

Claudine Blanchard-Laville and Philippe Chaussecourte, in Chapter Four, provide an important set of perspectives on the psychic world of teaching and learning in classrooms. Their contribution summarises the application of psychoanalytic ideas, used "in a clinical style", to the relations of education. They introduce notions of the psychic space, and a methodology of observational studies, clinical groups, and writing, to help professionals make better and deeper sense of experience, including transference and countertransference dynamics. Balint-style, professional practice analysis groups meet regularly to process experiences in the classroom and with clients, connecting the professionals' personal histories and critical incidents in their work with the other.

In Chapter Five, Laure Castelnau and Claudine Blanchard-Laville provide one of two case studies, using the above methods. We are introduced to the difficulties encountered when a pupil, named Zohar, unexpectedly moves classes. There is a careful chronicling of pupil and teacher interactions in the classroom and an in-depth consideration of the quality of the psychic space, and why the processes involved are so disturbing to both teacher and pupil alike. Anne Bastin and Philippe Chaussecourte, in Chapter Six, provide us with a second case, that of "Margot's red shoes". We enter into a consideration of transference and countertransference dynamics, once more, between teacher, pupil, and primary carers. Jacki Cartlidge, in Chapter Seven, shows us how psychoanalytic thought can illuminate pedagogical practice when working with "non-traditional" adult learners in second chance education. She uses Donald Winnicott to illustrate the importance of playfulness in teaching and learning, and the role of transitional space and objects, like "White Horses", in bringing learning to life. Primitive aspects of the psyche can be engaged and experience might be transformative.

Alper Sahin, in Chapter Eight, interrogates the notion of the countertransference in Turkish school settings. He challenges too loose an application of clinical terms in non-clinical settings, and seeks to develop the idea of "transferential responses", as an alternative, in which a consideration of unconscious processes remains possible and can lead to more effective understanding of pupil behaviour. He contends that by making teachers aware of their "transferential res- ponses", the whole management of the school, as well as relationships between teachers and pupils, can be improved. Alan Bainbridge, in Chapter Nine, engages with the interplay of past and present in the narratives of trainee teachers. He highlights how early experien- ces in education, for aspiring professionals, can have a powerful impact, if often unconscious. He proposes that educational biograph- ical narratives can be used to illuminate how the past effects the present and present past, in teacher education, for the benefit of all concerned.

Celia Hunt and Linden West summarise, in Chapter Ten, many years of using learners' lives, and a psychodynamic framework, in teaching and research. Celia uses the ideas of Karen Horney in creative writing to help mature students identify some of the defences that cause blockages in writing, learning, and relationships. Linden's approach is influenced by object relations and the necessity of considering the dynamics of self and other, cognition and emotion, in encounters with education, both formal and informal. Intimate biographical material is introduced from the narratives of particular young parents participating in informal programmes. These are young mothers who have struggled against histories of abuse and suspicion in relationships. What can make the difference, Linden asks, between risk taking and fuller experience of selfhood, in artistic activity, on the one hand, and resistance, acting out, and self-denial, on the other? Linden uses biographical approaches to chronicle good enough relationships between tutors and learners, but also how the visual arts can serve, in the case of a young woman called Gina, as a container for projections of difficult, disturbing emotions, which may then be worked on, artistically and narratively, to be introjected in transformative ways.

Anna Zurolo, in Chapter Eleven, offers the first of two chapters on the application of psychoanalytic theory to education in Italy, focused on professional development. She describes psychoanalytically informed interventions, such as role-play, used to facilitate teacher development in difficult school settings in the south of the country. She argues that these approaches can encourage profounder forms of professional learning and reflexivity. Italy provides the context for Chapter Twelve, too, where Nunziante Cesàro and colleagues use creative activities to enable trainee psychologists to begin to learn more effectively from experience.

This section concludes with Chapter Thirteen, and Olivia Sagan's longitudinal, unstructured biographical narrative research among students with a history of mental illness. We are taken into especially complex territory, conceptually and research-wise. Her study demonstrates how artistic activity can enable more coherent and meaningful narratives to be composed. The symbol of a continuum is developed, one that represents processes of healing and repair, and of movement from more paranoid–schizoid modes of functioning towards the depressive position. The very ability, or freedom, echoing Arendt and

Bion, to "think" a continuum, to make connections across time and space, in creative ways, using art, for instance, lies at the heart of transformation.

We then, in the concluding chapters, engage with the potentially transformative but also frequently constraining nature of education. In Chapter Fourteen, Larry Green uses forty years of experience working as a psychotherapist in Canada to offer a view of transformative learning as a sort of existential crisis, where individuals oscillate in a space he calls "liminality", between who they are and what they might become. He notes, for transformation to occur, that individuals must be able to deal with being broken and then mended. Tony Brown and Mark Murphy, in Chapter Fifteen, use a psychosocial lens to inform their understanding of higher education and its discontents. They challenge the current neo-liberal influence on education policy and call for a pedagogy that acknowledges the importance of relationships. They combine psychoanalysis with critical theory, using Axel Honneth and his idea of recognition as an important bridge. Learning, of any significant kind, indeed selfhood, freedom, and even democracy, too, depend on people feeling sufficiently recognised at an intimate, group, and whole community level.

In the final chapter, we bring together some of the overarching themes of the book: of how clinical derived concepts can illuminate what lies beneath the surface of things. Building connections between clinical insights and the classroom matters, given that, ultimately, psychoanalysis deals with neuroses that apply to human beings as a whole rather than those deemed ill or abnormal (Honneth, 2009). And we argue that psychoanalysis helps to fill a gap in understanding of the apparently mundane and everyday as well as the extraordinary and transformational. If Frosh (1989) posed a question—in demonstrating how psychoanalysis can be unique in understanding levels of behaviour and its meanings—as to why, for example, Jack hit Jill (that he had no way, like many males, of expressing rage and he believed, unconsciously, that women deserve to be hit), we pose a similar question in relation to education and psychoanalysis. We ask why and what Gina learnt (she is the subject of Linden's reflections in Chapter Ten). This cannot be explained, we suggest, by reference to neuropsychology alone, or to pedagogic ideas, or conventional motivational theory, but requires in-depth understanding of the life, relationships and meaning making of an experiencing, potentially agentic but deeply anxious subject; a subject able, eventually, to move from acting out and hostility, to feeling herself to be an artist for the first time in her life. This is movement requiring containing others to be alongside, love, in a non-narcissistic sense, and also good enough space for story-telling and playfulness. We also require some understanding of mechanisms like projection, introjection, and reparation if we are to make any sense of why and what Gina learnt.

We end on a positive note by providing examples of new and creative work—using auto/biography with psychoanalytic sensibilities—in different professional settings and classrooms. We note, in fact, the emergence of biographical and observational research of a clinical style, and its use in illuminating professional encounters, classroom turbulence, and/or troubling change processes in adulthood. We draw a parallel between such research and the analytic process itself, including the necessity of grounding understanding in the complex particulars, subtleties, and semantics of individual lives. Yet, we argue, this does not leave us trapped in particularities: we can see in such lives more general truths about human experience, including the fundamental importance of good enough relationships and self-respect. Gaps, in short, of comprehension as well as of practice, are challenged in the many spaces we call education. The book represents, we believe, an essential contribution to bridging many gaps, not least in its evocative challenge to reductive accounts of education and of being a learner.

References

Aichhorn, A. (1951). *Wayward Youth*. London: Imago.

Appel, S. (Ed.) (1999). *Psychoanalysis and Pedagogy*. Westport, CT: Bergin and Garvey.

Bainbridge, A. (2012). On becoming an education professional: the past in the present. Unpublished Doctor of Clinical Science thesis, University of Kent.

Berger, P. L., & Luckmann, T. (1966). *The Social Construction of Reality: A Treatise in the Sociology of Knowledge*. London: Penguin.

Bibby, T. (2011). *Education – An Impossible Profession? Psychoanalytic Explorations of Learning and Classrooms*. London: Routledge.

Bion, W. R. (1962). *Learning from Experience*. London: Heimann.

Britzman, D. P. (2003). *After-Education: Anna Freud, Melanie Klein and Psychoanalytic Histories of Learning*. Albany, NY: State University of New York Press.

Britzman, D. P. (2009). *The Very Thought of Education: Psychoanalysis and the Impossible Professions*. Albany, NY: State University of New York Press.

Chaussecourte, P. (2009). Approche clinique d'orientation psychanalytique. Réflexions d'après-coup. Unpublished note de synthèse d'habilitation à diriger des recherches, Université Paris Ouest Nanterre La Défense, Nanterre.

Dirkx, J. (2011). Romancing tales from the dark side: crisis, emotion, and the construction of meaning in transformative learning. Paper presented to the 9th International Conference on Transformative Learning, Athens, 27–29 May.

Ecclestone, K., & Hayes, D. (2009). *The Dangerous Rise of Therapeutic Education*. London: Routledge.

Ferenczi, S. (1949). Psycho-analysis and education. *International Journal of Psychoanalysis, 30*(4): 220–224.

Freud, A. (1930). Four lectures on psychoanalysis for teachers and parents. In: *The Writings of Anna Freud, Vol. 1* (pp. 73–136). New York: International University Press.

Freud, S. (1925f). Preface to Aichhorn's *Wayward Youth*. S.E., *19*: 273–277. London: Hogarth.

Friedman, L. (1999). *Identity's Architect: A Biography of Erik H. Erikson*. New York: Scribner.

Frosh, S. (1989). *Psychoanalysis and Psychology: Minding the Gap*. London: Macmillan.

Frosh, S. (1991). *Identity Crisis: Modernity, Psychoanalysis and the Self*. London: Macmillan.

Frosh, S., Phoenix, A., & Pattman, R. (2005). Struggling towards manhood: narratives of homophobia and fathering. *British Journal of Psychotherapy, 22*(1): 37–56.

Furedi, F. (2004). *Therapy Culture: Creating Vulnerability in an Uncertain Age*. London: Routledge.

Giddens, A. (1999). *Runaway World*. London: Profile Books.

Greenhalgh, P. (1994). *Emotional Growth and Learning*. London: Routledge.

Hinshelwood, R. D. (2009). Do unconscious processes affect educational institutions? *Journal of Clinical Child Psychology and Psychiatry, 14*(4): 509–522.

Hollway, W., & Jefferson, T. (2000). *Doing Qualitative Research Differently*. London: Sage.

Honneth, A. (2009). *Pathologies of Reason: On the Legacy of Critical Theory.* New York: Columbia University Press.

Hunt, C., & West, L. (2006). Learning in a border country: using psychodynamic ideas in teaching and learning. *Studies in the Education of Adults, 38*(2): 160–177.

Hunt, C., & West, L. (2009). Salvaging the self in adult learning. *Studies in the Education of Adults, 41*(1): 68–82.

Illeris, K. (2007). *How We Learn: Learning and Non-learning in School and Beyond.* London: Routledge.

Klein, M. (1975). *Love, Guilt and Reparation and Other Works, 1921–1945.* New York: Free Press.

Krathwohl, D. R., Bloom, B. S., & Masia, B. B. (1964). *Taxonomy of Educational Objectives; The Classification of Educational Goals. Handbook II: The Affective Domain.* New York: Longman

Lave, J., & Wenger, W. (1991). *Situated Learning: Legitimate Peripheral Participation.* Cambridge: Cambridge University Press.

Leader, D. (2011). *What is Madness?* London: Hamish Hamilton.

Lortie, D. C. (2002). *School-Teacher: A Sociological Study.* Chicago, IL: University of Chicago Press.

Merrill, B., & West, L. (2009). *Using Biographical Methods in Social Research.* London: Sage.

Salling Olesen, H. (2007). Professional identities, subjectivity and learning: be(coming) a general practitioner. In: L. West, B. Merrill, P. Alheit, & A. Siig Andersen (Eds.) *Using Biographies and Life History Approaches in the Study of Adult and Lifelong Learning* (pp. 125–141). Frankfurt: Peter Lang.

Salzberger-Wittenberg, I., Williams, G., & Osborne, E. (1983). *The Emotional Experience of Learning and Teaching.* London: Karnac.

Sayers, J. (1995). *The Man Who Never Was. Freudian Tales.* London: Chatto and Windus.

Smith, L. (1998). Biographical method. In: N. K. Denzin & Y. S. Lincoln (Eds.), *Strategies of Qualitative Enquiry* (pp. 184–224). London: Sage.

Tennant, M. (1997). *Psychology and Adult Learning.* London: Routledge.

Vygotsky, L. S. (1978). *Mind in Society: The Development of Higher Psychological Processes.* Cambridge, MA: Harvard University Press.

Weber, K. (2007). Gender, the knowledge economy and every day life. In: L. West, B. Merrill, P. Alheit, A. Bron, & A. S. Andersen (Eds.), *Using Biographies and Life History Approaches in the Study of Adult and Lifelong Learning* (pp. 91–108). Frankfurt: Peter Lang.

West, L. (1996). *Beyond Fragments: Adults, Motivation and Higher Education.* London: Taylor and Francis.

West, L. (2001). *Doctors on the Edge: General Practitioners, Health and Learning in the Inner-city*. London: Free Association Books.

West, L. (2007). The radical challenges of families and their learning. In: L. West, P. Alheit, A. S. Andersen, & B. Merrill, B. (Eds.), *Using Biographical and Life History Approaches in the Study of Adult and Lifelong Learning: European Perspectives* (pp. 221–239). Hamburg: Peter Lang.

West, L. (2009). Really reflexive practice: auto/biographical research and struggles for a critical reflexivity. In: H. Bradbury, N. Frost, S. Kilminster, & M. Zucas (Eds.), *Beyond Reflective Practice* (pp. 66–81). London: Routledge.

West, L. (2010). Apprendre et le sujet apprenant : point de vue psychanalytique dans la recherche auto/biographique. *Cliopsy, Revue électronique*, 4: 21–36.

West, L. (2011). Crisis, ambivalence and ambiguity in transformative learning: challenging perspectives from auto/biographical narrative research. Paper presented to the 9th International Conference on Transformative Learning, Athens, 27–29 May.

Youell, B. (2006). *The Learning Relationship: Psychoanalytic Thinking in Education*. London: Karnac.

CHAPTER TWO

To think or not to think: a phenomenological and psychoanalytic perspective on experience, thinking, and creativity

Lene Auestad

Introduction

Juxtaposing Bion's and Arendt's reflections on "thinking" as an activity provoked by experience, the chapter aims to question the preconditions for openness to the differences of new situations encountered. Both theorists illuminate how thinking rests on some social conditions, how the individual is not self-sufficient as a producer/perceiver of meaning. Where Arendt's philosophical account emphasises the necessity of a space between people for meaning and thinking, Bion's psychoanalytic theory conveys the essential importance of an inner space and the presence of a receptive other. The theme of thinking and its dangers is explored through two stories that have informed psychoanalysis. First, King Oedipus, questioning why a plague is destroying his city, discovers that he has unknowingly caused the disaster by marrying his mother and killing his father, and reacts with horror. He became a king because he freed the city from the terrible sphinx through guessing its riddle. Second, Nathaniel seeks to find out who the figure of the Sandman is, and his obsession with this theme seems to lead him into madness. Ambivalence with regard to the value of enquiry is common to both the Greek myth/play and Hoffmann's gothic fairy tale. It is argued that the acquisition of a conceptual framework involves an epistemic closure as well as enrichment, and that thinking rests jointly on a fundamental felt security and willingness to risk one's supporting frameworks.

"Thoughts are a nuisance," says Bion's patient in *Learning from Experience*; "I don't want them" (1962b, pp. 34–35). "Thinking", writes Arendt in *The Life of the Mind*, is "equally dangerous to all creeds and, by itself, does not bring forth any new creed" (1977, p. 176). Both these writers present theories of what thinking is, and about the risks associated with thinking; why we would sometimes not want to think. The purpose of this chapter is to question how "learning", conceived not as mechanical reproduction, but as a process of creative engagement with material, comes about, using Arendt's philosophical account of thinking with Bion's psychoanalytic account. They both illuminate how thinking is not a necessary component of a human life, though it would be a poor one without it; how it has a potential to undermine the existing social and mental frameworks on which we rely for support; and how thinking, as an activity arising out of experience, depends on some social conditions for its existence.

To explore this theme, I shall first present two pre-psychoanalytic tales which have been central to psychoanalytic thinking: Hoffmann's story of *The Sandman*, as read by Rand and Torok (1994), and Sophocles' *King Oedipus*, primarily as seen by Bion. In these interpretations, both the play and the fairy tale are concerned with the theme of enquiry and its potential dangers.

The Sandman

In Hoffmann's fairy tale *The Sandman* (1816), which forms the basis for Freud's essay "The 'uncanny'" (1919h), the harmony of Nathaniel's family is disturbed on evenings when his father receives an unknown visitor, and the children are rushed to bed, being told that the Sandman is coming. The answers the hero receives to his questions about the Sandman's identity do not satisfy him, and, hiding in his father's room, he discovers that the visitor is the lawyer Coppelius, a family friend feared and hated by the mother and children and treated with admiring subservience by the father. The two men perform some mysterious work involving a fire, and when Nathaniel is discovered, Coppelius wants to throw burning coals into the boy's eyes, but his father intervenes and prevents it.

In Rand and Torok's reinterpretation of the nature of the uncanny, based on their reading of Hoffman's story, damage to the eyes, rather than providing an image of castration, represents an epistemic loss. The authors' emphasis is on the effects of secrecy in the family, which "disrupts the intimacy and familiarity of the home" (1994, p. 189). When attempting to ask about the Sandman, Nathaniel is told by his mother, "When I tell you that the Sandman is coming, it only means that you are sleepy and can't keep your eyes open any longer, as though someone had sprinkled sand into them" (ibid., p. 193). His sister's nurse, on the other hand, informs him that the Sandman "is a wicked man who comes to children when they refuse to go to bed and throws handfuls of sand in their eyes till they bleed and pop out of their heads" (ibid.). The point is that the mother and nurse's explanations reveal the element of wilful deception involved in their stories; "The expression they use, 'to throw sand in someone's eyes' (*Sand in die Augen streuen*) is the German equivalent of the English 'to throw dust in someone's eyes', meaning to mislead, to dupe or trick" (ibid., pp. 194, 196).

As the story evolves, Nathaniel falls madly in love with the doll Olympia, thus failing to realise that she is a piece of mechanical clockwork rather than a human being. As in his childhood, the hero is deprived of the insight those around him possess. The implied threat in the nurse's story, "If you try to look, you will be blinded" (ibid., p. 196) is, in the end, made true, as Nathaniel's search for the truth ends in madness and he throws himself out from a tower while in a delusional state. In Rand and Torok's interpretation (ibid., p. 198), the figure of the Sandman stands both for the ongoing fraudulent activity in the family and for the fact that its existence is covered up.

"From the idea of 'homelike, belonging to the house', the further idea is developed of something withdrawn from the eyes of strangers, something concealed, secret", wrote Freud (1919h, p. 225), concluding that the uncanny is something "familiar and old-established in the mind which has become alienated from it through the process of repression" (ibid., p. 241). Rand and Torok's argument is that *The Sandman* provides a less than perfect illustration of Freud's thesis. In Hoffmann's story, the uncanny is not the return of something

Nathaniel himself has repressed, but the return of the secrets his family has kept from him (1994, p. 202). Thus, we should think of repression here as happening primarily on a social level.

King Oedipus

In Bion's interpretation of the Oedipus myth, the hero's persistent search to discover the truth is at the core of the story. Oedipus "represents the triumph of determined curiosity over intimidation and may thus be used as a symbol for scientific integrity" (1963, p. 49). Bion draws a parallel between this narrative and those of the Garden of Eden and the Tower of Babel: curiosity, in all these stories, has the status of transgression; it amounts to encroaching upon the territory of the gods. "The punishment in Eden is expulsion from the garden: in the Babel story the integrity of the language is destroyed. . . . The exile theme common to both stories is discernible in the exile of Oedipus" (ibid., pp. 82–83).

Enquiry, in all these instances, is associated with potential danger. In the Oedipus myth, the hero's enquiry is about himself. The riddle posed by the Sphinx, a creature who, in its sexual ambiguity, can be seen as representing both his parents, is about the nature of man, and the answer to Oedipus's questions about the cause of the plague and the identity of the murderer of King Laius is no other than the questioner (see also Shengold, 1989). Originally Egyptian, the Sphinx as presented in this story is known from the legends of Oedipus, occurring in tragedies from the fifth century (March, 2008, p. 272). As a divine creature, it was arrogant in its certainty that a mere human would be incapable of grasping his own nature, of knowing himself, but the story differs from the biblical myths in that Oedipus is victorious. Oedipus guesses the answer to the riddle, whereupon the sphinx dies. There is an ambiguity in the story about whether knowledge is good or bad: on the one hand, we witness a victory of reason; the sphinx simply dissolves once its secret has been discovered; on the other hand, there is the presence of the notion that insight into the true state of affairs might be too devastating to bear. The end of the story, where Oedipus blinds himself, is interpreted by Steiner (1985) along these lines: as an instance of self-mutilation signifying a shying away from the truth. The truth is too gruesome to face, and he pokes his eyes out so as not to have to see it. In this version, the story echoes the theme of the nurse's prophesy in *The Sandman:* "Do not look, or you will be blinded." But the ending could also be interpreted differently, more in line with the symbolic significance of blindness in antiquity; in poking his eyes out, Oedipus becomes like the blind seer, Tiresias. He might be regarded as having abandoned the world of appearances in favour of the world of spiritual truth, thus no longer being prey to the deceptive theatre presented to his senses.

To Oedipus's crucial question, "Who among mortals made me?", Tiresias responds, "This very day will make and then dissolve you" (Sophocles (2004, p. 63). This is a repetition of his earlier question to the oracle before leaving Corinth, to which the response did not state the identity of his parents, but, instead, told him the prophecy that he would kill his father and marry his mother. Precisely because he leaves Corinth in an attempt to avoid fulfilling the prophecy, he walks right into the trap set up for him by the gods.

Tiresias, like the gods, knows what is going to happen. But the gods, being immortal and invulnerable, are not in a position to empathise with human beings. Oedipus is acquainted with some of the facts, but he fails to understand them before it is too late. The situation can be compared to Bion's (1963, p. 50) example of reversible perspective drawings, where the perceivers look at the same thing and yet see two different things. The image can be used to illustrate the distinction between meaning and truth. There is the perspective of the eternal truth of the gods, and there is the meaning of the event to human beings. The human spectators, fallible interpreters endowed with character flaws, neither omnipotent nor omniscient, are able to grieve for the fate of the hero, which could have been their own.

Arendt on thinking

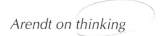

The reason for recounting the stories of the Sandman and of Oedipus was to show how their depiction of thinking and enquiry as potentially dangerous activities strike a theme that has intrigued psychoanalysts. Yet, if thinking is not clearly distinguished from an instrumental activity, this point is easily missed entirely. Conceived as an activity of radical questioning, its potential becomes clearer. In thinking, states Arendt, I am "'two-in-one'—I am conducting a dialogue

[handwritten at top: thinking - dialogue of two / cognition + reasoning — can be done 'alone']

[handwritten in left margin: Thinking = quest for meaning, not truth]

with myself, but it is a dialogue in which other people are represented" (1951, p. 476). Hence, thinking presupposes the human condition of plurality. This is not the case with what she calls cognition and logical reasoning, as these activities can be performed by "Man in the singular". Thought is distinguished from cognition by the fact that it has no utility function; it has neither an end nor an aim outside itself. Cognition, on the contrary, always pursues a definite aim, and it comes to an end once this result is achieved. It is the intellectual work of fabrication, including those of science and workmanship (Arendt, 1988, pp. 170–171). Thus, Arendt does not identify "thinking" with specific professions or layers in society; "inability to think," she writes, "is not a failing of the many who lack brain power but an ever-present possibility for everybody—scientists, scholars, and other specialists in mental enterprises not excluded" (1977, p. 191). Arendt distinguishes logical reasoning from both thought and cognition. Deductions from axiomatic statements and subsumption of particular instances under general rules are activities that obey the laws of logic. Hence, they are characterised by a total absence of freedom; logical laws, to the mind, carry the same force of compulsion as do natural laws to the body. Arendt equates logical reasoning with "brain power" or "intelligence" (1988, p. 171), thus an inability to think is distinct from a lack of intelligence (1971, p. 423).

Reason, to Arendt, seeks meaning rather than truth. Taking over from Kant the distinction between reason (*Vernunft*) and the intellect (*Verstand*), she declares that thinking, belonging to the faculty of reason, is inspired not by the quest for truth, but by the quest for meaning (1977, pp. 14–15). Questions of truth are answered by the evidence provided by the common sense that belongs to the realm of appearances. Questions about meaning, to the contrary (ibid., pp. 57–59) are meaningless to common sense, since common sense makes us feel at home in the world so that we feel no need to question what appears in it. Yet, thinking has one characteristic in common with action: freedom. Arendt states that "both action and thought occur in the form of movement and ... freedom underlies both: freedom of movement" (1968, p. 9). Thinking, although it cannot replace action, is another way of moving in the world of freedom. Thinking takes place in solitude, but in the dialogue of thought other people are represented. Thus, thinking is a state of inner plurality, in which I have a conversation with myself. In loneliness, this two-in-one collapses into one; it

[handwritten annotation: Loneliness = loss of internal conversation, back to one]

is a state of being one person deserted by all the others (1976, p. 476); "man loses trust in himself as the partner of his thoughts" and the confidence in the world required for experience (ibid., p. 477).

This is a description of what takes place in totalitarian societies. Whereas tyrannies, to Arendt, destroy the public sphere and, thus, the capacity for action, totalitarian states destroy the private sphere as well, and, thus, ruin the capacity for thought. Totalitarian movements are characterised by a mixture of cynicism and gullibility, more cynicism higher up and more gullibility further down in the ranks, though the members share a strict principle of authority (1976, p. 382). The elite is distinguished by its members' total contempt for facts and reality, their ability to understand a statement of fact as a declaration of purpose (ibid., p. 385). Think of the proto-genocidal logic involved in processes where a segment of the population is declared as inferior, and then unliveable social conditions are created for this segment, whereupon the leaders point to the results and say; "Look how these people live. It proves we were right, that they actually are inferior." If we imagine a state of affairs where the neighbour has suddenly disappeared, and everyone knows, seemingly instinctively, that they are not to ask any questions, to proceed as if nothing ever happened, and pretend that she never existed, we can begin to discern the outlines of a situation where fear is instigated as an attack on thought, memory, curiosity, imagination, creativity—or mental freedom. An act of physical extermination would be followed by an attack on memory, where victims are to be wiped out from the minds of those who knew them and from the consciousness of the surrounding world. An internalisation of coercion takes place, based on the feeling that some things are too dangerous to be thought about. Thus, creativity is severely restrained; one's thoughts can no longer move around freely for fear of what they might encounter. Prevented from receiving confirmation from others, one is put in a state where one's senses become untrustworthy. "Even the experience of the materially and sensually given world," writes Arendt, depends on contact with others, "without which each of us would be enclosed in his own particularity of sense data" (1976, pp. 475–476). "Only because . . . not one man, but men in the plural inhabit the earth can we trust our immediate sensual experience" (ibid., p. 476).

Hoffmann's story of Nathaniel can be read as an expression of a similar totalitarian situation existing in the family. The hero's attempts to enquire are answered with threats: "Do not ask questions, or else . . .", and his understanding is thwarted. His senses fail him, and he is drawn into a land of shadows, unable to distinguish deceit, in the shape of the doll, Olympia, from the real and genuine, embodied by his human fiancée, Clara. Since this is a gothic fairy tale, no path proceeds towards enlightenment; the reader is left more or less in the same position as its hero, unable to draw a clear line between his hallucinations and what is happening objectively.

Experience and thinking are undermined when human beings are prevented from engaging in meaningful contact with others. Arendt's account of totalitarianism is not only intended as a historical description. It ends on a note of warning, stating that in a social situation where people are made superfluous as human beings, when they are placed outside of a context where they can exchange opinions, exercise judgement, and act together with others, a totalitarian temptation is created. When meaning is not upheld interpersonally, the world becomes inhuman, like a desert, from which ideology might provide an escape, appearing "like a last support in a world where nobody is reliable and nothing can be relied upon" (1976, p. 478).

Bion on thinking

Like the bird-mother who feeds the baby bird with food she has digested, Bion's mother nurtures her infant with digested experience, leading to the growth of an ability to think. While the bird's digestive organs grow on their own, the growth in the infant's capacity for thinking presumably results from first a mimicking and then an elaboration of the mother's interpretative activity. Bion starts from the premise that thinking is based on a negative realisation: it comes into being when there is a preconception of a good object and the expectation of its appearance is unfulfilled;

> The model I propose is that of an infant whose expectation of a breast is mated with a realization of no breast available for satisfaction. This mating is experienced as a no-breast, or "absent" breast inside. . . . If the capacity for toleration of frustration is sufficient the "no-breast" inside becomes a thought and an apparatus for "thinking" it develops. (Bion, 1962a, pp. 111–112)

Bion - thinking can result from absence of breast

If the painful experience of this absence cannot be tolerated,

> What should be a thought, a product of the juxtaposition of pre-conception and negative realization, becomes a bad object, indistinguishable from a thing-in-itself, fit only for evacuation. . . . [The psyche] operates on the principle that evacuation of a bad breast is synonymous with obtaining sustenance from a good breast. The end result is that all thoughts are treated as if they were indistinguishable from bad internal objects. (Bion, 1962a, p. 112)

Bion bases this description on Freud's (1911b) distinction between the pleasure principle and the reality principle. It is in accordance with the pleasure principle that bad states are not felt, but are replaced by hallucinatory wish-fulfilment; thus, absence as negativity is replaced with a positive phenomenon. Only if the absence of the breast is held on to does it become a thought.

The theory could be used to state that thoughts are, by their nature, about what is absent, but a different point could also be made: an expectation of something other than what is has to be present. In order to describe a situation as characterised by the absence of something, one must expect this something to be there. Awareness of such subjective contribution to one's perception is lacking in the latter example, where the painful material has become a concretely felt, independently existing entity, a beta-element subjecting one to attack. Thus, a collapse in the self–other relation has entailed a collapse in subjectivity. Bion describes a third way of relating to, or handling, reality, also a kind of collapse in subjectivity, though not psychotic in the psychiatric sense. "This involves the assumption of omniscience as a substitute for learning from experience by aid of thoughts and thinking" (1962a, p. 114).

Bion states that, in this case, a moral distinction between right and wrong replaces a factual one between true and false, and adds that the morality engendered is a function of psychosis. His description resembles Arendt's analysis of ideological reasoning, and, based on the latter, we can clarify the meaning so as to state that it is not the case that moral judgements replace reality-testing, because the distinction between the two is, in fact, blurred in such a way that neither one can correct the other. Within this logic, factual findings cannot correct moral prescriptions because they are subordinate to them, but these prescriptions are, again, merely functions of natural or historical laws, and, thus, a moral critique of the factual circumstances is as impossible as a fact-based critique of the moral system, since neither perspective is granted sufficient independence from the other to articulate a different point of view.

Bion's greatest contribution to psychoanalytic thinking is his theory of containment, where he articulates how meaning, thinking, and subjectivity originate in an interpersonal constellation:

> Normal development follows if the relationship between infant and breast permits the infant to project a feeling, say, that it is dying into the mother and to reintroject it after its sojourn in the breast has made it tolerable to the infant psyche. If the projection is not accepted by the mother the infant feels that its feeling that it is dying is stripped of such meaning as it has. It therefore reintrojects, not a fear of dying made tolerable, but a nameless dread. (Bion, 1962a, p. 116)

While Arendt dwells on the necessity of a social space, a space *between* people, for meaning and thinking, Bion elaborates on the requirement of an inner space and on the historical and, possibly, renewed presence of a receptive other. In their different ways, they convey how assigning meaning to experience, in the intimate sphere as in the public sphere, rests on a collective effort. The starting point for both these paths of reflection is how meaning is destroyed, in Arendt's case, from without through the collapse of a public, political space, and, in Bion's case, from within through a collapse of a psychic space. These seemingly similar processes are intertwined. It is interesting to note that Freud, when attempting to explain the concept of the censor, employs the example of political censorship in Russia.

> I will try to seek a social parallel to this internal event in the mind. Where can we find a similar distortion of a psychical act in social life? Only where two persons are concerned, one of whom possesses a certain degree of power which the second is obliged to take into account. . . . This censorship acts exactly like the censorship of newspapers at the Russian frontier, which allows foreign journals to fall into the hands of the readers . . . only after a quantity of passages have been blacked out. (Freud, 1900a, pp. 141–142, 529)

Freud is, in effect, saying "take this political phenomenon, of tyranny, and try to imagine it as taking place on an individual level". Bion's description of nameless dread goes further in conceiving of

[handwritten margin note: feelings made tolerable OR nameless dread through containment]

how the social reaches into the soul of the individual. Not only is meaning distorted and covered up, it is thoroughly destroyed. The object of refuted containment has acquired an additional quality by being refuted; it has become meaningless, indigestible, that-which-cannot-be-thought. Bion's analogy of witnessing not so much the remnants of a past civilisation as a primitive catastrophe (1957, p. 88) paralleled the political situation that gave rise to Arendt's thought, where human beings had not simply been killed on a massive scale, but an attempt had been made to destroy their humanity before killing them and to eradicate the memory of them in the aftermath. The situation was not one in which one could simply pick up the pieces of past Western thought and gather them together again; a thorough effort at rethinking was required.

Thinking and experience

Psychoanalysis can be seen as an effort to reinstall or recreate meaning, to think about the unthinkable. But, as a conceptual scheme, it is also socially determined. This means that it is guided by power structures, as we saw in the quote by Freud, but another point in the context of thinking is that as long as you are operating within a conceptual scheme, you are making sense, but once you start to test the limits of that conceptual scheme, you risk meaninglessness.

Thinking is, as we have seen, essentially disruptive. It "brings out the implications of unexamined opinions and thereby destroys them"; thus, it liberates the faculty of judgement. It has a political function only in times of crisis; "When everybody else is swept away unthinkingly by what everybody else does and believes in, those who think are drawn out of hiding because their refusal to join is conspicuous" (Arendt, 1977, p. 192). The story of Anton Schmidt, a sergeant in the German Army, who, for five months, supplied the Jewish underground in Poland with forged papers and military trucks until he was arrested and executed in March 1942, shows that "under conditions of terror most people will comply but *some people will not*" (1994, pp. 231–233). Examples that such actions are possible are needed for the worldly preservation of meaning.

The stories of thinking that interest Bion, the Garden of Eden, the Tower of Babel, and the myth of Oedipus, all end in expulsion, *e.g. vocabulary in maths gives framework, but also limits thinking to its own concepts + not the gaps?*

pointing towards his interest in the potentially stifling quality of the group. Arendt's ideal type, Socrates, the thinker *par excellence*, was, as we know, finally executed for corrupting the youth of Athens. Yet, his example is two-sided, since his thinking was always dialogical; he always thought *with* someone, yet he was also got rid of by the community.

A twofold quality can be discerned in teaching and learning as well. In learning, acquiring a conceptual scheme, one is enriched with a capacity to experience reality through its concepts, but the process also serves to set up a barrier against that which cannot be grasped through them. Thus, in teaching someone a conceptual scheme, one is also teaching them where not to look. One is simultaneously, to a greater or lesser extent, saying, "We will throw sand into your eyes".

To appeal to Arendt's clarifying distinctions, cognition can be taught, but thinking cannot. Thinking cannot be copied, or passed on like a piece of knowledge, only inspired. Around the age of fourteen, I had a teacher who, in the context of speaking about the French Revolution, started asking, "What are the preconditions required for a revolution to take place?" Rather than saying "This is the truth because it says so in the book", he was taking a step back and wondering why. I mention this because it was a kind of revelatory experience to me, where I thought, "He is standing up there and actually thinking." In doing so, he was creating a space in which such activity could take place.

To Arendt, conscience is a result of the experience of thinking itself (1977, p. 189). When Socrates debates with himself, he is engaged in a dialogue with an inner friend, his *daimon*. At the end of his life, when imprisoned, and deciding not to take the opportunity for escape offered by his friends, he declares, "Since my *daimon* has remained silent, I know I am doing the right thing." Although Arendt tends to overlook the emotional basis of such inner dialogue, she has a keen eye for how it might be lost under destructive social conditions. Towards the end of the play, in an hour of need, Oedipus calls out for his *daimon*, asking where it has gone (2004, p. 97). Thinking psychoanalytically, one could say that he is calling out for an inner object to come to his support. The word *eudaimonia*, misleadingly translated as happiness, means, literally, living in peace with one's *daimon*, that is, a harmonious co-existence of the various parts of the soul, or, stated in psychoanalytic terms, a good relationship to one's inner objects.

Finally, I have aimed to imply that Arendt has something essential to add to an idea of containment extended in a social sense: that is, an epistemic point about perspectival plurality. A distinct form of humanism inheres in her emphasis on the irreducibility of the different positions people occupy and the potential for extended vision each participant's perspective lends to all. According to Hecht, the translator of *King Oedipus* (2004, p. xx), the hero is the person to whom the riddle of the sphinx does not apply. Having had his feet pinned together as an infant, Oedipus was, in fact, handicapped; he never walked upright on his own two feet without the support of a walking stick. An Arendtian interpretation of this fact could be that the place in the world he occupied as a result of his deformation allowed him to see what everyone else overlooked. What to everyone else would be too obvious to notice, walking upright and unsupported, was not obvious to him; thus, he was the only one who was capable of guessing the riddle.

Whether a teacher is capable of taking up a perspective that comes from the sideline—in terms of culture, class, gender etc.—depends, I think, jointly on a basic security and a willingness to take a risk. Bion's concepts illuminate how this security is an unconscious state of affairs and how it is unconsciously communicated. The element of courage required to put one's concepts into play and risk one's frameworks of support is fruitfully explored in Arendt's political existentialism.

References

Arendt, H. (1968). *Men in Dark Times*. San Diego, CA: Harcourt Brace.

Arendt, H. (1971). Thinking and moral considerations. In: *Social Research*, *38*(3): pp. 417–446.

Arendt, H. (1976). *The Origins of Totalitarianism*. San Diego, CA: Harcourt Brace.

Arendt, H. (1977). *The Life of the Mind*. San Diego, CA: Harcourt Brace.

Arendt, H. (1988). *The Human Condition*. Chicago, IL: University of Chicago Press.

Arendt, H. (1994). *Eichmann in Jerusalem*. New York: Penguin.

Bion, W. R. (1957). On arrogance. In: *Second Thoughts* (pp. 86–92). London: Karnac, 1984.

Bion, W. R. (1962a). A theory of thinking. In: *Second Thoughts* (pp. 110–119). London: Karnac, 1984.

Bion, W. R. (1962b). *Learning from Experience*. London: Karnac.

Bion, W. R. (1963). *Elements of Psychoanalysis*. London: Karnac.

Freud, S. (1900a). *The Interpretation of Dreams*. *S.E.*, *4–5*. London: Hogarth.

Freud, S. (1911b). Formulations on the two principles of mental functioning. *S.E.*, *12*: 218–226. London: Hogarth.

Freud, S. (1919h). The "uncanny". *S.E.*, *17*: 219–256. London: Hogarth.

Hecht, J. (2004). Introduction. In: *Three Theban Plays* (pp. vii-xxii). Ware, Hertfordshire: Wordsworth.

Hoffman, E. T. A. (1816). *The Sandman*. Available electronically: www.fln.vcu.edu/Hoffmann/sand_e.html

March, J. (2008). *The Penguin Book of Classical Myths*. London: Penguin.

Rand, N., & Torok, M. (1994). *The Sandman* looks at "The 'uncanny'". In: S. Shamdasani & M. Münchow (Eds.), *Speculations after Freud* (pp. 185–203). London: Routledge.

Shengold, L. (1989). *Soul Murder*. New York: Fawcett Columbine.

Sophocles (2004). *Oedipus the Tyrant*. In: *Three Theban Plays* (pp. 49–105). Hertfordshire: Wordsworth.

Steiner, J. (1985). Turning a blind eye: the cover-up for Oedipus. *International Review of Psycho-Analysis*, *12*: 161–172.

CHAPTER THREE

Anxiety, psychoanalysis, and reinvigorating education

Anastasios Gaitanidis

Introduction

In this chapter, I examine how the psychoanalytic understanding and treatment of anxiety can provide the basis for a radical re-thinking of the current educational system. I begin by highlighting the problematic assumptions embedded within the seventeenth and eighteenth century idea of liberal education (*Bildung*), along with its desire to preserve the students' autonomy and their ability to think critically. I then move on to examine the recent developments in education that contribute to the abolition of the students' critical abilities and reinforce their passive acceptance of their individual and social fate. I argue that this is accomplished by the current system's promotion of a form of pseudo-education (*Halbbildung*), which can be characterised as "psychoanalysis in reverse", that is to say, a type of education which attempts to repress and stifle students' anxieties, instead of encouraging the critical exploration of the underlying conflicts and tensions that give rise to them.

In this respect, the current educational system can only be trans-formed if it adopts the psychoanalytic belief that anxiety is a produc-tive indication that students are intensely dissatisfied with specific individual and social conditions that render them impotent to experi-ence anything as immediate and alive. For this reason, I propose the creation of a new, psychoanalytically informed educational system which will support the autonomous development of the students' ability to "hold" their anxiety so as to critically examine and effec-tively challenge its individual and social origins.

The development of the idea of liberal education (Bildung)

Let us begin with an account of the historical changes that led to the creation of the current educational system. With the advent of moder-nity and the age of enlightenment, the identity of experience in the form of a life that is articulated and possesses internal continuity was endangered. The emphasis on the importance of the function of reason was imposed on a traditional culture which had a critical potential embedded in its close relation to nature as well as in its scep-ticism, wit, and irony. In this culture, the elderly were the main "educational" resource because they embodied a continuity of consciousness, an understanding based on a coherent remembrance of the past. A relatively homogeneous existence gave traditional life the basis of judgement, and the wisdom of the elderly was respected for the experience it contained. However, this experience was also based on a narrow and dogmatic world view as it resisted anything innov-ative that could transform and upset its directives. Thus, the educa-tion of the intellect was simultaneously a liberation from, and a threat to, this way of life, a release from the chains of dogma and supersti-tion and a danger to the continuation of a shared culture of lived expe-rience which had negative implications for judgement itself.

For this reason, enlightenment thought aimed to replace the judge-ment of experience with reasoned judgement. This task was assigned to the idea of transformative, comprehensive education, or *Bildung*, operative in seventeenth- and eighteenth-century liberal thought. Thus, rational judgement was meant to be achieved through the culti-vation or development of individuals into completely self-determin-ing persons, who are integrated and in harmony with their society, and at home within it. In this sense, comprehensive education has always been a form of re-education, an attempt to replace the tradi-tional experience of a coherent existence based on a mimetic, close relationship with nature that has been lost with a higher, rational unity of moral individuals who pursue their own ends and realise their potentials, using their own understanding without irrelevant external influences. On the basis of this, people were meant to be able confidently to work their way out of the unthinking ordering of their "animal" existence and state of barbarism, and establish a law-governed social order capable of just and fair action.

This demand for reasoned judgement and self-determination is strongly present in the work of Immanuel Kant, who, in 1784, responded to the question "What is Enlightenment?" by answering "autonomy" or "emancipation from self-imposed immaturity". By autonomy, Kant meant intellectual and moral autonomy. On the one hand, he wanted individuals to get out of the influence of the "wise" elders, priests, and aristocrats and to think for themselves. On the other hand, he wanted them to rise above their desires and act in accordance with moral and intellectual norms that they themselves created by exercising their reason. For Kant, moreover, norms formulated in this way would be universally applicable. Thus, from the Kantian perspective, the role of education was to create "autonomous" individuals who will be able to overcome their racial, gender, and social situations as well as their "natural" inclinations and desires so as to formulate rational and moral judgements.

However, at the very heart of this liberal idea of education there was a notion of culture that separated the rational and moral from the natural and restricted the cultural to the rational. It also produced a division between mental and manual labour. This separation was the product of the liberal ideology's belief that nature needed to be mastered by beginning to treat and perceive it as though it consisted of extrinsic objects to be manipulated and controlled. The idea of a temporary and playful or mimetic identification with the environment was eclipsed by an identification that grasped the object from a calculated distance. What is important to understand here is that this mastery over nature was accomplished through self-sacrifice. In order to set ourselves apart from nature—so as to control it all the more—we had to learn how to renounce what we shared with nature, that is to say, we had to repudiate the sensuous and material aspects of the self (see Adorno & Horkheimer, 1986).

Our intellectual freedom was purchased, therefore, at an enormous cost: the internal and external domination of nature. However, as Freud (1915d) astutely pointed out in his account of the "return of the repressed", mutilated nature returned in distorted form to haunt us. Sensuous contact with the environment suppressed by civilisation, for instance, touch and smell, became repulsively alien to us. The subject that was the product of this liberal education betrayed its uncompromising inflexibility in its reaction, for example, to animals, women, and the human body. The "badness" that was therefore attributed to this natural "other" was, in actuality, a projection of what remained unsatisfactorily repressed and what threatened to disrupt the self's identity. Borrowing Freud's (1919h) idea of the "uncanny" (*das Unheimliche*), we can argue that what seemed abominably alien was, in fact, all too familiar. The *unheimlich* characteristics that returned to haunt our mind were the very things that were repressed within this mind. What we despised was really what we secretly longed for (that is, the repressed mimetic closeness to nature).

The liberal idea of education, therefore, which turned on a pedagogic separation of aspects of human existence and presented culture as something disengaged from nature, the body, and practical aspects of daily life, did not always develop or enhance the capacity for judgement. Divorcing itself from the experience of the body and its natural and social determinants, it often suppressed intellectual capacities even though it had its basis in a culture of rational judgement.

However, despite its problematic character, this liberal idea of education does not contain only the means to damage culture, but is also capable of reinstating the capacity for reflection. More specifically, due to the separation of the intellectual from social conditions, an independent culture has been developed since the advent of the idea of *Bildung*, establishing the importance of critical examination. In a fragment published as the *Theory of Bildung*, one of the most significant proponents of liberal education, Wilhelm von Humboldt (2000 [1793–1794]), states that *Bildung* is about linking the student's self to the world in the "most general, most animated and most unrestrained interplay". However, he also argues that it is crucial that the student "should not lose himself in this alienation, but rather should reflect back into his inner being the clarifying light and comforting warmth of everything that he undertakes outside himself" (von Humboldt, 2000[1793–1794], p. 58).

It is this emphasis on self-reflexivity that has the potential of providing a glimmer of hope for genuine autonomy. It is not the autonomy of someone living in a direct and sensuous way, and it does not guarantee the radical transformation of the world, but it at least provides a degree of intellectual freedom. This enables students to refuse to blindly adapt to society's laws, since it develops their capacity for self-determining judgement, encourages their desire to establish a critical distance from prevailing social perspectives, and fosters their need to be honest and decent with themselves and others.

The decline of Bildung and rise of Halbbildung (half-education)

If liberal education reflected the idea of providing the kinds of cultural experiences to students that fostered their desire to think critically, then a recent development in education, which Adorno (1972) termed *Halbbildung*, translated as "half-education", produces the desire to comply with the current cultural and social directives. Half-education is that which is left when the conditions of autonomy inherent in liberal education are discarded and integration and conformity become the central focus. This type of education provides students with a set of presumptions that filter their actual existence, offering them a way of dealing with their anxiety by smoothing over any contradictions and tensions generated by a thoughtless adaptation to the social whole. It achieves this by convincing students that the existing social structures will never change while providing stimulation for their tedious and powerless existence.

External institutions like the mass media have contributed to the students' sense of powerlessness and uncritical acceptance by becoming the major influence over both the content of general education and its pedagogical practice. Increasingly, thoughtless adaptation occurs as much outside the formal institutions of teaching and learning as within them. As Adorno (1972) remarked,

> What happens in the cultural domain is not the ... lack of *Bildung* [but] is *Halbbildung*. ... [T]he pre-bourgeois conception of the world ... was destroyed. ... Nevertheless, the a priori of the essentially bourgeois concept of culture – autonomy – had no time to develop. Consciousness goes immediately from one heteronomy to another. The bible is replaced ... by the television. (p. 99)

and it can just as well be said to have replaced the knowledge conveyed by school teachers or university lecturers. The mass media command the students' undivided attention and their readiness to participate to a far greater degree than any teacher's or lecturer's clever or ingenious teaching plan. Thus, teachers and lecturers feel compelled to use multi-media presentations for the good reason that it has become necessary for them to be "entertaining" so as to be accepted by students who believe that the only knowledge worth having is the one that has "entertainment value" attached to it. However, by following this trend, they deny the students the kinds of experiences that could develop their critical and self-reflexive capacities.

In this respect, the mass media type of information provided in contemporary education becomes the mortal enemy of the educational process. It encourages a form of superficial knowledge that produces hatred and resentment against everything that is "too deep" or "too complex". Thus, the systematic and in-depth exploration of a field of knowledge which enhances the students' capacity for memory and critical thinking has been replaced by the selective, disconnected, interchangeable, and ephemeral state of adhering to what is "fashionable" and "trendy".

Consequently, the students' memory becomes very weak, as they can only remember what is immediately present. It is as if they live a life where the memory of a previous event is instantly replaced by the actuality of the next one. Absence and lack are not recognised or tolerated, since they are constantly negated by an eternal presence. Thus, their actions are motivated neither by a sense of who they were in the past, nor by what they are missing in the present, nor by what they would like to be in the future, but by a pseudo-immediacy which ultimately signifies a collapse of critical consciousness into the mass consciousness of our consumer society.

The educational values of "hardness" and "coldness"

Here, psychoanalysis should be utilised to examine the active exclusion of critical consciousness and the generation of psychological blocks to memory and self-reflexivity. It could also help us understand how the educational ideal of "hardness" (i.e., the belief that the student can only achieve a strong moral character if s/he manages to endure the maximum degree of pain and hardship), in which many might believe without reflecting about it, is completely erroneous.

This is because this process of instilling discipline and moral strength can become a screen-image for masochism that, as psychoanalysis has established, can easily turn into sadism and produce subjects who are incapable of feeling guilt for the pain they are inflicting on others. As Adorno (1998) states in his essay, "Education after Auschwitz",

> Being hard, the vaunted quality education should inculcate, means absolute indifference toward pain as such. In this the distinction between one's own pain and that of another is not so stringently maintained. Whoever is hard with himself earns the right to be hard with others as well and avenges himself for the pain whose manifestations he was not allowed to show and had to repress. (p. 199)

Moreover, psychoanalytic ideas should be used to examine how the educational system's endorsement of "coldness" (i.e., its promotion of emotional distance and lack of empathy) produces students who are deeply indifferent towards whatever happens to everyone else except themselves. For example, the educational system in its present form places far more emphasis on the students' successful completion of a series of competitive examinations than on the development of their ability to empathically relate to others, promoting, thus, the relentless pursuit of their own individual interests against the interests of everyone else. This has settled into the character of students to their innermost core and contributes to the modern subjects' lack of concern for other people's distress and a sense of isolation through the creation of an unquenchable appetite for competition. The only reaction to this process is the so-called "lonely crowd", "a banding together of people completely cold who cannot endure their own coldness and yet cannot change it" (Adorno, 1998, p. 201). It is no accident, therefore, that there is a proliferation of "reality" television shows like *Big Brother*, *The Apprentice*, *The X Factor*, etc., that blatantly illustrate how extremely narcissistic and emotionally distant individuals have to be to pretend to get along with each other and work as a team so as to win the television competition.

Thus, modern groups are formed through coldness, that is, through the absence of libidinal investments, in contrast to Freud's (1921c) belief that groups are created through the establishment of intense libidinal bonds between its members. In the reduction of intersubjective relationships to indifferent connections between objects,

coldness results in the development of a consciousness that is characterised by "a rage for organization, by the inability to have any immediate human experiences at all, by a certain lack of emotion, by an
overvalued realism" (Adorno, 1998, p. 198). As such, modern subjectivity is devoid of emotional resonance and incapable of recognising
difference or the value of affectionate bonds.

However, as the current educational system plays such a crucial
role in the creation of this "unemotional" subject, it can also attempt
to invert this process by working against the psychological and social
preconditions that produce this character structure. In order to accomplish this, its teaching practices should be altered in such a way as to
discourage the naturalisation of hardness and coldness as educational
virtues. One might think that this can be accomplished by giving more
warmth and love to students. However, students who have no idea of
the coldness and hardness of social life are then truly traumatised by
the cruelty of it when they must leave their protected educational
environment. If anything can help against hardness and coldness,
then it is the students' understanding of the conditions that determine
them and the attempt to fight those conditions.

The psychoanalytic treatment of anxiety

But how could this be achieved? Here, again, the psychoanalytic
understanding and treatment of anxiety can provide the basis for the
students' attempt to fight the conditions which produce the symptoms
of hardness and coldness. This is because psychoanalysis refuses to
frame anxiety in the "negative", that is, as a bothersome affect that
needs to be repressed or abolished since it disrupts the "normal" functioning of the modern ("hard" and "cold") subject. Instead, anxiety is
perceived as a valid response to internal and external conditions that
generate conflict/tension. In this respect, the presence of anxiety is
a "positive" indication that something is "moving" (or about to
"move") within the "hard" and "cold" subject that should be properly
"held" and analysed during the therapeutic process. This "positive"
aspect of anxiety will also become apparent in the following discussion of Freud's theory of anxiety.

In his second theory of anxiety, Freud (1926d) proposes that the
ego is "the actual seat of anxiety" (p. 93); it alone can produce and feel

anxiety, because, in its attempt to respond to the conflicting demands of its "three tyrannical masters" (the external world, the id, and the superego), it produces three corresponding types of anxiety: realistic, neurotic, and moral. As Freud (1933a) puts it, "[the ego] feels hemmed in on three sides, threatened by three kinds of danger, to which, if it hard pressed, it reacts by generating anxiety" (p. 77).

Anxiety as a reaction to these three dangers on the part of the ego results in repression: the ego excludes the repressed from its "great organization" so that, even when the danger situation changes, the now restricted ego cannot undo the earlier repression, and "the new impulse has no choice but to obey the compulsion to repeat" (Freud, 1926d, p. 154). The beginning of anxiety is, in this way, returned to or restated at its middle (i.e., the ego) immersed in its multiple dangers: internal and external; real, neurotic, and moral.

This middle, however, is equally the anxiety of beginning, not only an account of "the compulsion to repeat", but also an inducement of a movement forwards. In part, this concerns Freud's understanding of the creation of "free mobile ego" in terms of a process of remembering through which the bringing into consciousness of the three different sources of anxiety enables the overcoming of these anxieties. Yet, the attainment of a "free mobile ego" is not the result of a one-off, momentarily performed act of becoming aware of the origins of anxiety. This requires a protracted and strenuous process of remembering in which one attempts, against persistent resistance, to appropriate retrospectively the sources of anxiety that block one's memory and result in the compulsive repetition of neurotic patterns of behaviour.

Therefore, if the aim of psychoanalysis is to restore a "free mobile ego", then the five psychoanalytic meanings of resistance/repetition can themselves be seen to yield the meaning of this restoration, this movement forwards: three ego resistances (knowledge resistance, transference resistance, and the gain from illness), id resistance, and superego resistance (the following account is taken from Freud, 1926d, pp. 158–160). Knowledge resistance, the easiest to overcome, implies that movement forwards is not a question of knowledge: one may come to know of a source of anxiety which produces repression without thereby overcoming it and, thus, might still engage in repetitive patterns of behaviour. Transference resistance means repeating the neurotic pattern of behaviour in relation to the analyst, acting it out symptomatically instead of overcoming it. The authority of the analyst here is both essential to moving the analysand beyond repetition and potentially dangerous in that this authority could reinforce this repetition so that relation to an external authority is again substituted for taking a relation to one's own authority. The third ego resistance is "the gain from illness", by which the symptom is assimilated into the ego and results in unwillingness to relinquish the satisfaction or the substitute relief which the symptom affords. Thus, the ego prefers to console itself with the "familiar" repetition of the symptom instead of engaging in the painful recollection of the sources of its anxiety.

The id resistance follows after the ego has decided to give up its resistance but "still has difficulty in undoing the repressions", because the power of the compulsion to repeat—the attraction exerted by the unconscious origins of its anxiety—has still to be overcome. The "period of strenuous effort" required to achieve this is called "working-through". "Working-through" is the pivot that decides whether the analysis is successful or unsuccessful, whether it overcomes the lure of the unconscious origins of anxiety, and ushers in a "freely mobile ego" movement forwards.

The fifth resistance, "the last to be discovered", comes from the superego and also inhibits successful analysis, set out in the idea of "working-though", because of the need for guilt and the desire for punishment. The guilt, the "moral" factor, might be unconscious and it might require an alternative ego ideal—"prophet, saviour and redeemer" (Freud, 1923b, p. 50)—which analysis does not permit the analyst to provide. For Freud (1923b) admits that

> Since the rules of analysis are diametrically opposed to the physician's making use of his personality in any such manner, it must be honestly confessed that here we have another limitation to the effectiveness of analysis; after all, analysis does not set out to make pathological reactions impossible, but to give the patient's ego *freedom* to decide one way or the other. (p. 50)

However, it is this continuous and systematic refusal to profoundly interfere with the analysand's *freedom* and ability to "hold" his/her anxieties by offering consolations, reassurances and promises of salvation that makes psychoanalysis such an exemplary practice of autonomous emancipation. And it is by adopting the psychoanalytic belief that the individual's anxiety should neither be consoled nor repressed that the educational system could facilitate the students' understanding of the origins of their anxiety, which can potentially lead them to overcome their "hard" and "cold" character structures. As Adorno (1998) puts it,

> When anxiety is not repressed, when one permits oneself to have, in fact, all the anxiety that this reality warrants, then precisely by doing that, much of the destructive effect of unconscious and displaced anxiety will probably disappear. (p. 198)

In this case, anxiety is a productive signal that the "hard" and "cold" character structure of the modern student/subject is no longer working properly, and that s/he is close to understanding the unbearable truth that his/her character formation attempts to conceal. As such, anxiety (when it is appropriately "held" and analysed) is the most powerful educational affect for exploring the psychological contents petrified by hardness and frozen over by coldness and their social determinants (see also Lewis, 2006).

Conclusion

I hope that I have successfully demonstrated how the psychoanalytic understanding and treatment of anxiety can provide the basis for a radical transformation of the educational system. This system will no longer attempt to console or repress the students' anxieties but will enable them—through the autonomous development of their "holding" capacity—to uncover, "work through", and alter the individual and social conditions which produce these anxieties.

However, is it possible to establish a psychoanalytically inspired learning culture which would allow students to "hold" and creatively explore their anxieties when recent developments in education regard "student satisfaction" as the only relevant measure of teaching quality? In other words, how could students be encouraged to examine the reasons behind their dissatisfaction with the "cold", instrumental logic of the market when these recent developments suggest that teachers and lecturers should be "service providers" who need to keep their students "satisfied" by fulfilling their "consumerist" demand for accumulation of educational assets so as to increase their marketability and future employability prospects? In a recent article for the *London Review of Books*, Collini (2010) succinctly summarises this dilemma:

> I would hope the students I teach come away with certain kinds of dissatisfaction (including with themselves: a 'satisfied' student is nigh-on ineducable), and it matters more that they carry on wondering about the source of that dissatisfaction than whether they 'liked' the course or not. This is another respect in which the 'consumer' model is simply misleading, an error encouraged by the prevalence in current edspeak of the category of 'the student experience'. (p. 24)

These thoughtful remarks seem to indicate that it is absolutely crucial for us to resist the application of this "consumer" model of education that promotes this superficial category of "student experience". They also imply that a genuine "student experience" should not be based on the renunciation of the students' "dissatisfaction" with the current educational and social systems and the anxiety they produce. In this respect, a psychoanalytic understanding of anxiety can provide the guidelines for a new education not based on renunciation and repression but on insight, an education to be worked out in the future.

References

Adorno, T. W. (1972). Theorie der Halbbildung. *Gesammelte Schriften, 10*(2): 93–121.

Adorno, T. W. (1998). Education after Auschwitz. In: *Critical Models: Interventions and Catchwords* (pp. 191–204). New York: Columbia University Press.

Adorno, T. W., & Horkheimer, M. (1986). *The Dialectic of Enlightenment*. London: Verso.

Collini, S. (2010). Browne's Gamble. *London Review of Books, 32*(21): 23–25.

Freud, S. (1915d). Repression. *S.E., 14*: 141–158. London: Hogarth.

Freud, S. (1919h). The "uncanny". *S.E., 17*: 219–256. London: Hogarth.

Freud, S. (1921c). *Group Psychology and the Analysis of the Ego. S.E., 18*: 67–143. London: Hogarth.

Freud, S. (1923b). *The Ego and the Id. S.E., 19*: 3–66. London: Hogarth.

Freud, S. (1926d). *Inhibitions, Symptoms and Anxiety. S.E., 20*: 77–174. London: Hogarth.

Freud, S. (1933a). *New Introductory Lectures on Psycho-Analysis. S.E.*, 22. London: Hogarth.

Kant, I. (1784). An answer to the question: what is enlightenment? In: H. Reiss (Ed.), H. B. Nisbett (Trans.), *Kant: Political Writings* (pp. 54–60). Cambridge: Cambridge University Press, 1991.

Lewis, T. (2006). From aesthetics to pedagogy and back: rethinking the works of Theodor Adorno. *Interactions: UCLA Journal of Education and Information Studies*, 2(1): 1–17.

Von Humboldt, W. (2000[1793–1794]). Theory of Bildung ["Theorie der Bildung des Menschens"]. In: I. Westbury, S. Hopmann, & K. Riquarts (Eds.), *Teaching as a Reflective Practice. The German Didaktik Tradition* (pp. 57–61). Mahwah, NJ: Lawrence Erlbaum.

CHAPTER FOUR

A psychoanalytically orientated clinical approach in education science

Claudine Blanchard-Laville and
Philippe Chaussecourte

Introduction

The existence of educational sciences in the French university system dates from 1967. Education science currently has the status of a fully autonomous university discipline with the legitimacy to hire its own teaching and research staff. Studies in the field start in the third year of the bachelor's degree—what in France is called the *licence*—and extend to the doctoral level. There are some 14,000 students in the discipline with teaching and research staff numbering around 500.

All the educational sciences programmes in France have components of psychology and applied sociology linked to education, and quantitative and qualitative methodologies. The programmes also very frequently contain courses in pedagogy, the history of education, educational ideologies and/or studies of educational systems and institutional approaches to teaching and evaluation. There are also often courses in the history and philosophy of education, anthropology, comparative studies in education and didactics, as well as a great variety of optional subjects that are often linked to a local context.

It could be said that the education sciences form a sort of disciplinary hub in the same way that the medical and political sciences and, in recent years, psychology, do. Recently in France, a new approach has emerged in the field of the education sciences that has involved the development of what we call a clinical approach with a psychoanalytical orientation. Before offering a definition of what the clinical approach involves, we need to say something about the links that already exist between psychoanalysis and pedagogy.

The connections between psychoanalysis and pedagogy

There are many undeniable connections between psychoanalysis and pedagogy, particularly if one considers broader and "humanising" connotations of "education". We make specific reference to a text by Freud, *The Future of an Illusion* (Freud, 1927c), which was the source of great debate in France in the educational milieu of the 1980s. In fact, education, understood in the sense of pedagogy, made its entrance quite early into the history of psychoanalysis; the two domains were understood to be closely connected. In 1908, the question of the application of psychoanalysis to pedagogy was posed for the first time by Sandor Ferenczi at the First International Congress of Psychoanalysis in Salzburg (Ferenczi, 1908 (1968)). Freud, too, suggests a link between psychoanalysis and education, directly, several times in different texts, which are cited here in the chronological order of their first editions: "Introduction to Pfister's *The Psycho-analytic Method*" (Freud, 1913b); "The educational interest of psycho-analysis", also in 1913, in this case in the review *Scientia* (Freud, 1913j, pp. 189–192); "Some reflections on schoolboy psychology" (Freud, 1914f); in the Preface to August Aichhorn's book, *Wayward Youth* (Freud, 1925f); and in an excerpt from the 34th Lecture of the *New Introductory Lectures on Psycho-analysis* (Freud, 1933a). One other noteworthy indication of the potential importance of linking the fields is found in the *Review of Psychoanalytical Pedagogy*, which lasted for a period of eleven years (from 1926–1937) in Berlin and Zurich (Cifali & Moll, 1985; Milhaud-Cappe, 2007). It is also worth mentioning that Anna Freud, who was a teacher (from 1914 to 1920), contributed several articles to the *Review*.

Since the creation of educational sciences in France in 1967, some university-based researchers in the discipline have contributed to the development of the psychoanalysis–education theme. A number of them are committed to using psychoanalytical knowledge to shed light on the unconscious dimension of pedagogical processes. They are, of course, aware of the questions and doubts that exist about the application of psychoanalytic notions and concepts outside the field of classic psychoanalytical practice. In 2005, Blanchard-Laville, Chaussecourte, Hatchuel, and Pechberty published, in the *Revue Française de Pédagogie,* an evaluation of the epistemological case for using psychoanalysis in research on teaching and learning. This provided a range of francophone research influenced by psychoanalysis since 1987. Prior to this publication, another evaluative summary (Filloux, 1987) focused on the whole period from the beginning of psychoanalysis. In 2009, some of these epistemological questions were revisited (Chaussecourte, 2009a) and we are presently working on a publication entitled "Psychanalyse, éducation et formation" commissioned by the publishers Dunod. We are, therefore, strongly engaged in the development of the movement to connect psychoanalytic insights to education and have contributed the notion of a clinical approach with a psychoanalytical orientation to this process.

A psychoanalytically informed, clinical approach to the educational sciences

Our understanding of the "clinical approach" corresponds to the meaning the social sciences generally attribute to the term: that is, a methodological style and, more widely, a way of knowing. In discussions with practitioners in the fields of the medical and health sciences, with reference to the notion of the "clinical", it seems that there are recurrent difficulties arising from different definitions of the term and the cultural diversity to which they relate. When the term clinical psychology was introduced in France (Lagache, 1949), psychiatrists, referring to the etymological sense of the adjective "clinical" (what is observable at the patient's bedside), felt an attempt was being made to appropriate aspects of their professional field. In addition, within medicine, clinical psychiatry was obliged to redefine and reconsider its position in ways that might be considered more "genuinely scientific". At the same time, the distinctions and similarities between clinical psychiatry and clinical psychology are more familiar to psychiatrists and clinical psychologists (who regularly encounter one another in health-care institutions, for instance), if not necessarily clear to other researchers or a wider public.

To clarify, for us, when we are considering a psychoanalytically orientated clinical method, our focus is primarily on the unconscious mind—unconscious here being understood from a psychoanalytic perspective. The subject in psychoanalysis is a kind of theoretical construction, whose unconscious prevents him or her from being totally "master in his own house" (Freud, 1916–1917). This is a subject whose mind has many demands, impulses, phantasies, and its own mechanisms of defence. To understand the subject, the clinician-researcher must base, in large part, their understanding in psychoanalytical theory and case study. Even though, as in the case of the educational sciences, the situations being dealt with are different from conventional psychoanalysis, the clinician–researcher must work intuitively, drawing on both theoretical and practical understanding, and cultivating what can be called the "third ear" (Reik, 1976). Thus, a special sensitivity is required in cultivating awareness and understanding mental phenomena.

When the clinician–researcher leaves the structure of the psychoanalytic space, they encounter more of a social dimension. The subjects they deal with might have difficulties in their complex professional lives, and their responses and thoughts need to be analysed; or the subjects, by being members of professional groups, institutions, or other organisations, might struggle with unconscious processes that are a feature of collective life, too. These unconscious processes can develop, without the individual necessarily being aware, in the group as well as in individual minds. We need to remember that talking about unconscious processes, in the Freudian sense, not only applies to the unconscious, in the general meaning of the term, that which is unknown or hidden, but also to processes whose effects are unknown to subjects themselves. Those processes, even when discovered, or when subjects are partially aware of them, might continue to influence behaviours with a power and intensity which remains obscure or uncontrollable.

Objectives and specificities of psychoanalytically orientated clinical research

Our clinical approach to research, based on the previous rationale, centres on one or more people in dynamic interaction. The first objective is to understand the basic dynamics of psychological functioning in such interactions. According to this perspective, the clinician–researcher watches and listens attentively to the speeches and behaviours of the subjects s/he is trying to investigate in order to observe and describe individual experience. The clinician–researcher uses clinical interviews, clinical observation, case analysis, clinical groups, etc. to this end. One of the specific dimensions of the clinical approach is the consideration of the position and role of the clinician–researcher in relation to the observed subject. This interaction creates a tension that might get in the way of the research relationship. Then, s/he is in a space of intersubjectivity: in a position that Revault d'Allonnes (1999) has defined, appropriately, as "privileged and fragile" at one and the same time. Contrary to other scientific approaches, where the contribution of the subjects at the heart of research can be minimised or controlled, the clinical approach values the subjects' subjective engagement and the effects of this in terms, for instance, of the countertransference effect on the researcher (Devereux, 1967). This subjective engagement provides a useful resource for building important knowledge. The subjectivity of the researcher is completely integrated as part of the investigation: it is "grist to the mill" for studying psychic phenomena between people. However, it should also be noted that there are differences of opinion (as in psychoanalysis more widely) about the importance to be attached to analysing the countertransference (Green, 2002; Widlöcher & Miller, 2003). Another dimension of the clinical approach is that the subject is regarded as a whole, distinct person. None the less, the approach does not abandon all thought of generalisation. It can identify, from singular cases, mental mechanisms or mental organisation that might be common across a number of cases, and move towards a conclusion that they can be ubiquitous phenomena.

Our research is, thus, not about applying psychoanalysis directly to educational studies, but, rather, about constructing a new approach, supported by epistemological enquiry. And it is important to underline the fact that praxis and theorising are strongly, and dialectically, linked together. Our approach allows us to discover the way psychic processes can organise themselves and influence a subject in professional situations: as such, our studies generate hypotheses about the consequences of this for professional functioning. Castelnau's and Bastin's case studies below (Chapters Five and Six, respectively) illustrate our approach to research with reference to their classroom experiences. The studies were developed at the Paris Ouest Nanterre University, France, among the team of the Clinique du rapport au savoir.

The contribution of Claudine Blanchard-Laville is at a clinical and theoretical level. She makes use of Bion's ideas and has found important ways of thinking about the roots of the capacity to think and learn (Blanchard-Laville, 1996). Significantly, she offers several key notions to describe psychic aspects particular to the teaching environment: such as the notion of the mental space of the classroom, the idea of didactic holding, and the concept of the didactic transfer. She has been able to show in her research that, in relation to the teacher's learning, his/her psychic positioning in the teaching profession, and/or to his/her subject, in the didactic transfer, is of crucial importance (Blanchard-Laville, 2011a).

It is very important to recognise professional mental anxiety derived from the "simple" business of building and maintaining these didactical links. To be a teacher, you must, day after day, be connected: at first, to pupils, and later to their parents; then to colleagues from the institution, and to the hierarchy of the institution. Such a job requires a person to engage in intersubjective and unconscious relations of diverse types and to maintain these relations for many hours. The groups of pupils might not be like us, are not as we expected and hoped them to be; but, on the contrary, they might confront and confuse the teacher in her role. As teachers, we need to learn how to react and how to defend ourselves when facing such pupil reactions. These interactions and responses are significant: partly because relations and their muddles are ubiquitous; partly because, for we teachers, in our social role, they are an inevitable part of enabling learners to enter into a relationship to knowledge, and/or to the knowledge we have "chosen" to teach, and of which we are the representatives. In the teaching space, the way we connect to others, and the connection built up in our own psychic development, will find expression: it will reveal what is deeply inside us in relation to ourselves, but also to others. Blanchard-Laville, as noted, terms this the didactic transfer: the particular way each teacher projects this double connection into the teaching mental space; that is his/her own connection to knowledge and his/her own connection to the group of pupils. These dynamics will give a particular tone to the atmosphere of a classroom. They can also be a source of misunderstanding (Chaussecourte, 2009b). In addition, beyond these intersubjective "dual" interactions with each pupil, we need to take into account the group dimension that all teachers face: something that teachers can ignore, especially in the first years of their teaching career (Yelnik, 2006). However, teachers have to build a good enough psychic envelope to assure a didactic holding which is sufficiently secure for their pupils. This is essential if pupils are to negotiate successfully their ambivalent relations with the subject being taught (Blanchard-Laville, 2001).

We shall now discuss the formative practices of the clinician–researchers that are fundamental in the clinical approach. We have developed two types of group situations in the clinically orientated training of professionals who work in caring, in the teaching profession, and in social work. Some groups have the objective of encouraging professionals to analyse their own practice, immediately after their professional activity, and using their subjective states as a key resource. Others have the objective of understanding different forms of subjective experience and response, but through psychoanalytic observation of other practitioners.

Frameworks and understanding in professional practice analysis groups

In the groups of practice analysis (the type of group that Anne Bastin and Laure Castelnau describe below), each of the professionals can offer to tell a story about a recent situation in his/her professional practice that might be giving concern. First, the participant presents his/her version of the situation to the group. Then, the group asks questions, the objective of which is to clarify the facts and to develop the story in more detail or depth. Third, group participants will form some hypothesis and propose some connections—between the situation and their own more personal experience, for instance—which will allow the person presenting to begin to engage with some of the underlying issues and the consequences of any decisions taken. The presenter might feel both reassured—thanks to empathy shown by the group—and also decentred because of the questions posed. But this also provides opportunities to engage with what might be underlying aspects of his/her professional functioning. The exchanges within the group can help him/her to progressively distance him/herself from the situation, and to understand more of what might inhibit effective functioning. Two or three situations are presented in each session. During the following meeting, each of the presenters can, if they wish, revisit their situation and any progress that might have been made between the two sessions.

This group process is underpinned by a set of rules which are made explicit at the first session and whose role is essentially to guarantee that everyone's words are welcomed without being judged and/or disrespected. Everyone is free to participate and can bring to the session a story about a situation, as long as s/he accepts that s/he needs to attend the sessions regularly. No written notes are taken. There is a strong insistence that participants are not judgemental, but build on what they felt when listening to the story. Moreover, the confidentiality and the anonymity of the persons and situations are strictly contained within the group, and participants are asked not to discuss this outside the group. The group sessions are not recorded.

Therefore, a process of transformation of professional behaviour can be achieved when the work of collaborative thinking in the group is done, and based on an iteratively developing understanding of professional situations. It is important that the frame established by the group leader contains the emotions that might emerge in the stories: this provides emotional care for the professionals who participate (Blanchard-Laville, 2008). The testimonials from many of those who have participated indicate how the work can lead to a form of lightening of the mental weight they have to carry in their daily working life. Consequently, their sense of professionalism is able to grow, since it becomes less affected by anxiety that can, sometimes, easily overwhelm.

These spaces for the clinical analysis of practice are ones where the professional experience of participants is in transition: they are spaces where new intersubjective experience can be lived as participants articulate different, developing senses of their professional subjectivity and share their thoughts and feelings about this, over time, which can, in turn, reinforce a positive dynamic.

It could be said that these places might be where professionals have an opportunity to access a kind of professional depressive position, in a Kleinian sense, where complexity and ambivalence can be tolerated. Alternatively, when people are on their own, in their place of work, they are pushed into more of a paranoid–schizoid position, where tension and conflicting thoughts can lead to "scapegoating" or idealisation, not least because of provocations in the external environment, which can be experienced as abusive. Experiences of sharing their emotions and feelings in the group works according to an appropriate rhythm: as situations are engaged with and revisited, in slower and mindful ways. Sensitivity towards the rhythm of the group allows participants to restore some sense of inner security. The work is not based simply on positive reinforcement, repression, or the denial of difficulties. The professional who shares his/her experience can recognise the deep emotions that can come to the surface in a moment of storytelling and group exploration, and this is where containment by the group leader is so important.

The sharing of subjective experience by each professional is also part of the second approach we want to describe. This has the objective of training people for psychoanalytic observation work (Houzel, 1995).

Psychoanalytic observation training

The main idea that shapes this approach is to allow participants to feel and elaborate their subjective responses when they observe a particular situation. The selected site for the observation is a teaching situation, essentially because, for the trainers among the academic participants of the course, such observation work can encourage rethinking about their own relation to knowledge. This relation to knowledge is particularly energised for the majority of those who take the opportunity to return to study in the university.

The main organisational principles of the approach are as follows: first, each participant in the group (there are about a dozen people), agrees to observe a teacher for one hour. The observation is done without notes being taken, without visual or sound recording, and without the collection of any other materials. Second, the observer writes a report after the observation, as precisely as possible, about all that has been observed, giving details too about his/her own feelings and any associations s/he might have had. Third, the report is read in a seminar supervised by an "education clinician" and an elaboration of the possible psychic dimensions takes place. This process is based on the phases of infant observation developed by the psychoanalyst Esther Bick, at the Tavistock Clinic in London (Bick, 1964) and has been adapted by Chaussecourte (2003).

Our approach is designed to adapt to the university context, with reference to the type of participants—professionals involved in care, teaching, and social work—and the need to operate during one semester. The objective, which can be described as "psychoanalytic", is to discern some of the psychic qualities of a teacher, which might have been unconsciously mobilised in her relationship, for instance, to the subject she teaches (in this case, mathematics). The objective is also to engage with the didactic transfer (Chaussecourte, 2006a) by observing and writing reports on a regular basis, preferably at the same time and the same day each week over a prolonged period, thereby enabling some of the psychic phenomena involved to be identified and thought about.

Within the observational method, some variations can be noticed. The more common have to do with the choice of subject taught, the level of the class, or type of institution. The variations are questioned within the group and very often before the observation takes place. More subtle variations can appear. Observers will notice different things, including the non-verbal elements of situations. They might notice particular features, for example, the clothes people wear, or the noises and smells of a situation, alongside the positions and postures of different characters, and might also note some variations in the vocabulary used in the identifications of the observer (as pupil, teacher, or parent). The observers will be able to notice these variations within the group. The additional observations of other group members can enable a participant to appreciate more of their own style of mental functioning, with all their regularities and particularities.

The last point we want to make about such a training approach is to underline how important the three phases are to elaborating clinical understanding. Houzel linked these three phases characterising Bick's original observational approach with infants—and which are inherent and carefully respected in our work—to the three successive phases of activity of thinking as explained by Freud (1911b). Freud defines three functions: attention, memory, and judgement. According to him, the phases define the activity of thinking itself and precede a fourth phase: action. It is easy to associate the three functions of thinking with the three phases of the observation of babies as well as the work of groups: the hour or act of observation corresponds to the function of attention, the writing of the report corresponds to the function of memory, the weekly update corresponds to forming judgements (Houzel, 1989, p. 34).

To conclude, the theoretical research and the clinical structure for professionals described in this chapter come together in a distinct diploma: the Développement de Compétences en Formation d'Adultes-Formation à l'Intervention et à l'Analyse des Pratiques (Development of Abilities to Train Adults—Training to Intervene and Analyse Practice). This university training, where for more than ten years the psychoanalytical clinical approach has been nurtured, is about the transmission of research ideas but also about learning from experience (Blanchard-Laville, 2011b). Our objective, using the framework, is to train existing professionals, to help them find ways of relating their new understanding to their professional practice, and to constantly re-create and/or invent clinical approaches which can sustain them in their roles and in managing the intense emotional and psychic demands made on them in their work.

References

Bick, E. (1964). Notes on infant observation in psycho-analytic training. *International Journal of Psycho-Analysis, 45*: 558–566.

Blanchard-Laville, C. (1996). Aux sources de la capacité de penser et d'apprendre. A propos des conceptions théoriques de W. R. Bion. In J. Beillerot, C. Blanchard-Laville, & N. Mosconi (Eds.), *Pour une clinique du rapport au savoir* (pp. 17–49). Paris: L'Harmattan.

Blanchard-Laville, C. (2001). *Les enseignants, entre plaisir et souffrance*. Paris: PUF.

Blanchard-Laville, C. (2008). Effets d'un cadre clinique groupal sur le travail du penser des participants. Approche psychanalytique. In: M. Cifali & F. Giust Desprairies (Eds.), *Formation clinique et travail de la pensée* (pp. 87–105). Bruxelles: De Boeck.

Blanchard-Laville, C. (2011a). À l'écoute des enseignants. *Violences dans le lien didactique Revue de Psychothérapie Psychanalytique de Groupe, 55* (Angoisse et violences dans les groupes, les familles et les institutions): 147–162.

Blanchard-Laville, C. (2011b). De la transmission à la professionnalisation. Le pari de la clinique d'orientation psychanalytique dans une formation d'analyste de pratiques à l'université. In: M. Cifali & T. Périlleux (Eds.), *Les métiers de la relation malmenés* (pp. 85–100). Paris: L'Harmattan.

Blanchard-Laville, C., Chaussecourte, P., Hatchuel, F., & Pechberty, B. (2005). Recherches cliniques d'orientation psychanalytique dans le champ de l'éducation et de la formation. *Revue Française de Pédagogie, 151*: 111–162.

Chaussecourte, P. (2003). Observations cliniques en sciences de l'éducation. Microanalyses et observations directes de pratiques d'enseignant(e)s de mathématiques. Unpublished Thèse de doctorat, Paris X Nanterre, Nanterre.

Chaussecourte, P. (2006). Dans la classe de Mona: une observation clinique directe d'une enseignante de mathématiques. In: J.-S. Morvan (Ed.), *Espaces éducatifs et thérapeutiques: approches cliniques d'orientation psychanalytique* (pp. 129–157). Paris: Fabert.

Chaussecourte, P. (2009a). Approche clinique d'orientation psychanalytique. Réflexions d'après-coup. Unpublished Note de synthèse d'habilitation à diriger des recherches, Université Paris Ouest Nanterre La Défense, Nanterre.

Chaussecourte, P. (2009b). Le transfert didactique, un faux ami? In: C. Cohen & N. Sayac (Eds.), *Questionner l'implicite – Les méthodes de recherche en didactiques* (pp. 137–144). Lille: Presses Universitaires du Septentrion.

Cifali, M., & Moll, J. (1985). *Pédagogie et psychanalyse*. Paris: Dunod.

Devereux, G. (1967). *De l'angoisse à la méthode dans les sciences du comportement*. Paris: Flammarion, 1980.

Ferenczi, S. (1908). Psychanalyse et pédagogie. In: *Psychanalyse* (Œuvres complètes – Tome I 1908–1912) (pp. 51–56). Paris: Payot, 1968.

Filloux, J.-C. (1987). Psychanalyse et pédagogie ou d'une prise en compte de l'inconscient dans le champ pédagogique. *Revue française de pédagogie, 81*: 69–102.

Freud, S. (1911b). Formulations on the two principles of mental functioning. *S.E., 12*: 218–226. London: Hogarth.

Freud, S. (1913b). Introduction to Pfister's *The Psycho-analytic Method. S.E., 12*: 327–331). London: Hogarth.

Freud, S. (1913j). The claims of psycho-analysis to scientific interest. *S.E.*, *13*: 165–192. London: Hogarth.

Freud, S. (1914f). Some reflections on schoolboy psychology. *S.E.*, *13*: 241–244. London: Hogarth.

Freud, S. (1916–1917). *Introductory Lectures on Psycho-analysis*. *S.E.*, *16*. London: Hogarth.

Freud, S. (1925f). Preface to Aichhorn's *Wayward Youth*. *S.E.*, *19*: 273–277. London: Hogarth.

Freud, S. (1927c). *The Future of an Illusion*. *S.E.*, 141–197. London: Hogarth.

Freud, S. (1933a). 34th Lecture: Explanations, applications and orientations. In: *New Introductory Lectures in Psycho-analysis*. *S.E.*, *19*: 136–157. London: Hogarth.

Green, A. (2002). Démembrement du contre-transfert. In: J.-J. Baranes, F. Sacco, M. Aisenstein, S. Bolognini, F. Duparc, A. Ferro, A. Ferruta, & F. Guignard (Eds.), *Inventer en psychanalyse, construire et interpréter* (pp. 131–161). Paris: Dunod.

Houzel, D. (1989). Penser les bébés, réflexions sur l'observation des nourrissons. *Revue de médecine psychosomatique*, *19*: 27–38.

Houzel, D. (1995). Observation des bébés et psychanalyse, point de vue épistémologique. In: M.-B. Lacroix & M. Monmayrant (Eds.), *Les liens d'émerveillement. L'observation des nourrissons selon Esther Bick et ses applications* (pp. 108–116). Ramonville Saint-Agne: érès.

Lagache, D. (1949). Psychologie clinique et méthode clinique. *L'évolution psychiatrique*, *1*: 155–178.

Milhaud-Cappe, D. (2007). *Freud et le mouvement de pédagogie psychanalytique 1908–1937*. Paris: Vrin.

Reik, T. (1976). *Ecouter avec la troisième oreille; L'expérience intérieure d'un psychanalyste*. Paris: Epi.

Revault d'Allonnes, C. (1999). Psychologie clinique et démarche clinique. In: C. Revault d'Allonnes (Ed.), *La démarche clinique en sciences humaines* (pp. 17–33). Paris: Dunod.

Widlöcher, D., & Miller, J.-A. (2003). Débat. Psychiatrie, sciences humaines. *Neurosciences*, *1*(1): 10–18.

Yelnik, C. (2006). *Face au groupe, discours de professeurs*. Paris: L'Harmattan.

CHAPTER FIVE

Zohar's late arrival: a clinical analysis of teaching practice

Laure Castelnau and Claudine Blanchard-Laville

The subject of my (LC) research is the transmission of unconscious phenomena from the teacher's point of view in the teaching space. The focus is on understanding how the introspective
work I undertook with a clinical analysis of professional practice
group, followed by written work, enabled me to analyse a professional situation which had concerned me as a teacher. The research
processes presented here took place over several periods of time.

I begin by presenting what is involved in belonging to a clinical
analysis of professional practice group, and by describing the main
elements of the process that supported my research over the three
periods of time elaborated below. Later, I develop hypotheses about
what might have been played out between the teacher I was and the
pupil I call Zohar.

The clinical analysis of professional practice group

This form of clinical analysis of work-based problems, conceptually
derived from the ideas and practice of psychoanalyst Michael Balint,
is outlined in Chapter Four, above, by Blanchard-Laville and Chausse-

courte. The group meetings take place every three weeks and each lasts two and a half hours. The group is directed by a leader specifically trained for this work within the framework of a professional Masters degree. During each meeting, two or three participants explain professional situations, which are then explored as a group. The speakers are encouraged to bring as much spontaneity and improvisation to their accounts as possible, factual details and inner feelings are solicited, with the other participants being allowed to request clarification, in order to throw light on the institutional context and what is professionally at stake within the situation described. At the instigation of the leader, the group then moves to a phase of associations, encouraging, wherever possible, links to the professional situation described in the teaching as well as the personal history of the speaker. At the following meeting, those participants who have described situations are invited to comment on their work experiences since the last discussion, and to share with the group the emotions, introspection, and ideas which have stemmed from the previous meeting's work. One characteristic of the setting derives from a hypothesis that, between the two meetings, the participant continues his or her psychic work, often unconsciously, which can result in subsequent modification of his or her link to the events being studied.

Each participant committed to this way of working, in giving an account of their professional situation to the group, benefits from the opportunity of understanding how these problematic personal practice experiences can be understood by making specific links with self and others, and by examining the types of psychic organisation underlying professional behaviours. These elaborations permit professionals to "unearth", momentarily or in the longer term, their professional functioning in those most significant scenarios which we all tend to repeat in personal or professional life, becoming established for each of us as an unconscious and seductive core within our professional behaviour (Blanchard-Laville, 2011, p. 140). During participation in this group, I talked several times about difficult situations I had experienced with a pupil in my class, a boy of eleven whom I call Zohar. He had problems with learning, in his attitude to school, and in his relationships with other children and adults in the school.

The research work

During the year following my participation in the professional analysis group, I wrote a journal "One year with Zohar in my class", written when the boy was no longer my pupil. It is organised chronologically from September to June and presented as a record of real events (those I remembered at the time), mainly class incidents that had caused tension between Zohar and myself. I refer to the period of writing the journal following that year as time t_1. I then wrote a second document, based on the re-reading of this account, using a more theoretical perspective, in an attempt to understand the nature and effects of psychical processes during that school year. The first re-working of the journal, that is the second written draft, becomes time t_2, and the present, during this analysis of the two former periods with a later perspective on events, I refer to as time t_3.

The research material

When I re-read my journal from the viewpoint of a follow-up, in order to consider theoretical perspectives, I decided that I should leave it just as it was, as a testimony to certain events occurring during time t_1. Any interference entailed the potential risk of modifying the content of my account, rather than using it to chronicle my changing understanding of my relationship with Zohar. This is why I chose to add in t_2 so as to distinguish any new text from the original. Re-reading, and my engagement with others in the analysis group, had initiated some important changes in comprehension that could be clearly chronicled by reference to the different texts.

In taking up this work again in this chapter, in time t_3, I intend to study certain elements in the two distinct writing times, t_1 and t_2, and to try out certain hypotheses on the place each of them represents in my psychic elaborations, at their time of writing, on just what was involved for me as the teacher then, within the classroom.

Arrival of Zohar in my class

The initial journal (t_1) starts by recounting the arrival of Zohar in my class.

Zohar arrived in my class several days after the beginning of term. He was late. The headmaster accompanied him, with his mother, and introduced us briefly prior to the new pupil settling in. A table and space had to be found.

That particular year (. . .), in order to free up a teaching job, we had to distribute all the CM2 pupils into two classes. Every day that passed seemed to bring a new pupil at that level: we were approaching thirty pupils per class, a limit which seemed symbolically impossible to exceed (. . .) This uncertain situation worried me.

The start-up activities of the class had already been completed. The pupils had received their exercise books, the information forms to fill in, the school rules, and time had been spent discussing what we would do together throughout the year. Zohar arrived while the pupils were at work. We took the time to get to know each other, then the pupils continued working while I helped Zohar settle in. I gave him exercise books and invited him to get to work.

These three paragraphs at the beginning of the journal indicate from the start my place in this story: I give the account of the school teacher, an account listing the facts and concentrating on the difficulties met, difficulties due to the overloading of classes and the pupil missing the start of term. These preliminary paragraphs underline, for the teacher that I was, the real constraints that form an obstacle to Zohar's satisfactory integration into his new class.

The constitution of the psychic group package

However, I also say more than that: I show a teacher creating the psychic space in which the class activities will take place. This memory underlines, in a certain way, the usual activities at the start of the new school year. Various kinds of objects are circulated: notebooks, forms, the school rules, which every pupil receives, but which the class then takes time to read together. The personal details of each pupil are recorded in the appropriate forms. As part of this, a group identity is constituted through everyone expressing their needs, which can become a group project at the start of the year. One senses that these objects exchanged are not only material, but that they could constitute in some way psychic objects. Blanchard-Laville, in her work (2001, pp. 221–248), has theorised the constitution by the teacher of what she considers to be a group psychic envelope necessary for the creation of psychic spaces in teaching. According to her, this envelope is "a kind of container, creator of the psychic space of the class, a container both dynamic and an organiser for the psychic turbulences within this space" (ibid., p. 221). This notion of an envelope permits the representation of a matrix within which the teacher concurrently actualises both his or her own relationship with knowledge and his or her links to the pupils. It is proposed (Blanchard-Laville, 2001) that the double link thus established by the teacher in a teaching situation be called a "didactic transfer", using the hypothesis that the link concerned contributes to shaping the psychic space, which affects the pupils' learning, in an individual way, for each teacher.

Blanchard-Laville and her team have concentrated in the main on the conditions for establishing this psychic envelope, and, in particular, on the non-verbal elements emanating from the teacher: the psychic posture, voice, and the subtleties of which it is composed, the manner of looking at pupils, or not looking, which are all elements that can be seen to ensure psychic continuity for them; and conversely, when pupils or the class group do not feel this continuity sufficiently, their capacity for learning is impeded.

Zohar and the psychic teaching space

Zohar's arrival in this context, or, more precisely, my own account in time t_1, seems to constitute an attack on this psychic space. I recall that this pupil arrived "late" and question if his arrival represents some kind of unconscious threat to the group psychic envelope that I was trying to establish.

A year later (t_2), interrogating the journal in the first research text, I wrote:

> My welcome on that day was no doubt brief and lacking in warmth. It seems to me that I failed to distance myself from the unfavourable circumstances surrounding the arrival of Zohar: the staggered arrivals, too many pupils, his being late . . .

The second text, during time t_2, reveals a shift in attitude towards the pupil by the teacher I was: she is still aware of the material conditions surrounding Zohar's arrival, conditions felt to be unfavourable. But she now realises that her welcome to him "lacked warmth". These lines bear witness to a certain conceptual distancing of herself from the difficulty experienced in welcoming this pupil, and an enhanced understanding of what this "poorly welcomed" pupil might be feeling. I hypothesise that a mechanism of projective identification was initially at work. This psychic mechanism was first described by Melanie Klein as a defence mechanism which a person makes use of in order to protect her/himself from anxiety, by unconsciously projecting on to the other some elements s/he is uncomfortable with. Zohar was the repository for a range of anxious projections: he was a threat that needed to be defended against. This psychic mechanism, as Klein noted, exists to protect the person from anxiety. In effect, I was unconsciously projecting on to Zohar some elements I was uncomfortable with. He was a repository for my anxieties about being overwhelmed as a teacher, and also that the class might be overwhelmed, too. Zohar was, therefore, carrying, via projective identification, a great deal of negative energy.

The work in the practical analysis group permitted me to start moving away from the view I then had as the class teacher; the writing of the journal seemed to strengthen the defence mechanisms, with the effect of exonerating me from responsibility for Zohar's difficulties, which were, of course, real. It was later, during time t_2, that a memory of my own schooldays came back to me that, no doubt, helped me to feel empathy for Zohar's difficulties. This is apparent in the second stage of my writing.

> When I was 14, I joined a new school when the family moved. After a week, just when I was beginning to feel accustomed to the new situation, I had to change classes in order to continue a Latin option. I tried to convince my parents to abandon the language in order to avoid the change, but they refused, so that, unfortunately, I had to join the new class where it took time to integrate and, above all, to start working.

This memory shows two moments of separation, one of which remains in the background. It is the second separation that appears difficult, whereas the first school separation with which I was confronted when joining a new school is mentioned only briefly. It looks as though the second separation was "catastrophic" for me, whereas

I had been able to absorb, emotionally and psychically, the difficulty of the first separation.

The return of this school memory, while I was trying to reflect on Zohar's arrival at the school, no doubt permitted me to reach a different understanding of the feelings of strangeness experienced by this pupil on his arrival. The psychic elaboration I undertook during time t_2, by including the account from the journal, allowed me to reach a certain capacity for empathy towards Zohar's feelings by making contact with a split part of me, the pupil part.

But, in time t_3, I make another hypothesis: through a projective identification mechanism, might I be projecting elements of my own psychic reality into this situation, putting Zohar in the role of having to carry my part of the "pupil in difficulty" in a situation of separation, just as though, unconsciously, I was asking him to (re)live this traumatic situation in my place?

The account I give in time t_1 of the "creation" of the class, in its first few days, should be examined in the light of the above hypothesis: might it be an idealised account of a group where all doubts, all sufferings, are split off and projected on to one pupil, who, in some way, becomes a scapegoat for the whole group? Thus, the group could enjoy unmitigated pleasure. The time t_2 account shows that my "capacity for reverie", as theorised by Bion, and to which I will return below, is threatened by this pupil and indicates that the first account I wrote embodies the attack I felt.

The relationship with knowledge

I wish to return to the question of the place I gave Zohar, in the context of the links I established with this pupil. In conceptualising *didactic transfer*, Blanchard-Laville (2001, pp. 193–219) theorised the dual links between teacher and class, links with the pupils, but also links with the knowledge to be taught. I quote here an extract from the time t_1 journal concerning Zohar's relationship with knowledge and the hypotheses that might be inferred from the teacher's relation with knowledge.

> The beginning of term was forgotten. Rapidly, it became apparent that Zohar was not following the class rhythm. He seemed lost, often

complained that he did not have what he needed to work, in particular
the necessary sheets of paper. As this repeated itself, I took a closer look.
I discovered that he had only one exercise book where everything was
piled in together, one thing following another and in turn, history, geography, and science, with no separations. So it was impossible for him to
trace documents, texts, maps, summaries . . . I looked at this exercise book
unable to believe my eyes. Nothing seemed to make sense. I recall panick-
ing: I wondered if this boy really had a place in the class.

When I re-examined the journal in time t_2, I wrote:

Zohar came from another town. He had not finished the year in his former
school: I know now that he left well before the summer holidays, and
ignorant of the fact that he would not be returning. Zohar used the same
exercise book for history, geography, and science, whereas other pupils
passed from one exercise book to another. History can be understood as a
subject with markers in time, whereas geography is applied to markers in
space. It seems to me now that that the "history" of Zohar's family had
disrupted his "geography": the family had moved rapidly because of
personal circumstances judged serious enough to justify the departure. I
make the hypothesis that history and geography are traumatically mixed
for Zohar.

In the journal, Zohar's requests concern what the teacher does *not*
give him: "the necessary sheets of paper". I now conceive this to be a
form of paranoid–schizoid functioning, in which the exercise book
and the bits of paper have a central place. The exercise book serves
here as a passive receptacle: it fails to hold Zohar's objects of knowledge, and even less to transform them. There is no space here for
"maternal reverie", which undermines any capacity to learn new
things. The capacity for reverie, as theorised by Bion (1962), is the
function exercised by the mother towards her baby: first, when she
absorbs the elements the baby splits off and projects into her, in an
attempt to be rid of the feelings of anguish, hate, and psychic fragmentation. Second, when she is not destroyed by the baby's anger, but
shows that she is capable of converting the projected beta elements
into detoxified alpha elements. This theory of the capacity for reverie,
where learning takes place, is transposed here into a function that
the teacher can use with her pupils. For Zohar, the beta elements
remained, untransformed, and the reverie in the learning environment does not take place.

Blanchard-Laville, coming from a Bionian perspective, emphasises the importance of understanding of "the psychic subsoil in which a subject's relation to knowledge takes root" (1996, p. 21). In this memory, it is indeed on the stage of knowledge that "something" is played out between Zohar and the teacher. I sense that the very objects of the knowledge transmitted—the history and geography—are "red-hot". They are impossible to handle, since they touch closely on deep-seated anxieties in the pupil, both personal and familial. Transmission of new knowledge becomes impossible in such a situation. In the teaching space, a scenario is played out between teacher and pupil exchanging muddled requests and defensive anxiety (Blanchard-Laville, 2001, p. 151).

Conclusion

In this chapter, I have attempted to show that Zohar's presence threatened my ability to contain the group and constituted an unconscious threat to the group psychic envelope that I, as a teacher, wished to create for my class. When I expressed, in the original journal, my own question about whether this boy had "his place in my class", I no doubt had a negative answer in my head. Zohar might have communicated to me some aspects of fear, maybe of failure and unacceptability, as well as messiness in relation to the situation he found himself in. I have attempted to show how his unconscious fears might have reverberated with fears which belonged to me. Blanchard-Laville emphasises that teachers should interrogate their professional practice and personal history, and how it could get muddled with those of pupils, in particular by engaging in the clinical analysis of professional practices. I have attempted to show how, thanks to the various support structures, I was able to develop, in a particular way, my own "capacity for maternal reverie", after the event, by working on reworking my understanding of the complex interactions taking place during that school year. In this way, I was able, not least by writing this chapter, to restore meaning to previously enigmatic school situations. This ability mirrors some of the acceptance and support I received from the tutoring and group feedback over the whole period. This acceptance and support enabled me to reintroject certain feelings that I had been unable to metabolise alone, and to become, in turn, more capable of activating my alpha function.

References

Bion, W. R. (1962). *Learning From Experience*. London: Karnac.

Blanchard-Laville, C. (1996). Aux sources de la capacité de penser et d'apprendre. À propos des conceptions théoriques de W. R. Bion. In: J. Beillerot, C. Blanchard-Laville, & N. Mosconi (Eds.), *Pour une clinique du rapport au savoir* (pp. 17–49). Savoir et formation. Paris: L'Harmattan.

Blanchard-Laville, C. (2001). *Les enseignants entre plaisir et souffrance*. Paris, PUF.

Blanchard-Laville, C. (2011). Pour un accompagnement clinique groupal du travail enseignant. *Nouvelle Revue de Psychosociologie*, 1(11): 131–147.

CHAPTER SIX

Margot's red shoes: when psychic reality challenges teaching

Anne Bastin and Philippe Chaussecourte

This chapter highlights how psychoanalytic theory can be used in the study and understanding of the relationships and psychic processes at work in the educational experience of a primary school teacher. The material has been discussed and analysed between Philippe and myself, Anne, but I will use the personal pronoun, since much of the writing is mine and derives from a developed process of investigating psychic interactions in the ordinary teaching setting of my own class. While participating in a professional practice analysis group, I have presented situations giving rise to professional anxiety concerning a particular pupil that I call Margot. Her situation was evoking strong echoes in my own personal story. The group gave me the opportunity to work through the unconscious phenomena that resonate between pupil and teacher, generating misunderstandings inherent to the educational setting (Blanchard-Laville, 2001).

In order to deepen my understanding of the psychic phenomena at work, within a university research setting, I devised and implemented an observation framework. This is composed of two complementary processes: writing and talking. The individual writing process consisted of a psychoanalytically informed research monograph based on direct observation of the little girl in my class during a school year.

The talking process refers to the group work, which offered an appropriate space to share professional difficulties, to be listened to, and to disentangle some of the muddle of the teaching situation. I will first describe some theoretical elements for understanding the case study, before presenting the teaching situation, and a particular episode with Margot is analysed.

Theoretical background

My theoretical background is that of French clinical research undertaken within a psychoanalytically informed approach in the field of education and training. As explained in Chapter Four, written by Philippe Chaussecourte and Claudine Blanchard-Laville, this approach acknowledges psychic reality, unconscious phenomena and processes, and attempts to characterise, understand, and explore their expression in educational contexts. The major psychoanalytical concepts that have been used to illuminate the selected episode are Bion's "thought-thinking apparatus", Winnicott's concepts of "good enough mother", "omnipotence", and "self", as well as Klein's "projective identification". These are explained below.

Bion developed the complex notion of thinking as distinct from disparate thoughts, drawing on a model of the digestive system (Bion, 1962). There is insufficient space to discuss this comprehensively, but I will highlight the aspects especially relevant to my study. In order to give a "digestible" summary, I refer to Bion's biographer, Gérard Bléandonu. In his book on Bion's life and work (1990), Bléandonu explains that, as Bion perceived it, when all goes well, and the newborn baby receives milk from the mother and processes it in her/his digestive tract, s/he receives at the same time feelings of security, wellbeing, and love. Yet, when babies become aware of a "missing breast", as inevitably at times they must, they need to evacuate what is now experienced as a "bad breast". In this sense, they will be projecting their intolerable affects or "beta elements" into the mother. If all is well, the mother welcomes and transforms them, using her empathic emotional and conceptual understanding of what her baby is experiencing. In this way, she is exercising her "alpha function", that is, she is making these affects tolerable and so it becomes possible for her baby to reintroject them as digestible "alpha elements". Hence, in the process, with the milk, the infant receives good internal objects. And, if the mother observes that her baby has several needs, she will select the more urgent or important one out of her/his "mess of distress". She will also transmit, at the same time, a way of coping that the newborn baby can internalise, which will, little by little, lead her/him to think for her/himself. In the case study, I give hints on how a teacher might use and develop her "thought-thinking apparatus" in order to cope with the psychic challenges arising in class.

Another important point of theoretical reference is Winnicott (1971), with his concepts of "good enough mother", "omnipotence", and "self". According to Winnicott, the real dependency of a baby on her/his environment is one of the central characteristics that will determine her/his emotional development. He established three stages of dependency: absolute dependency, relative dependency (a stage in which primary school children normally are), and independence. In order for a child to successfully reach the third stage, they need to have been given a "good enough environment" from the beginning of life. The concept of "good enough mother" refers to the capacity of a mother (not necessarily the infant's own) to repeatedly enter into contact with the baby's "omnipotence" and give sense to it. The infant creates the mother's breast (and the world) thanks to omnipotent phantasies, and this illusion is necessary for her/his psychical development. It allows the little one to experience frustration in a constructive way and gradually acquire the reality principle. A mother's adequate adaptation to her infant's needs will strengthen the child's weak ego and enable her/him to symbolise and support the construction of a true self (Winnicott distinguishes between true and false selves: the latter is more of a defensive structure, a kind of false adaptation to relationships and an environment). The function of the self is to organise and integrate experience. Winnicott considers that the true self can already exist in the mother–baby dyad. A defensive structure of the false self also develops with normal as well as pathological aspects. There is always a mix of these elements (Winnicott, 1965, 1968, in Abram, 1996). I will try to demonstrate how providing such a good enough environment can be considered as a significant part of a teacher's task.

Finally, Klein's concept of "projective identification" has proved illuminating in developing the present study. It is important to emphasise the fact that such processes are unconscious. Rycroft (1968) defines projective identification as the

> process by which a person imagines to be inside some object external to himself. This again is a form of defence since it creates the illusion of control over the object and enables the subject to deny his power-lessness over it and to gain vicarious satisfaction from its activities. (ibid., p. 76)

Despite being a defence, it is important to add, following Hanna Segal, that this type of identification has "manifold aims" and

> has its valuable aspects. To begin with, it is the earliest form of empa-thy and it is on projective as well as introjective identification that is based the capacity to "put oneself into another person's shoes". (Segal, 2006[1964], p. 36)

Some aspects of projective identification will appear in the case study analysis.

These concepts belong to the field of psychoanalytical clinical prac-tice and, arguably, therefore, cannot be simply transposed on to the field of education. They are, none the less, invaluable heuristic tools for research on unconscious teaching and learning processes. Some of these concepts have, more specifically, proved fruitful to a better understanding of what transpired between Margot and me, her teacher. Part of the process of elaborating and analysing the problem is now presented, written, as noted, in the first person.

Research process

As a primary school teacher, I have been confronted with professional deadlock and unease that contradicted my conscious behaviour. Within a rigorous research setting, my initial purpose was to give meaning to what was happening in my own classroom. Finding out that some of the phenomena encountered had structural charac-teristics helped me consider the situation more clearly and broadened my questioning. My professional experience has convinced me that unconscious phenomena do not stand waiting quietly outside the classroom door, a fact that affects both teaching and learning abilities.

My observations were recorded in a class log while, in parallel, I was attending a professional practice group in which I could share the difficulties I was facing. The study consisted of a combination of these two complementary processes: the writing and the talking group work. The dynamics of this approach have generated what Balint (2000[1957], p. 301) might have called a "limited though considerable change of personality", a constructive change that has challenged my professional identity and practice.

The writing process

The use of monographs about pupils for training purposes, acknow-ledging the role of the unconscious, has been shaped by Fernand Oury, a primary school teacher and founder of institutional pedagogy, who resisted the idea that schools should be run on a military model (Oury & Vasquez, 1967). The role of writing was of central importance in developing a more psychoanalytically informed understanding, with writing at the core of sense-making in an academic setting.

The core material of my monograph (Bastin, 2009) was a class log on Margot that I carefully kept. Step one consisted in writing down salient facts related to the little girl I observed in the class and in the playground, during a break, or after the class. In step two, when the school day was over, I recorded my spontaneous reactions to these facts, unelaborated feelings and thoughts. Between step two and the next written step, I reported, in my professional practice analysis group, some of the difficulties that emerged in my relationship with Margot, and tried to process them with the group's help. The final step was a rewriting process, through which I reconsidered the situa-tion in question, as well as my understanding of it, in a developed, psychoanalytically informed way. This last phase could have been endless, but I decided to put an end to the rewriting at the close of the school year. The present chapter can, however, be considered a further step in the process: writing this chapter takes into account the previous steps, yet also invites me to re-examine the entire case study.

The group work

In the professional practice analysis group (Blanchard-Laville, 2011), we were invited to share our professional difficulties and voice our emotions and thoughts. It was a group consisting of teachers, social workers, and educators. We used to meet every two months for three hours during the school year. There were eight participants and we did not know each other at work or outside the group. The leader, a highly skilled and qualified facilitator, trained in group analysis, provided an ethical, caring environment. No notes were allowed to be made or used for the presentation of situations. Group rules were agreed and included adherence to confidentiality, mutual respect, and responsibility. The feedback given by the members of the group to the presenter was aimed at increasing the understanding of what might be happening, with factual questions or personal emotional reactions, but no advice given. Each group participant presented over two consecutive sessions. In the first session, the presenter would describe a current incident giving cause for thought or distress. In the following session, s/he would share with the group what had happened between the sessions, both in external reality and on a psychical level. Recalling some elements that had been worked through in the group helped me gain some psychical relief as well as deepen my understanding of my professional difficulties. At that time, I had been teaching in primary schools for nine years, after a long period working for an American bank and the legal department of a large French company. Quite simply, but powerfully, Margot reminded me of my young sister, for whom I had been appointed legal guardian in my early twenties. Personal analysis (a further dimension of the process), my class log, and the professional group—enhanced and consolidated by sustained writing—helped me cope with strong unconscious phenomena activated in my relationship with this little girl.

Background to the case study

In the year that I undertook the study of Margot, the professional environment and the people constituting it were all new to me. The primary school, composed of ten classes, was located in the suburbs of Paris. I was in charge of a Year Three class (children aged seven to eight). In my class, six pupils out of thirty had special educational needs. I began holding one of them, Margot, in my mind from the summer preceding our first school year together: her former teacher drew my attention to this pupil—alongside certain others—as someone needing to be "handled with care" because of a delicate family situation and difficult school experience. Her parents had been denied custody of Margot. Consequently, her elder sister (aged nineteen or twenty) had been designated as Margot's legal protector and they both lived at their grandmother's house. It was the first time in my professional experience that I had encountered a situation like this. Due to her school achievements being considered poor, it had been decided that she would repeat her Year Three with me. The whole year was to become dotted with family events that disrupted the child's schooling. In September, I met Margot's elder sister, whom I will call "Celine". She told me that the judge had chosen her as Margot's legal protector for her "youth capital". In spring, Margot announced that Celine was expecting a baby "on the 24th of July", and that she was living with her boyfriend. Looking very happy, she added: ". . . this way I'll be looking after my little sister!" I did not know clearly who was looking after Margot.

I would also learn that the baby was a boy, a nephew for Margot. Meanwhile, there had been many administrative problems in relation to her, including an issue over school insurance, and also with school lunches, which were managed by the town hall. I asked to meet Margot's grandmother. She spoke about her daughter's (that is, Margot's mother's) problems, as well as about her adult son's handicap and their material dependency on her. She asserted that she was now Margot's legal guardian. This complex background was sometimes reflected in what Margot said. In everyday school life, Margot would speak to me during break, or before and after class, always smiling, confiding events that were often a mix of the dramatic and ordinary. "My mother fell this morning in the kitchen and we called the emergency medical service." Or "Look, my dog put a ball in my schoolbag so that I don't forget her!" Then, she would let the ball roll around in the class during a lesson . . .

An episode with Margot

I now report a very short episode that took place in February of that year.

Step one: factual notes

This morning, Margot looks restless. I see her making large gestures and wanting to speak a lot. We are correcting a maths exercise. Walking between the aisles of tables I notice that she has found the correct answer and quickly conclude that she has understood the lesson. She puts her hand up and talks "nonsense". It makes me unhappy and I send her to the blackboard in order to correct what I believed she had done right in her exercise book. But she walks awkwardly, limping, the red boot on her left foot half on. She looks all bothered, writes something on the blackboard, then turns back to look at me. I am so overwhelmed that I cannot recall what she has written down.

Step two: notes on my immediate reactions and questions

This morning I find it difficult to cope with her agitation and her interventions that I consider inappropriate. I want to give her the opportunity to show herself in the light of a successful pupil and correct an exercise that she had got right, but she accentuates her neglected and "imbalanced" aspect. Perhaps this sends me back to the little girl I once was? Yet, I imagine I had been quite the opposite: invisible, inaudible, but sharing something of this "imbalance". Could Margot be a caricature of the pupil I once was that I was ashamed of? I consider that acting stupid could be a defence. Did she try to provoke, to test something in me, and what? To what extent could I accept her, love her? Or did she have a role to play in front of the class as a pupil repeating her year? Perhaps a parallel can be made between Margot's elder sister and the situation I was once in myself. As a "tutor", would I not want to see this young "plant" grow up straight? (In French, the word *tuteur* means legal guardian, study tutor, and garden stake.)

In the final stage of my study, that is, the reflexive work consisting in writing this chapter, I am now much more aware of the echo between Margot's family story and my own history. Sometimes faint, sometimes strong, it had most probably aroused immediate, empathic feelings towards this little girl and, at the same time, caused much turmoil. Despite being relatively aware of psychic processes, I felt totally disorientated in the face of the unconscious staging of repressed wounds that suddenly burst into an apparently ordinary class situation. Keeping the class log helped to set down on paper the confusion taking hold of me in that situation, which I could not really digest. I liken this material to Bion's "beta elements", which are expelled from me and processed in written words on what I might call the "paper-mother", the blank page. This process of writing, as well as the group, helped me transform chaos into something less strange, more digestible. I gave an account of the particular incident of the shoe to my seminar group because I was struck by my attitude and mixed feelings of guilt, distress, and anger. By the end of the school year, I wrote the following account of the episode.

Next step: a more clinical analysis

> Am I seeing in Margot a younger sister of mine or am I projecting on to this pupil the child I believe I was? I wish that Margot would grow up and stop speaking "nonsense". I would like her to write the correct answer on the blackboard and at the same time I exposed her to possible mockery from the other pupils by not anticipating that she would limp towards the blackboard. Why didn't I simply tell her that her boot was not properly attached without feeling upset? Why didn't I concentrate on the school work? I think I would have acted differently with another child and I dislike this. Regarding the maths exercise, I make the hypothesis that if I had felt I mastered the subject matter better, I would have been more interested in the didactical content and centered on the task that was pushed into the background. What would have happened if it had been a French or an English lesson (subject matters in which I feel more confident and therefore less anxious in front of pupils' difficulties)? The question of the teacher's "link with knowledge" is also raised here (a concept constructed and used in psychoanalytically orientated education studies by the team at Paris Nanterre University, France).

Today's interpretation

The experience shared and developed in this chapter marks a formative turning point in my awareness of the complexity of the teacher's role. After such a process, I believe, in a similar situation, that I would think, feel, and act differently, and would consider other aspects of the interaction and the environment. I would certainly confirm that writing, together with the group analysis, sustained me psychically, enabling me to engage in thinking as well as find a more appropriate professional stance. At first, I did not realise that the link between Margot and me could be seen as projective identification (Klein, 1952): I was seeing her and her family situation through the filter of my own life story. It made me lose grasp of a present reality in which Margot, struggling with my confusion and her own feelings, would accumulate the "mistakes" mentioned above (in talking "nonsense", in going to the blackboard limping, and in not writing an appropriate answer). She was behaving so differently from the child I had imagined her to be, and my reactions were inadequate given what I now consider to be an idealised perception of teachers and teaching. The defence mechanisms at work to protect myself in the class from intrusive emotions and memories that I could not deal with partly comprised this idealisation of the profession, but also of the pupils. There was a profound discrepancy between my phantasies and reality. We can imagine that, in order to assert her individuality, Margot was somehow compelled to exaggerate her clumsiness so that I could see the little girl she really was. I also wonder to what extent her attitude might be identified as self-sabotage.

Yet, I would also add that this unexpected confrontation with "shared reality", as Winnicott calls it, awoke ambivalent feelings in me. I was aware of the affection I had for Margot and my conscious motivation in inviting her to go to the blackboard was to enhance her self-esteem. In fact, I reprimanded her and sent her back to her seat. This was nothing to do with pedagogical matters, neither was it focused on the mathematical task in hand. Similar reactions occurred over the year, events resonating with parts of my own life history, which remained deeply sensitive. There was internal conflict because of feelings of helplessness and inadequacy that Margot evoked alongside a struggle to avoid causing her pain. Sharing and working through the material in an appropriate environment allowed me to learn from it. This is similar to the kind of experiential understanding that Salzberger-Wittenberg, a Kleinian psychoanalyst, tried to convey to a group of teachers during a first course at the Tavistock Clinic in London, on "Aspects of Counselling in Education" (Salzberger-Wittenberg, Williams, & Osborne, 2004):

> Of course, everyone knows about feelings of insecurity, but we tend to pay lip-service to these, hide them, ignore them or ride rough-shod over them. . . . Knowing about them from within ourselves increases

our perceptiveness and understanding of others. It made the group of teachers identify and sympathise with those they taught . . . (p. 5)

I cannot stand completely in Margot's shoes, so to speak, but I can formulate potentially useful interpretative propositions derived from further reflections on the countertransference and transference dynamics in my encounter with Margot. These have taken me to a view that Margot could have been unconsciously in four difficult places, two belonging to reality, and two reflecting her teacher's phantasy. The first two relate to Margot as an actual child and pupil; the others to the teacher's phantasised younger sister or daughter, alongside the "pupil-self" of the teacher (a concept developed by Blanchard-Laville (2001) referring to the pupil whom the teacher phantasises s/he has or might have been). The mix of roles may have been fundamental: I was at the same time the actual teacher and a woman coping with day-to-day reality, as well as, in a sense, the imaginary elder sister and mother to Margot. Furthermore, since unconscious phenomena tend to venture into external reality most powerfully at times of anxiety, it is clear that my fears and expectations unwittingly lay beneath and gave energy to this problematic dynamic. What belonged to me, and what to Margot, had become hopelessly entangled. I agree, in these terms, with Salzberger-Wittenberg's observation, that

> We never completely outgrow infantile wishes and attitudes and they are bound to some extent to invade our private and intimate relationships. It is important, however, that we strive to become aware of them so as to minimize their interference in our professional life. (Salzberger-Wittenberg, Williams, & Osborne, 2004, p. 41)

In becoming more aware, Margot might have been afraid of being abandoned again, or of not being loved by her teacher, and she might have been anxious about failing once more in her school achievements. I recall being anxious about being overwhelmed by the feelings aroused because of Margot's family situation. And I might have feared that I would fail to help her as a teacher. I can imagine that Margot might have been searching for some kind of unconditional love from me, and some form of reparation for her present family situation. As for me, I could have been seeking to offer Margot some of the symbolic reparation she sought, repairing in the process my own past, one being repeated, in all its messiness, in front of my own eyes, and evoking feelings of helplessness and anger. Some of the internal conflicts that we were both confronted by could have been articulated by Margot like this: "I would like my teacher to be a good mother for me but she is not my mother and never will be." Whereas I could have said, "I would like to 'save' Margot but she is neither my little sister nor my daughter and never will be; I cannot and I must not do so." On a more institutional as well as professional level, this has raised the question of a teacher's responsibility: where is the happy medium, the *well-tempered holding* (Blanchard-Laville, 2001), between excessive involvement and undue neglect?

Little by little, all the turmoil subsided. Margot became a pupil among other pupils again, and I, as Winnicott might have described it, became more of an ordinarily failing and mending teacher, analogous to the good enough mother: I hope I now provide a good enough environment for all the pupils again. These changes seem to include, in Margot, stronger feelings of internal security, knowing that she was accepted, understood, and taken care of by her teacher. She became more attentive and able to learn. Perhaps she was able to engage in thinking: "At school, I am in my place, I am a child of my age, allowed to develop and play safely, and I am a pupil free to think and concentrate on school activities." Similarly, given my own psychical release, I could write, "I am sensitive to the well-being of the child who has been entrusted to me but have no feeling of guilt regarding her situation. I am only responsible for her at school, as the child she is, and as the pupil she is."

Prospect

To conclude, even if only a small part of the psychical processes at work in an educational setting has been considered here, I can state that the research has transformed my perception of teaching and the relationships at its core. The work of writing, combined with the group, has operated as a container both for me and also Margot, not least because I have learnt to develop my own capacity for containment in professionally appropriate ways. Salzberger-Wittenberg has addressed the issue of the relationships between social workers and their clients, and described professional containment as:

What is essential to the client is the caseworker's willingness to *try* to understand how he feels, to be prepared to listen and respect him as a unique personality. Her actions, as well as her words, will show the client whether she is really concerned about him and in touch with the adult and infantile parts of this personality and whether she has the courage and integrity to face emotional pain. Abilities in this direction are of as much, if not more, importance to the client than her technical skill, though ideally, of course, they will all go together. (Salzberger-Wittenberg, Williams, & Osborne, 2004, p. 163)

I have tried to understand how Margot felt and to face the emotional pain arising in the situation (hers and mine). The attitude described above might, indeed, apply as accurately to teachers and their pupils, but how can this be achieved? Bion's digestive model of the thought-thinking apparatus alongside the idea of a mother's ability to welcome and digest her baby's intense archaic bodily feelings and emotions—the capacity, in short, for maternal reverie (Bion, 1963)—offers an illuminating understanding of the whole process. The writing and group were my container. And if it is possible, which I believe it is, to draw a parallel between Bion's model of the mother–infant relationship and that of the teacher–pupil, if the teacher can transform messy thoughts and feelings into thinking, s/he can make it available for the benefit of her/his pupils. Imperceptibly, this clinical study made an impact on my professional identity: de-idealising the teaching profession made it less persecutory for me, reducing both phantasies of omnipotence and helplessness. More room was made for available for individuality and creativity. Being a good enough teacher, as Blanchard-Laville says, paraphrasing Winnicott, turned out to be a sound and demanding enough aspiration.

Psychical realities and external realities will, none the less, continue to collide, even in the most ordinary-looking teaching settings, and professionals will face vicissitudes they have not necessarily been prepared to handle. Anxious feelings might be repressed or creatively transformed. Understanding defence mechanisms can be crucial, and teachers helped to recognise, accept, and transform them. More often than not, when faced with unconscious disruptive phenomena, arising in professional situations, responses can be reductively dismissed by the teacher or/and by the professional team as personal failure, which adds to the intensity of the ordeal. Blanchard-Laville's research findings have challenged this simplistic association between professional suffering and personal incompetence (Blanchard-Laville, 2002). Each imperfect, yet potentially significant, shift in a teacher's psychic growth—if the conditions exist to learn from experience—can offer some release and even progression for an entire profession. It is possible to alleviate worrying teacher–pupil relationships and liberate the teaching space, while placing at the heart of these interactions an understanding of their deeply human dimensions.

References

Abram, J. (1996). *The Language of Winnicott: A Dictionary of Winnicott's Use of Words*. London: Karnac.

Balint, M. (2000[1957]). Appendix I. In: *The Doctor, his Patient and the Illness* (pp. 297–314). New York: Churchill Livingstone.

Bastin, A. (2009). Margot, une élève ordinaire. Monographie. In: C. Blanchard-Laville & P. Geffard (Eds.), *Processus inconscients et pratiques enseignantes* (pp. 19–42). Paris: L'Harmattan.

Bion, W. R. (1962). A theory of thinking. *International Journal of Psychoanalysis, 43*: 4–5.

Bion, W. R. (1963). *Elements of Psychoanalysis*. London: Karnac.

Blanchard-Laville, C. (2001). *Les enseignants entre plaisir et souffrance*. Paris: PUF.

Blanchard-Laville, C. (2002). Plaisirs et souffrances des enseignants. In: A. Picquenot (Ed.), *Il fait moins noir quand quelqu'un parle. Éducation et psychanalyse aujourd'hui* (pp. 45–54). CRDP de Bourgogne.

Blanchard-Laville, C. (2011). Pour un accompagnement clinique groupal du travail enseignant. *Nouvelle revue de psychosociologie, 1*(11): 131–147.

Bléandonu, G. (1990). *Wilfred R. Bion. La vie et l'œuvre. 1897–1979*. Paris: Dunod.

Klein, M. (1952). Notes sur quelques mécanismes schizoïdes. In: M. Klein, P. Heimann, S. Isaacs, & J. Rivière (Eds.), *Développements de la psychanalyse*. Paris: PUF, 2009.

Oury, F., & Vasquez, A. (1967). *Vers une pédagogie institutionnelle*. Paris: Maspero.

Rycroft, C. (1968). *A Critical Dictionary of Psychoanalysis*. London: Penguin, 1995.

Salzberger-Wittenberg, I., Williams, G., & Osborne, E. (2004). *The Emotional Experience of Learning and Teaching*. London: Karnac.

Segal, H. (1964). *Introduction to the Work of Melanie Klein*. London: Karnac, 2006.

Winnicott, D. W. (1971). Transitional objects and transitional phenomena. In: *Playing & Reality* (pp. 1–34). London: Tavistock/Routledge, 1991.

CHAPTER SEVEN

White cliffs, white horses: on playing and auto/biography

Jacki Cartlidge

"Whatever I say about children playing really applies to adults as well"

(Winnicott, 1971, p. 46)

This chapter extends a discussion that I developed in a recent article (Cartlidge, 2011), using the theories of Donald Winnicott, psychoanalyst and physician. The starting point was research carried out for my PhD, which involves engaging with the educational biographies of a small number of non-traditional learners in and around Dover, in the South East corner of Kent. By "non-traditional learners", I mean people, some of whom are older returnees to education, who, for a range of reasons, are deemed to have "failed" at school, either in their own perception, or that of the educational authorities. I argue that "playing", as Winnicott employs the term, is potentially crucial in understanding their experiences of learning and of managing transition. I also discuss the potential for using psycho-analytic insights, alongside an auto/biographical narrative approach, to illuminate complex processes in teaching and learning. By auto/biography, I mean the sense of how we might draw on our own lives to make sense of others, as well as theirs to make sense of our selves, in both research and teaching (Stanley, 1992)

At the core of this chapter is a case study of someone I call Liz, a non-traditional learner, now a teacher, from a working-class family in Dover. The study traces the development of Liz's biographical narrative and her writing around this. Interpretatively, I draw on Winnicott's ideas on significant others and relationships, on playing and creativity, to understand more of her own learning as well as that of her students, a group of educationally unconfident adults. Liz uses fiction and literature to facilitate deeper forms of playing among them, in ways that mirror her own experience, both in the past and also the present.

Winnicott, it should be noted, insists on the present participle "playing", rather than the noun "play" (1971, p. 45) because he wants to move away from what he sees as the psychoanalyst's preoccupation with content towards more of a focus on the actual qualities of the child/adult playing and relationship. For Winnicott, playing and creativity, as well as self-development, are intrinsically linked.

The use of narrative and steps into auto/biography

I want to explain, before moving to the case study, aspects of what I term an auto/biographical narrative research methodology. The approach has incorporated the use of writing and literature alongside biographical narrative interviews, as well as an interrogation of my own experience, as a means of better understanding transitional processes in myself as well as others. Fiction has always been one of the good objects in my own life, in helping me in processes of meaning making. Elements of auto/biography are clearly redolent in the case study, as one life—including the life of the researcher—intertwines with another, often in largely unconscious ways. I encourage the use of fiction and literature in working with others, creating a multi-disciplinary approach, challenging conventional boundaries between fact and fiction, the use of literature, and biographical narrative material.

Auto/biography, with the slash, can be attributed to Stanley (1992), a feminist sociologist. Merrill and West (2009) define the term auto/biography as "the inter-relationship between the construction of our own lives through autobiography and the construction of the others' lives through biography" (p. 5). Miller defines this kind of imaginative endeavour as "a set of ideas, skills, metaphors and multi-disciplinary perspectives focused on making sense of personal social and psychological experience through narrative life history" (2007, p. 167).

Miller, among others, recognises the position of the researcher when using an auto/biographical approach. It is impossible to tell stories of others without being aware of how one's own story impinges on the research. Miller recognises the "artful nature" of the construction of biography, but our own lives can be a rich source for connectedness with others, as my wider doctoral research, including the case study, makes clear.

I should also add that the biographical narrative interview style adopted was largely unstructured, as well as longitudinal. It was, in its own right, designed to create a good enough space for playing in storytelling about lives, for bringing into the exercise the imagination and the heart, alongside reflexivity. Recordings were fully transcribed (using oral history conventions) and then used as a basis for further exploration and iteration in subsequent interviews. The whole process enabled some deeper forms of communication and auto/biographical connection to develop.

Liz and her background

Liz, the main subject of the chapter, has lived in Dover all her life. She is a non-traditional adult learner in her own right. Matthew Arnold's (1867) poem "Dover Beach" captures some of the difficult ebb and flow of her educational biography:

> Listen! you hear the grating roar
> Of pebbles which the waves draw back, and fling,
> At their return, up the high strand,
> Begin and cease, and then again begin
>
> (Arnold, 1867)

Liz's biographical narrative material is located against the troubled cultural background of Dover. This is an ancient town, known as the "Gateway to England", with its symbolic white cliffs. It has faced armies of invasion and has been fortified, settled, and developed over millennia. Today, it is a big ferry port, an exit to Europe and around thirteen million travellers pass through every year. Less well known are its now abandoned coalmines, many of which extended out under the sea. Mining began in the late nineteenth century, but all are now closed. Work associated with the ferry port provides contemporary employment, but has been in decline since the 1980s. Liz talked of her great-grandfather walking with his family across Kent to find employment in the mines, while her own father was a builder. Liz is now a teacher of English and sociology in a college of further education, which traditionally, among other things, provides educational opportunities to students who might have struggled at school.

I have included in the text some extracts from Liz's biographical narrative as well as her associated writing: they offer glimpses into her background and provide space for her "voice". She is the child of a working-class family, born in the 1970s, when the mines were closing and employment was difficult. Liz's cultural background, which includes failure in a public examination called the 11 plus (designed to select children for the more academic education provided by grammar schools, which still exist in Kent), is significant in that she is able to identify with her struggling, often unconfident students and they with her.

After the first interview, Liz was excited by the process and voluntarily added a written response, which eventually, as will be seen, became an important part of a classroom exercise with her students.

> Home was a small terraced house: front room; middle room; scullery; outside toilet; three bedrooms and a tin bath hung on the wall in the back yard. Opening the front door, I was always met with a particular smell that told me which day of the week it was: *Lux Soap Flakes*—Monday; *Robin Starch*—Tuesday; stew—Wednesday and so on. On Saturdays it was Welsh cakes; sponge; bread pudding; mincemeat pies; lemon meringue. Mum and Gran's baking day.

She went on, in detail, to describe sampling the baking and climbing on to [Great] Gran's lap to practise her English and to be told stories. What emerges from the extract and the transcripts more generally is of a whole family who create space for Liz: for playing, with storytelling at its heart.

Liz's evocation of a loving home environment is set at a time when the family was extremely hard pressed financially:

I wonder at however we got through that winter. Dad was a master brick-layer and due to the severe frosts and snow he was unable to work for much of that time. Being self-employed meant that he did not receive any state . . . [benefit] It is an example and testimony to the protection and security my parents gave me. *They did not allow their adult world to impinge upon my child's world of wonder and excitement.* I was cocooned from harsh realities—and yet at the same time I cannot say that I was wrapped in cotton wool. (My italics.)

I have italicised what might be a key sentence. Money was always scarce, but Liz's abiding memory—however open to interpretation, given that interpretations are never complete—is of a sense of suffi-cient warmth and security. She stresses that she was not "cocooned" and that her parents were sufficiently adaptive to encourage her in her playing but also to understand some of the realities of living in diffi-cult times.

Winnicott and Liz

Liz comes across as a secure and confident person, resilient, commit-ted to education as a means of progress and self-fulfilment. Never-theless, she still recognisably retains her working-class identity, living close to the house she grew up in. For her, educational aspiration does not include rejecting her family or culture of origin; rather, combining this with her identity as a teacher.

Winnicott's understanding of the importance of relationship in playing—and the risk-taking this involves—has helped me under-stand Liz's narrative. Winnicott considers that healthy "growth and development" (Winnicott, 1986, p. 62) rely on early relationships of sufficient reliability and security. Separation and individuation depends on the response of the other, on a sense of being seen, recog-nised, and loved simply for being. The infant can then begin to exper-iment and play without being overly anxious about the other. S/he can enter transitional space and begin a process of recognising and negotiating objects as separate from her/himself. Ego development is possible in such a context, in both the responses and eyes of the other and also the experiences of selfhood that play enables. Except, if this process is not good enough—and there is a perpetual anxiety sur-rounding the emotional availability of the other, for instance—the ego can be "feeble" (ibid., p. 63). We can apply such an analysis, perhaps, to adult experiences in a classroom, for instance: the quality of the relationship between a teacher and her students, as well as the space represented by play itself, can be a vehicle for important transitions in the sense of who we are and might be.

Transitional objects, teddy bears, and other special objects

Winnicott also sees what he calls transitional objects to be essential to healthy progression and development. The object might be a substitute for the breast in the first instance, and becomes the first not-me object that the infant encounters. As Winnicott, and many parents, are aware, a substitute adopted by the baby might be a thumb or finger in the mouth, a strip of satin or smooth material from an early blanket, or an object often associated with Winnicott, that of the teddy bear. Winnicott (1986) concludes that the object "is gradually allowed to be decathected, so that in the course of years it is not so much forgotten as relegated to limbo" (p. 6). Texture seems to be necessary and part of the transitional object's essence, possibly part of the initial auto-erotic association with the breast. Many neglected and worn teddies sit on shelves in the later years of the owners, important as symbols of strong affection and object relating, their original use outgrown; worn because as well as love they have been the recipients of the anger and frustration of their owner. They have served their purpose, but as transitional objects have helped the self with its negotiations with reality.

Transitional objects might be meaningful in adult development, too. Some students might have a special pen, or something similar, which is associated with a first successful piece of work. The object might ward off the anxiety remaining from prior unsatisfactory learning experiences but also generated in present struggles to separate from an existing identity. Transitional objects remain a defence against anxiety, and can manifest themselves in a range of scarcely noticeable forms: a catch-phrase a teacher has used, scribbled at the top of an exam script, the notes that signify learning and understanding a topic, loss of which can bring about extreme distress. A good enough and adaptive teacher will respond with intuitive empathy to what, to others, might appear trivial. And, perhaps, particular forms of storytelling and writing, as other examples, might serve as good enough, highly cathected objects, which allow space to be claimed, risks taken, and identities negotiated.

A secure sense of self

I have suggested that Liz is a relatively secure and confident person. Winnicott argues that "trust and reliability" (1971, p. 127) are essential factors in relationships with significant others in nurturing the capacity for playing. The space between subject and object "can become an infinite area of separation, which the baby, child, adolescent, adult may creatively fill with playing" (ibid.). Failure to accomplish this stage successfully Winnicott identifies as deficiencies in ego development. Yet, he also argues that therapists and teachers can offer ego support to fragile selves. The work of a teacher, like Liz, can be crucial, in Winnicott's schema, in "giving ego support where it is needed" (1986, p. 63). It is during playing, Winnicott argues, that "the individual child or adult is able to be creative and to use the whole personality" (1971, p. 63). This can take place in the classroom, if certain preconditions exist and particular relational qualities are encouraged. Forms of teaching and learning that can evoke the imagination, via writing, poetry, and/or autobiography, could combine with processes of projective identification (in which it is possible for students to identify and feel valued by a significant other), all of which combine to overcome potentially paralysing anxiety and resistance to experiment. Education can raise deeply embodied, felt questions about who we are, might be, and whether we are good enough, which might reach back to earliest experience and touch the most primitive levels of personality. Projective identification, on the part both of the teacher and her students, in which imaginative and often unconscious connections are made between one and other, can be important. Liz's own narrative resonated, deeply, with those of her students: she was like them, but also different.

Her educational experience at eleven left her with a deep sense of deficit in terms of formal academic qualifications. Notwithstanding, in her storytelling, a passion for education, a love of learning for its own sake, remained. And the motivation to enter university might have been dormant, but was not extinct. I want to suggest (and this was explored in dialogue with Liz, over time) that her motivation was grounded in a positive sense of self, forged in earlier experiences, not least with her father. Over the course of the biographical narrative work, she described herself as "blessed" with her parents and family life, and as a child she had thought "that's what everyone has". Experience of teaching students from a similar background to hers has shown her how wrong this assumption was. When Liz's thirst for education re-emerged, for a range of reasons, it led her to take an Access to Higher Education programme, designed to give adults lacking formal academic qualifications a progression route to university. She went on to read English and Sociology at the University of Kent. Liz's father was highly significant in this narrative, meaning-making process across her life.

Playing and significant others

The term "significant other", from a psychoanalytical perspective, encompasses those who have played, and might continue to play, a key role in the stories we tell of who we are and might be. Liz's father was central in her narrative, and she described him as "the wisest man I've ever known" (Liz's written narrative).

He was an autodidact who left school at fourteen: he died seven years before she returned to learning and the Access to Higher Education programme. The impact and role of significant others can remain across a life, as what is intersubjective in origin becomes internalised as a good object, which might be activated in diverse ways, via memory in feeling as much as conscious thought. Liz constantly stressed her father's importance in encouraging her imagination and love of reading and learning. She vividly recalled him telling stories for her at bedtime. His living influence can be seen to be captured evocatively in the following passage. Here, she recalls a moment of imaginative connectedness between the two of them. She is four years old and on an outing to Dover beach:

> You've got this really rough day and he [her father] said "Can you see the white horses?" He got down, right down, he crouched down at my eye level. Of course it was the foam on the waves, and I said to him "Where?" and he said "Look, there's their manes." And do you know I could see

them. I absolutely remember that . . . I was about four years old and he said "This is the place where adventures begin" and, of course, I'm this little thing looking around at the ships and the trains . . . they're all going out . . . Coal and cargo . . . and I remember that as plain as plain, and they *are* white horses, that's what they were . . . Yes, he was incredible—the white horses, I'll always remember that.

Past and present intertwined in the storytelling. A small piece of coastline can be seen to be transformed into a whole world: here, with Liz's father, was the rhythm of imaginative playing, but without the rasping pebble-cadence of doubt in Arnold's poem. At this moment in the storytelling, she and her father were both bending down to the level of four-year-olds watching the white horses, both succumbing to the power of story. And it is this "white horses" moment—primitively evocative of the child in the adult—which Liz was to use to create space for imaginative playing and risk-taking among her own students.

Movement to the classroom

The "white horses" experience was developed by Liz and used as a kind of transitional object with her students. The biographical narrative interview method itself encouraged in Liz a growing awareness of the potential use of auto/biographical material in the classroom. After the interview, Liz wrote her own version of the incident; she turned it into a chapter incorporating the description of her home and the trip to Dover beach. Liz then adapted the chapter into a classroom exercise, leaving the ending open at the point she returned home with her father. She gave the adapted version to her students, asking them to supply and write up their own conclusion. They were directed to adopt the same voice, style, and tone to complete the whole chapter. And when their assignments were handed in, she gave them her own conclusion.

The results were astonishing in demonstrating a sensitive understanding, knowledge, and skilful use of language and a related engagement with a broad literature. The students were surprised that her chapter was written about life as late as the 1970s. They recognised similarities with their own experience, yet needed to investigate particular vocabulary, such as "scullery" (a word for kitchen). There were excursions into dictionaries, while D. H. Lawrence's novels were mined for his descriptions of sculleries in mining communities. Some were surprised by the history of mining in their community, yet they also recognised the localities involved. The students, as Liz reported, felt included and able to identify fulsomely with the material. She talked, too, of them identifying with her, while at the same time accepting her situation as other and separate. The attempt to continue in Liz's "voice", different from her everyday speech, became a subtle way of teaching them the appropriateness of different registers for the written and spoken word.

It is important to emphasise, as Liz perceived it, that the students had initially to be persuaded that it was possible to learn, creatively, in such a way. They were anxious about such relatively unstructured space: "they could not believe the freedom . . . it was almost frightening for them . . ." But such playing evoked, as Liz saw it, a more imaginative approach to their English studies. Knights and Thurgar-Dawson, in their book on *Active Reading*, theorise such as situation in the following way:

> A spiral of reading → writing → further reading, can also, within conditions of adequate security, be used to open up questions about the cultural situatedness of the self as at once addressee and agent. (2006, p. 66)

The students became active agents in the classroom and the quality of the psychic space seemed transformed. They produced their own magazine and began to think of themselves as writers for the first time in their lives. The momentum appears to have continued, and a number are applying for university places. Liz, at least, is a kind of envoy for the students, a messenger who embodies the transformative possibilities of education. It might be that, if interviewed in the future, these students could well cite Liz as a significant other. At the heart of the process, we might surmise, lie profoundly intersubjective encounters in which some projective identification is possible, where students may invest the other with aspects of themselves, and risks can be taken, imaginatively, with who they are and who they might become; where a teacher is felt to come alongside, knowing intuitively what it might be like in their shoes, while also different and other, like the good enough father; glimpses of what is, but also what might be.

Conclusion

I have applied Winnicott's ideas on playing to the past and present life of a teacher called Liz. Winnicott constantly stressed the link between playing, creativity, and more confident selves. Liz can be seen as a "good enough", "adaptive" teacher, with whom the students shared a transitional space, if only for a while. Primitive, highly cathected energies were generated in these relationships, between teacher and students, and between all involved and the creative processes of auto/biographical and fictional writing. Moreover, I do not think this situation is unique: the power of using biographical material in the classroom is well documented by Dominicé (2000) and also Hunt and West (present volume) illustrate the potency of creative writing in risk-taking and experiment. And, as West (1996) has chronicled, in depth, good enough relationships between a tutor and a student at university can facilitate subtle shifts in a student's sense of agency and the possibility for symbolic play. In the case of Liz, we have, I believe, an empathetic and adaptive teacher using fiction and writing for playing in energised, potentially transformative ways. My long teaching experience with adults and non-traditional learners contains many similar moments.

References

Arnold, M. (1867). Dover Beach. In: *The Oxford Library of English Poetry*, J. Wain (Ed.), Oxford: Oxford University Press, 1986.

Cartlidge, J. (2011). Playing and adults learning. *Cliopsy, Revue électronique*, 6: 53–60. Available at www.cliopsy.fr.

Dominicé, P. (2000). *Learning from Our Lives*. CA: Jossey-Bass.

Knights, B., & Thurgar-Dawson, C. (2006). *Active Reading*, London: Continuum.

Merrill, B., & West, L. (2009). *Using Biographical Research Methods in Social Science*. London: Sage.

Miller, N. (2007). Developing an auto/biographical imagination. In: L. West, P. Alheit, S. A. Andersen, & B. Merrill (Eds.), *Using Biographical and Life History Approaches in the Study of Adult and Lifelong Learning: European Perspectives* Vol 2 (pp. 167–186). Frankfurt: Peter Lang.

Stanley, L. (1992). *The Auto/biographical I*. Manchester: Manchester University Press.

West, L. (1996). *Beyond Fragments, Adults, Motivation and Higher Education; A Biographical Analysis*. London: Taylor & Francis.

Winnicott, D. W. (1971). *Playing and Reality*. London: Routledge, 1980.

Winnicott, D. W. (1986). Concept of a false self; *Sum, I am*; Varieties of psychotherapy; The concept of a healthy individual. In: C. Winnicott, R. Shepherd, & M. Davis (Eds.), *Home is Where we Start From: Essays by a Psychoanalyst*. New York: Norton, 1990.

CHAPTER EIGHT

Teacher's countertransference reconsidered

Alper Sahin

Introduction

The influence of psychoanalytic theory on school psychology is fast improving in Turkey. The impact of the Istanbul Psychoanalytic Study Group linked with the International Psychoanalysis Association (IPA) and founded in 1994 as the Istanbul Psychoanalysis Group has an important role in this process (Parman, 2011). The Educational Sciences Department of Maltepe University has also made significant contributions, with yearly conferences under the name of "School and Psychoanalysis" and publications on psychoanalysis and education. Maltepe University are pioneers in the area of psychoanalytic pedagogy in Turkey. This has led to many school psychologists and clinicians developing a growing interest in psychoanalytical concepts and their use in school settings. In this chapter, the reader will find one of these discussions that relates to the countertransference of teachers.

The quality of school learning partially depends on the relationships between the students and their teachers (Bloom, 1982). In order to improve the quality of this relationship, on the teachers' part, a deeper understanding of their emotions while working with their students is, therefore, necessary. Consequently, this chapter intends to investigate what might be a helpful way of defining and conceptualising the unconscious emotional responses, such as the countertransference of the teachers, within the classroom setting. In this chapter, the countertransference of teachers in the school setting will be discussed in terms of mourning and learning. In order to clarify, define, and explore the use of this term, two case study schools are presented. The reason why these two schools have been chosen is the problematic emotional atmosphere that formed around a single significant problem, which is the mourning behaviours of the students, teachers, and parents. Since the researcher is also the teacher trainer for the case study schools, the opportunity for close observation and interaction permitted a deeper awareness of the feelings of those involved. An important focus here is on the definition and use of countertransference in a non-clinical environment. Since the clinical setting is clearly defined by psychoanalytic principles and practices, any psychoanalytical concept used outside that setting must equally be defined carefully.

Psychoanalysis and pedagogy

The relationship between pedagogy and psychoanalysis has an old history. Some well-known psychoanalysts and psychoanalytic theoreticians were teachers at the very beginning of their careers (Cifali & Moll, 2003). In 1908, Ferenczi wrote an article, "Psychoanalysis and pedagogy", for the Congress of Salzburg (Ferenczi, 2006) where he pointed out that the current "conservative" approach to education was detrimental to young people and that it could be better organised on psychoanalytical principles. Furthermore, Anna Freud sought to use psychoanalytic theory in her teaching, as evidenced in the "Matchbox School" project, which she undertook with her collaborators, Erickson and Aichhorn (Midgley, 2008). After the project was over, she continued to work on psychoanalysis and pedagogy. Her famous conferences to parents and teachers stressed how the psychoanalysis of adults could help with the development of a healthy personality in children (Freud, 1930). Both Ferenczi and Anna Freud were concerned about the unrealistic pedagogical expectations teachers held about children, particularly in the area of the emotions. While their work taught that the application of psychoanalytic theory to pedagogy is no simple matter, it is of note that educators who are informed by psychoanalytical theory believe that it is an important perspective through which to understand human beings. Thus, it can be argued that there is still room for further work and research in this area, particularly in the investigation of patterns of interaction between students and teachers. This chapter focuses specifically on research on countertransference within the student–teacher relationship. In this sense, it is crucial to differentiate a classroom from a therapeutic setting where the neutrality of the psychoanalyst is a rule.

Does countertransference exist in the classroom?

According to Laplanche and Pontalis (1974), "transference" in psychoanalytic theory means the repetition of unconscious infantile patterns of interaction. In which case, every relationship will have a transferential aspect (Etchegoyen, 1999). Additionally, in the clinical setting, the concept of countertransference is used to gain deeper insight into behaviour and relationships. There are many views on countertransference. Freud (1915a) saw countertransference as the analyst's unconscious response to the analysand's transference. This was a problem, in that the analyst is not in control of their own unconscious, and this could derail the psychoanalytical process. Therefore, further analysis for the analyst was recommended to allow them to consider the origin of their emotional responses.

Laplanche and Pontalis (1974) defined countertransference as a set of unconscious reactions by the analyst in response to the transferences of the patient. In this case, it can be a useful clinical process. In a neutral analytical setting, the patient's infantile patterns of interaction are reactivated; they interact with the therapist's unconscious and become available for interpretation. In other words, countertransference occurs when the emotions projected by the patient into the therapist stimulate the unconscious of the therapist and evoke a set of feelings and reactions in him or her. When the therapist looks at his/her own thoughts, feelings, and reactions, this can provide insight into the patient's unconscious. In summary, analysts, through countertransference, can have a better understanding of the patient's unconscious with the help of their own. Laplanche and Pontalis (ibid.)

are clear that the use of countertransference should be confined to the psychotherapeutic setting, in which clear rules and boundaries apply: for example, in terms of time, neutrality of the analyst, free association of the patient, and payment. Etchegoyen (1999) also locates countertransference firmly within the psychoanalytic setting, bounded by the same rules. He also maintains that countertransference is a process that alerts psychoanalysts to their patients' transferences. Laplanche and Pontalis, and Etchegoyen, agree that outside of the clinical setting countertransference is lost within everyday communication.

However, Britzman (2009), a psychoanalyst and educationalist, holds a different view, and has sought to use notions of transference and countertransference in wider settings, such as the classroom. She maintains that an understanding of the transference–countertransference relationship between the student and teacher facilitates a better emotional atmosphere, which helps to create a better learning environment. She argues that the teacher's unconscious feelings, phantasies, and anxieties form a hidden dimension of what is happening in the classroom. Youell (2006) takes a similar view, pointing out that once the teacher is aware of the dimension of a dynamic unconscious, such as countertransference, they will be able to adjust their attitudes towards their students. The teacher's view of the student's behaviour will be less dependent simply on the transferential relationship and include a consideration of their feelings and responses.

This view of countertransference having a legitimate place outside the clinical setting needs to be evaluated and developed. It might be easy to accept the notion that the teacher's reaction to the student's transferences could be better understood by deploying the concept of countertransference, and, indeed, might help with the creation of a more effective teaching and learning environment. However, bearing in mind the advice of Laplanche and Pontalis, and Etchegoyen, is it legitimate to call this process countertransference? The psychoanalytic setting requires, among the previously mentioned boundaries, the anonymity of the psychoanalyst, which means that the patient does not know much about the psychoanalyst's personality. The situation is very different in teaching, as students remain with their teachers all year, in many different activities and roles. These include dealing with problems between students, carrying out disciplinary procedures, as well as having fun with them. This is not a clinical setting view of countertransference. It seems that countertransference might not the best term to use in this context. So, there is a question as to what term can be used.

The educational scientist, Bloom (1982), well known for his focus on cognitive aspects of learning did, however, also consider the affective aspects of learning. He points out that learning is facilitated by the positive emotional perception of previous learning experiences. Thus, what the teacher needs is a way of understanding the student's previous learning experiences and their emotional impact on, and meaning for, the students. Such understanding might lead to the creation of a better learning environment. From the psychoanalytic point of view the teachers' understanding of the students' emotional responses to learning is accessed via the countertransference. In this case, Britzman's (2009) proposal becomes problematic. The problem here is that the term countertransference does not exactly define the emotional situation of the teacher; rather, it defines that of the psychoanalyst. In other words, the meaning of the term countertransference becomes problematic due to the fact that it is applied to two different emotional settings.

Thus, a new term is suggested for conceptualising the attitudes of the teachers towards students, which is "transferential responses". Transferential response is a concept used exclusively for teaching and learning situations to distinguish from the "clinical countertransference", where the former relates to the intense emotional teacher–student interactions. The use of this term will enable psychoanalytical ideas to be used in education, but without the clinical connotations, since the school cannot be regarded as a clinic.

Now that an appropriate term has been suggested, its identification and application to the case studies is required. The examples provided consider the transferential responses of teachers in relation to the mourning of the students and parents within two case study schools. During the mourning process, the mourner loses interest in the external world (Freud, 1917e): this situation has an impact on the close circle of people around them. In the examples provided below, the intensity of this impact is very important. Therefore, the circumstances created by these two case schools allow the transferential responses of the teachers to be identified. It is intended to observe whether or not the mourning of the students and their parents block the learning of the teachers due to their transferential responses. Through these cases, it will also be possible to understand how the transferential response might differ from clinical countertransference.

Mourning and learning

In his work, "Mourning and melancholia", Freud (1917e) states that, during mourning, the world ceases to be interesting to the mourner as the person is aware of what has been lost and how the world has become poorer. The process of mourning is not easy and requires time and effort, with different cultures having their own mourning rituals that provide support for the mourners. These allow people not only to express their feelings, but they also set limits to the mourning and assign new functions to the survivors (Bowlby, 1980). However, the mourning that a child experiences for a lost parent varies considerably compared to that of the adult. The surviving parent's attitude seems to be an important variable for the attitude of the child, who might react strongly or withdraw, depending on the situation. Through the mourning process, the investment in the deceased person is gradually withdrawn. For a parent who has lost a child, the process is slightly different. Bowlby (1980) suggests that the parents of fatally ill children begin mourning when they hear the diagnosis. They have already experienced a loss, that of a healthy child. In the same way that a small child expects the deceased parent to return, so, too, the parents of a sick child expect that their child might regain health one day. The associated anger and denial disturbs the mourning process and causes complications, since reality is not accepted as it is. Additionally, unless it is not expressed in psychologically safe environments, such as psychotherapy or psychoanalysis, the anger towards the chronically ill or dead person might cause deeper problems, such as chronic depression or manic defences against depression. The people who accompany the mourner have a difficult position, since all the anger and disappointment that is for the lost or ill person might be projected towards them. In that case, the person who is offering support might feel angry and disappointed because of being offended in return for their good intentions.

An experience of the inability to learn

The research is set within two institutions where there is deep mourning due to the students who have lost their parents and parents who have lost the health of their children. The study focused on the interaction between the teacher with the researcher, and their interest in learning. The researcher was invited by the schools to train the teachers and to try to find out possible ways of solving problems that occur in the interactions between teachers, students, and parents. A common complaint of the school administrators and teachers was that they were unable to understand the responses of the students and parents. The researcher (a trainee psychoanalyst, who is also the teacher trainer) used psychoanalytic data gathering and analysing techniques such as interpretations of dreams, transferences, and his countertransferences, to gather information about the emotional experiences and learning of the teachers, to study the teachers' attitudes towards learning. The training, where the researcher had the role of facilitator, was designed around free discussion of any issues brought up by the teachers in the discussions.

When a researcher or teacher trainer is invited to an institution, s/he inevitably becomes a third party in psychoanalytical terms. While being an outsider has some disadvantages, a psychoanalytically orientated researcher has major advantages in terms of being able to identify and interpret patterns of emotional relationships in the situation. As Hunt (1989) points out, psychoanalytically trained specialists will be able to use their countertransferences to, potentially, reach a deeper understanding of unconscious aspects of the emotional life of the institution. Roquefort (1995) usefully differentiates three types of institutions in terms of their unconscious functioning: the psychotic, the perverse, and the neurotic. In the psychotic, words have no meaning, no law exists, and members cannot express themselves and establish relationships. In the perverse, the law is laid down, but no one obeys it. Any rules are discarded after a couple of months. In the neurotic, feelings of powerlessness and depression prevail, resulting in staff feeling hopeless and, therefore, resistant to change. Ultimately, they accept infantilisation.

All three types of functioning have a major impact on the learning environment. Britzman (2003) addresses another angle, teacher's defences against learning: learning is a destructive process that demolishes previous knowledge; thinking is the expression of "not knowing", and so prepares the way for learning. These two concepts are crucial, since they suggest that "not learning" is the result of "knowing and not thinking". In the case of teaching, the teacher's rejection or neglect of psychic communication with the student might result in a cold mechanical form of education. The teacher will be using limited knowledge about the student and there will be no space or opportunity to think about them. When the teacher is open to "not knowing", they are able to think about the emotional communication from the student and respond accordingly. However, this can be problematic, as the teachers do not know how to cope with the double burden of their own feelings of helplessness engendered by the institution and the feelings caused by students. They might respond by being cold and distant, and sometimes by being inappropriately friendly with the students. It is suggested that such reactions might be termed "transferential responses", since they are shaped by intense interactions with the students. The inability to think about the unconscious aspects of the teaching and learning relationship impedes effective learning, which requires attention to both cognitive and emotional knowledge. When the thinking process is blocked by emotional tension, teachers' learning ability is reduced. However, a psychoanalytically orientated trainer, with an understanding of countertransference and able to make effective interpretations, might also provide some insight.

In this sense, Bion's alphabetisation process, which requires thinking about the other's feelings by taking into account one's own, is an important tool to transform the transferences on the part of the institution. In this model, the baby reflects on to the care-taker unbearable affects through cries and other behaviours, and the care-taker tries to give meaning to these behaviours and to verbalise them for the babies and make comprehensible what seems meaningless. This transformation of what seems meaningless to something that is meaningful is achieved through the containing ability of the care-taker. Containing is a thinking process that allows reformulation of the problematic situation so that it facilitates discovery of problem-solving options. Thus, the expert might stimulate and facilitate the verbalisation and elaboration of thoughts within the teachers. In this way, unexpressed feelings could give rise to meaning by using language, and, thus, relate to the thoughts, behaviours, and other feelings. This results in an integration of conflicting aspects of feelings, behaviours, and thoughts, so that ability to cope with the problems is improved. The holding environment, an environment in which the teachers can understand their feelings and the reasons for their behaviours, created by the trainer, is used to enable the teachers to change, and it is hoped that this change will be reflected in their relationships with students. The following cases illustrate these interventions.

Case studies

Two cases will be discussed in this part of the study in order to explain the learning problems of the teachers that are related to transferential responses.

Case study 1

The first setting is a boarding school for orphans. The researcher was invited to provide training for the teachers after a bullying event among students. The administration and teachers were unable to provide suitable meanings for the behaviour of the students. They assumed that they had provided everything for an excellent learning environment. The school's aim for the training was to equip teachers with the skills necessary to deal with these problems and to prevent them reoccurring. The training programme used the technique of encouraging the teachers to work with their feelings. It took the form of a group interaction during which the teachers discussed their problems and feelings about the students.

The day before the researcher started to work with the teachers he had a dream:

> I was in a classroom rather like a living room with a lot of sunshine. Teachers were spread out chatting about a problem and met me with joy. They were thinking that I would put things in order.

One interpretation of this is that he had identified himself with the grandiosity of the institution and felt that he would solve all problems and put things in order. This possible interpretation is supported by another event.

The teachers forgot the appointment for the third session. They came to see the researcher once they heard he had arrived, and he then asked them about the significance of their forgetting the meeting. Although the group leader took responsibility for not reminding the others, the researcher persisted with the question. A teacher explained that there had been a flood (there was major flood in Istanbul that year). The researcher asked what the flood meant to them and they responded that the students had been kept in school, including weekends and holidays, for a month. The teachers stayed with them for day and night duties without a break. They felt overburdened and unsupported. One teacher explained how he could not see his own children during this period, while another talked of the difficulties of keeping students occupied for all that time. Initially, the teachers had been reluctant to talk and seemed anxious and tired. Once they started to talk, they opened up and became more animated. The researcher commented that they were flooded with the feelings of helplessness in the same way that their students were. The students felt helpless because they had been sent to boarding school after the death of a parent, leaving their family behind and not being able to go back and visit them. By forgetting the session, the teachers were projecting their feelings of neglect and hate towards the trainer (researcher), who also felt neglected and helpless. This meant that they were able to avoid thinking about their situation and, as a result, avoid learning. When encouraged to think about their forgetfulness, they were more able to understand their students. Their better attunement to the students might also enable the students, in turn, to think about their feelings and understand their own behaviour.

Case study 2

The second case study is based in a school for mentally and physically disabled children where it can be argued that the parents were in mourning over the loss of their children's health. The headmaster of the school contacted the researcher to ask for help for teachers who were having difficulties dealing with parents. Since the school was a part of a foundation for public benefit, the researcher agreed to work with this school *pro bono*. A group of fifteen teachers agreed to take part in the group. In the first year, the researcher met with volunteers on a monthly basis to work with their concerns, feelings, and thoughts. It appeared that the teachers were angry with the parents, whom they experienced as excessively demanding. They expected their chronically ill children to be cured, which, despite the teachers' best efforts, was impossible.

There came a point when the teachers declined to take part in any more sessions with the researcher, claiming that the process had raised too many dangerous feelings for them. The researcher sought to understand the meaning of this danger for them. They explained that they did not want to express their feelings, and some of the teachers even remained silent and distant. While some were happy with the process, the concerns of the rest of the group were perhaps summarised by one teacher, who said, "I find this kind of work dangerous because when we express our feelings we also lose control over them." Another teacher added, "It is a waste of time talking about feelings; it has nothing to do with what we do with the students." The researcher felt that the danger the teachers referred to was related to the articulation of their dangerous feelings. Since they did not know how to deal with negative feelings, their anxiety increased when they expressed these emotions. The general atmosphere of the meeting was now dominated by anger and a refusal to speak. However, the researcher gave a different view: "For my part, I realised how I was burdened with all the feelings of sorrow for children, for parents, and for us as well, because I think we are working with a very difficult group of children."

After that meeting, the researcher felt very angry towards the teachers, particularly because he was working for them on a *pro bono* basis. They were refusing the help he offered. His feeling was one of hatred, which he recognised was out of proportion to the situation. After thinking about this, he came to realise that he was feeling the hatred the teachers felt towards their students because he was willing to accept it. The transferential responses of the teachers that were stuck within them were projected on to the researcher. They made the researcher feel useless and as incapable as they felt in front of the accusing parents.

The feelings of the teachers were influenced by the transferential responses related to the mourning of parents and students, but were also accompanied by feelings of anger and hatred, which was the most difficult to express, since it creates guilt. That is why mourning is a very difficult process. The feeling of frustration, anger, and guilt towards the parents were part of daily life and, because they were so hard to face, got in the way of their learning from experience. Their transferential responses, here the unspoken hatred towards their students and parents, needed to be worked through in order for them to learn.

Learning and containing

The two institutions in the case studies above can be described in terms of Roquefort's (1995) categories as neurotic. Owing to the transferential responses, the teachers felt helpless and neglected and, accordingly, unable to think and learn. These cases can be understood using Bion's model (2005) of alphabetisation. Teachers might try to understand and make sense of what they get from students and offer to them meaningful knowledge, as care-takers do for babies. However, this process is not easy, since it requires that the care-takers reflect on their feelings. Thus, in the case of a school, first of all the teacher must work on their own transferential responses. The ability to think about thoughts and feelings creates an area of containment for the other. However, this presupposes the ability to contain one's own thoughts and feelings to begin with. In other words, thinking about feelings, behaviours, and thoughts creates an area of self-understanding and learning. In these cases, the inability to contain was caused by hatred, which was buried under other feelings, and, in so doing, this blocked any capacity for self-reflection and ability to consider feelings in relation to learning.

The problem here is, then, how to understand feelings such as "hatred" in terms of transferential response in contrast to a countertransferential relationship. Since countertransference is a specific term to describe the psychoanalyst's unconscious feelings stimulated by the presence of the analysand, it is a part of the psychoanalytic setting. Nevertheless, the notion of a transferential response is used to describe unconscious feelings of the teacher stimulated by the presence of the students in a classroom setting. These two settings have totally different interaction models, which, therefore, require a psychoanalytic approach that considers all situations as unique.

When Winnicott (1949) writes about countertransference, he takes hatred into consideration. He claims that a real relationship cannot exist unless it includes hate and love simultaneously. However, people usually consider hatred as a dangerous feeling, capable of ruining everything; therefore, it needs to be disavowed. However, as Winnicott points out, when hatred is denied, it is enacted in a variety of forms. As in the case of these schools, where the teachers cannot accept the existence of feelings of hatred and are, therefore, stuck. In that case, unexpressed hatred is enacted in the attitudes of the teachers towards the students as sadism or masochism, when the teacher refuses any help and rejects the opportunity to learn. It is important to note that feeling these emotions in their totality requires the ability to mourn. The teacher mourns for not being a great teacher, a saviour, resilient to everything, and then thinks about the reason behind why they have chosen this profession. So, the process of thinking about the unthinkable might help teachers to gain the ability to learn from their experiences by reducing defences against precisely this.

Conclusion

It should be noted that, in both the above cases, the teachers were never completely closed to learning, thinking, and feeling. Nevertheless, they needed the space and support provided by an expert who had committed to take time to listen to their stories. The goal of the research was to open a discussion of the relationship of psychoanalytic ideas to schools and to build a language of psychoanalysis for teachers, as Britzman (2009) suggested. In this sense, a new term, "transferential response" is suggested, instead of using countertransference, loaded as this is with specific meanings associated with psychoanalytic practice. In contrast, transferential response, still based on psychoanalytic theory, tries to define unconscious emotional responses of the teachers towards the attitudes of the students in a classroom setting. In order to specify transferential responses of the teachers, two case studies have been interrogated. It was found that the teachers' daily interactions with the students have strong effects on their emotional lives. Thus, transferential responses of the teachers negatively influence their own learning, unless, that is, there is an intervention from a psychoanalytically orientated expert.

References

Bion, W. R. (2005). *Second Thoughts*. London: Karnac.
Bloom, B. S. (1982). *Human Characteristics and School Learning*. New York: McGraw-Hill.
Bowlby, J. (1980). *Loss*. New York: Basic Books.

Britzman, D. P. (2003). *After-Education*. New York: State University of New York.

Britzman, D. P. (2009). *The Very Thought of Education*. New York: State University of New York.

Cifali, M., & Moll, J. (2003). *Pédagogie et Psychanalyse* (Psychoanalysis and Pedagogy). Paris: L'Harmattan.

Etchegoyen, R. H. (1999). *The Fundamentals of Psychoanalytic Technique*. London: Karnac.

Ferenczi, S. (2006). *L'enfant dans l'adulte* (Child in the adult). Paris: Petites bibliotheque Payot.

Freud, A. (1930). Four lectures on psychoanalysis for teachers and parents. In: *The Writings of Anna Freud, Vol. 1* (pp. 73–136). New York: International University Press.

Freud, S. (1915a). Observations on transference-love. *S.E., 12:* 157–170. London: Hogarth.

Freud, S. (1917e). Mourning and melancholia. *S.E., 14:* 239–258. London: Hogarth.

Hunt, J. C. (1989). *Psychoanalytic Aspects of Fieldwork*. London: Sage.

Laplanche, J., & Pontalis, J.-B. (1974). *The Language of Psycho-Analysis*. London: Norton.

Midgley, N. (2008). The Matchbox School (1927–1932): Anna Freud and the idea of a psychoanalytically informed education. *Journal of Child Pyschotherapy, 34*(1): 23–42.

Parman, T. (2011). *Brief History of the Turkish Psychoanalytical Study Group*. Available at: www.turkpsikanaliz.com/tr/hakkimizda.

Roquefort, D. (1995). *Le role de l'educateur: education et psychanalyse* (The role of educator: education and psychoanalysis). Paris: L'Harmattan.

Winnicott, D. W. (1949). Hate in the counter-transference. *International Journal of Psycho-analysis, 30:* 69–74.

Youell, B. (2006). *The Learning Relationship*. London: Karnac.

CHAPTER NINE

Prequels and sequels: a psychoanalytic understanding of developing a professional practice in an education setting

Alan Bainbridge

Introduction

A review of the research on the early careers of education professionals[1] reveals that the encounter with professional knowledge and practice involves an interaction between the past, with all its memories and phantasies, and the objectivity of an established professional practice (Connelly & Clandinin, 1988; Huberman, 1995; Jones, 2003; Ovens & Tinning, 2009). This dialogical relationship between the past and present reflects the psychoanalytic assumption that a dynamic unconscious influences how early life events contribute towards later dispositions. Within a traditional clinical context, it is the role of the therapist to jointly explore the influence of the past and to guide the patient towards an understanding of the present.

The research reported here applies this supposition to the early career development of education professionals. The implication that will be developed is that an awareness of past responses to education settings will have an impact on understanding how a professional practice might develop. This chapter provides a psychoanalytic discussion on how unconscious processes influence the interaction between the past and present in education settings. A discussion of the impact this has on the encounter with professional knowledge and practice will then lead to a justification for the research project that explores the use of narratives to encourage professional reflexivity.

The interaction with professional knowledge and practice

Bion (1961) conceptualises knowledge as K, the capacity to tolerate the anxieties related to learning, and that of minus K, which actively avoids and rejects new knowledge. He argues that defences are used to protect against the "attack" of minus K on new knowledge. Consequently, the ego can be put under unreasonable pressure to deal with contrasting internal and external demands, as new knowledge threatens the reality of existing knowledge, including what is known about the self. For those entering educational settings, this minus K attack is manifest when dealing with the required professional knowledge and this is often seen to be rejected in favour of practical experience. The personal knowledge that is brought to the profession is a lively muddle of expectations and anticipations, which Britzman (2003) argues will be used to defend against the complex and uncertain world of working in educational settings, thus making it challenging to accept and engage with new professional learning. Schleifer (1987) sees this defence against new ways of knowing in the context of Lacan's "passion for ignorance". This is not as a passive "not knowing", but the result of an active dynamic unconscious that seeks to defend against new knowledge. This passion for ignorance, or a desire to hold on to what is known, becomes a barrier to learning, for both the professional and the pupil. Both Felman (1982) and Schleifer (1987) suggest that because of this passion for ignorance, teacher "education" will be resisted and the best that can be hoped for is to create the conditions for learning and dealing with new knowledge.

New professionals have a tendency to focus on their own performance in educational settings, such as the need to maintain classroom control and the achievement of government imposed professional "standards". For example, student teachers act out what Gardner (1994) calls a "furore to teach", which is demonstrated as a desire to reject theory and focus only on their teaching experience; in doing so, they reduce the possibility of doubting their actions and prevent the inevitable encounter with new knowledge as they pursue the goal of becoming a "good teacher". Haworth (1998) remarks on how the conception of the good teacher is culturally bound, and, along with many other authors (Cameron & Baker, 2004; Connelly & Clandinin, 1990; Kagan, 1992; Nuthall, 2002; Webster-Wright, 2009), concedes that these notions are held extremely tenaciously and are resistant to change.

It is further argued that the process of becoming an education professional deserves special consideration due to the ubiquitous nature of education. Notwithstanding exceptional circumstances, everyone will have experienced some form of educational setting and, therefore, has a personal awareness of an assumed objective reality that these institutions represent. Consequently, those who choose to join the education profession will, unlike, many other occupations, have a good notion of what the role is like and what would be expected of them. Significantly, Britzman (2003) takes, as her starting point, the Freudian assumption that education inaugurates a crisis as it enhances the influence of the present external world on that of the past world, now represented by internal conflicts. This heightened level of anxiety increases the potential to mobilise the dynamic unconscious. In an education context, this offers up the possibility that memories and phantasies as to what it means to be a teacher, or indeed a learner, will be evoked and heightened by the effect of past or present transference relationships (A. Freud, 1930; Moore, 2006a,b; Pitt & Britzman, 2003; Youell, 2006).

Transference, countertransference, and education professionals

Transference is a central psychoanalytic principle that refers to the working of a dynamic unconscious: at its core is the idea that past unresolved conflicts or ways of relating are projected into new situations in the present. The countertransference relates to how one feels in the presence of an "other", and that these feelings might, indeed, not be yours but, in fact, belong to those of the other. What is important for the teacher to be aware of is to distinguish between any thoughts and feelings they are experiencing that are not theirs but might belong to the pupil. For Anna Freud (1930) this was of fundamental importance for teachers as she regards educational settings as being familiar places, therefore highly susceptible to the re-enactment of childhood memories and, hence, transference phenomena. The dynamics that this creates will have an impact on the relationship

between the teacher and pupil and, for this to be an effective relationship, the teacher also needs to be able to distinguish what feelings
and thoughts are his or her own.

Both Freud (1933a) and Anna Freud (1930) make the case that all
those who enter educational settings should first experience a period
of analysis to heighten their awareness of their own internal conflicts.
In fact, Freud considered the analysis of teachers or educators as a
"more efficacious prophylactic measure than the analysis of children
themselves" (1933a, p. 150). Anna Freud warns that, without analysis,
teachers could get stuck in transference dynamics that cast both
teacher and pupil back into their biographies and unresolved past
conflicts (see also Weiss, 2002a,b). She argues that if such an analysis
were to be undertaken, it would be more likely that pupil behaviour
could be understood in the context of the present intersubjective relationships. Britzman and Pitt (1996) see the need for teachers to understand their own internal conflicts as an ethical responsibility. They
argue that if teachers do not do this, then, as a result of the transference–countertransference, they will be continually leaving young
people with their own internal conflicts that are communicated within
the pedagogical encounter.

The present proposition is that the transference relationship and
associated countertransference occurs between individuals, but
Schleifer (1987) proposes a Lacanian adaptation on transference phenomena within educational settings. Her suggestion is that the transference is not so much a "shadow of something that was once alive"
(p. 805), but is instead the transference of discursive strategies from
one situation to the next. This has the impact of increasing the flexibility and applicability of the concept of the transference. Subsequently, it can now be applied, more broadly, to interactions between
the self and socially and culturally constructed structures and practices, such as those within education. This implies that transference
phenomena might be linked to both the knowledge and the authority,
of the objectified process of education itself.

The hypothesis offered here is that a full understanding of early
professional development requires an awareness of the influence of
the past. The necessity for developing such a reflexive outlook in
educational settings has been supported by many authors (Atkinson,
2004; Britzman, 1991, 2005; Moore, 2006a,b). The earlier suggestion,
from both Freud and Anna Freud, that teachers should receive psycho-

analysis to help them appreciate the origin and consequence of transference phenomena, is ultimately unrealistic. What this research sets out to do is to explore these relationships in education settings by identifying patterns of responding to education that are consistent over time. The premise is a simple one that, although based on psychoanalytic principles, does not necessarily require any deep understanding of psychoanalysis. The fundamental research approach has been to gather a number of narratives that represent past and present educational experiences.

Atkinson (2004) and Moore (2006a,b) recognise the important role that narratives can play in facilitating an understanding of the self. Narratives have a psychodynamic significance, as they are able to demonstrate how individuals are products of the interaction between their present social world and their past unresolved psychic conflicts (Pitt, 1998). Britzman (2000) argues that if beginning teachers can implicate themselves in their own narrative experiences of teaching and learning then this offers the possibility for insight and an opportunity to engage with past conflicts (Pitt, 1998). Therefore, the ability to be reflexive provides greater insight into the desires and fantasies that originate in the unconscious and, subsequently, make it more likely for professional experiences to be identified and owned.

This research project sought to develop the work of Atkinson, Britzman, and Moore by encouraging reflexivity through the use of narratives. In contrast to the above authors, this process involved the collection of two open-ended narrative interviews; the life story narrative, which drew on the life experiences before embarking on a career in an education setting, and the professional development narrative, which represents what has more commonly been collected by previous researchers, and that is an account of the participants' experiences once "in post". This approach was informed by psychotherapeutic sensibilities, where the telling of a narrative is situated in both the past and the present. Subsequently, information from both can be used to identify consistent patterns of relating that might have an influence on the development of professional understanding and practice.

The collection of narratives

The participants were recruited by means of an opportunistic sample, whereby a standard e-mail was sent to all schools that worked in

partnership with the author's university. To be recruited, the participants had to reply to the e-mail, after which they received more
details of the project, and they were then invited to an individual
meeting. At this meeting, an opportunity was provided to ask questions and to discuss and complete the consent forms. A date was then
agreed for the first narrative interview. All future interviews were
arranged by e-mail communication, where it was agreed that a non-
reply signified that the participant no longer wished to continue. Ten
participants were originally recruited, seven of whom (Chloe, Emily,
Grace, Jack, Lucy, Oliver, and Sophie—all pseudonyms) came to the
first interview and provided a life story narrative. Five continued to
provide professional development narratives and three (Lucy, Oliver,
and Sophie) also engaged with formative interviews. Of the remaining two that did not, one had resigned her post (Emily) and the other
(Jack) had moved school. Lucy and Oliver will be discussed later in
the case studies.

The initial interview was conducted early on in either their training or initial post and provided the life story narrative in response to
the single question, "Tell me the story of your life up until obtaining
this post". The second interview took place in the second term and a
professional development narrative was produced in response to the
question, "Tell me the story of your life since being in this post". The
narratives were analysed using three techniques to produce an education biography that represented the possible transference responses
to education. These responses would then form the basis of reflexive
formative interviews. The research had ethical approval from the
author's university, and confidentiality and anonymity were ensured
through the use of participant and workplace pseudonyms. The topics
discussed were those raised by the participants and the author sought
consent to continue their narratives if it was felt the material discussed
exposed them to sensitive issues.

Analysis

The initial analysis was informed by the Gestalt approach, with two
further techniques, the Narrative Process Coding System and Future-
Blind serving to triangulate this data.

Gestalt approach

The Gestalt approach (Hollway & Jefferson, 2000; Merrill & West, 2009) is grounded within a psychosocial view. It also closely mirrors the therapeutic encounter, where the analyst requests the analysand to "tell me about yourself and what has brought you here today", thereby initiating the telling of a life that contains conscious–unconscious and affective–cognitive material. Both Hollway and Jefferson (2000) and West (1996) take into account the importance of considering the whole data gathered and seek to find structure, coherence, and patterns and order inside this. Critically, the approach recognises the relationship between the researcher and participant and the need to become immersed in the data. The Gestalt-informed approach provided "individual experiences in context" that were developed from multiple re-readings and re-listening to the narratives where a number of themes were identified within the life story and professional development narratives. These were then compared and combined to produce a summary of responses in relation to educational settings.

Narrative Process Coding System (NPCS)

The NPCS was developed by Angus and Hardtke (1994) and Angus, Levitt, and Hardtke (1999) to analyse and explore narratives in therapeutic settings. The NPCS considers three narrative types, external, internal, and reflective. The external reveals the detail of the structure and content of the story, while the internal identifies (unconscious) emotional aspects. The external and internal narratives can, therefore, provide a situational context in conjunction with the narrator's experiential information. The NPCS also provides details on the reflective narrative. These are more analytical and are used to make sense of situations; therefore, they can serve to identify patterns or plans for future actions. In addition, the NPCS analysis involves the identification of narrative topics. The topics contain the details of the characters, plots, and future realistic or fictional goals. They can, therefore, provide insight as to the conscious cognitive "who", "what", and "why" of a narrative while also indicating future actions. NPCS narrative topics and types were identified from the life story and professional development narratives. This information was then collated to provide a summary of the "experience in context" in relation to the NPCS topics and types for each of the two narratives. These were then

compared and combined to produce a summary of responses in relation to educational settings.

Future-Blind

This technique is taken from the Biographic Narrative Interpretative
Method (BNIM) that has been developed from the work of Rosenthal
and Fischer-Rosenthal (cited in Wengraf, 2001). The process involves
the collection of very detailed interviews with the assumption that an
interrogation of these will reveal deeply hidden realities. One aspect
of the BNIM approach used in this research was to carry out a
"Future-Blind" analysis, during which a panel was presented with
either the chronological lived life or the sequential told life in successive segments. After each segment, the panel suggests hypotheses
about the life of the participant until a clear pattern can be agreed on
and confirmed by considering future segments. It is this pattern that
represents the consistent responses to education settings.

Formative discussions

This research sought to explore the effectiveness of using narratives
both as a research tool and also to afford opportunities for new education professionals to take a reflexive view of their practice by impli-
cating the impact of their past experiences and phantasies in the
present. As a result of considering the themes that emerged in all three
analytic techniques, an education biography for each participant was
developed. This biography identified ways of relating to education
that were common to both the life story and professional development
narratives. The final sequence of interviews, therefore, consisted of
open-ended discussions where the researcher highlighted the education biography and how this was operationalised in the life story and
professional development narratives.

Case studies

Two case studies are provided to highlight how the education
biographies were used to inform reflexive formative discussions that

implicated past responses to education settings within a developing professional practice. For brevity, the construction of the education biographies will not be included, just the formative discussion that resulted from themes contained within these.

Oliver

Oliver is in his late forties and he is training to teach on the Graduate Teacher Programme (GTP). Trainees on the GTP are employed as unqualified teachers by their training schools and, during the course of the year, they work towards gaining Qualified Teacher Status (the government approved qualification to work in state schools). He was academically able and "fast-tracked" at school and refused to follow the family tradition of attending an Oxbridge university, coming into teaching after working in the city. Oliver acknowledged that he found the formative discussions helpful and a "good reflective activity". The content of his education biography indicated that, in response to education settings, he had a controlling disposition. This can be illustrated from two formative discussions where Oliver provided further examples of how his desire to maintain a level of control had an impact on his professional practice.

An example of this was seen in relation to the requirements of the GTP. The course provided vast amounts of theoretical and organisational information; in fact, so much that even Oliver began to be swamped by this. His recollection is angry, and indicates how he began to feel deeply uncomfortable when it seemed impossible to control the situation. Oliver is also able to realise the significance of these wider controlling tendencies and worries if this might have a negative impact on his professional practice:

> If I'm honest, actually it's one of the things that worries me about being a teacher, being in control or not, because I would say that broadly speaking a classroom environment is not a particularly controlled environment is it? . . . well, I feel it's not, certainly not as controlled as I would like and um . . . certainly that's how I feel about it at the moment—and I just wondered whether that is a flaw for me in my ability to teach, actually, I'm not prepared to be as . . . uncontrolled or flexible or however you like to play it or explain it within the classroom environment . . .

Oliver also questions what useful information he could take from his involvement in the research process. I reflect the question back and ask if there is something he still wishes to talk about. What ensues next is a twenty-five-minute discussion centred on a particular class that Oliver has yet to be successful in managing. It appears that no matter what Oliver does, he is unable to keep this group under control and their academic results and behaviour are seen to reflect this. My assumption is that at this time (over halfway through his initial training year) the one class outside Oliver's control was sufficient to divert all his energies to this solution, irrespective of the impact on others.

The education biography also noted that Oliver carefully and intellectually reviewed the risks associated with education settings. He then subsequently made decisions that would protect him from the potential threats they represented. When the observation about Oliver using his intellect to manage risk was discussed, his response was very matter of fact.

> I guess it, it is sort of what I imagine most people do, but of course I don't have the benefit of your experience of seeing how other people live their lives. But yeah I just think—I suppose as I've been round again a relatively self-selecting group of people for most of my life. I mean obviously there are people here that are motivated differently but . . . most people I get on with I guess are pretty rational about what they do and why they do it . . .

His assumption that "all people" must be like him supports how deeply embedded this perception is: he finds it hard to imagine others not seeing the world as he does. He agrees the point, although somewhat grudgingly.

This gathering of useful information is what Oliver does to find out, control, and, ultimately, manage the potential risk that educational settings might pose. There is a sense that he just wants to understand his external world so that he knows what to do and then can get on with his job / task. He recognises this aspect of his personality and claims,

> I mean the only times I've ever been unhappy in a working environment have been the two times where I haven't been in control of my destiny and I absolutely hate that—absolutely hate it! I don't think there's a need for it . . . I think I'm smart enough to work out . . .

This clearly puts Oliver in control, as it is he who collates the information and considers what actions to take. He becomes anxious if this process takes too long and considered that, as GTP students, they

> ... faffed around for a hell of a long time, floundering, not really understanding what was expected of us, wasting a hell of a lot of time going down blind alleys ... what they would say is, "Ah! but it's all just the journey and part of the learning experiences that you've sort of got independent cognitive ability" and all this rubbish but I'm not convinced of that ...

This delay in providing the appropriate information only serves to hinder Oliver's mastery of the new situation and is not welcomed. He makes it clear that his role is to become competent quickly and to have an understanding of and a useful function in this setting:

> ... I guess the approach I take to anything is, if I've got something new to do, find out how to do it first and then decide is this something ... that I actually emotionally want to do, feel like doing, or whatever, yeah. First job is to work out how quickly you can be good at it in a mechanical sort of way ...

Oliver continues to provide additional evidence of his predisposition to control and reduce the potential risk inherent in educational settings. Significantly, Oliver left his unsuccessful first placement early, but was full of praise for the subsequent, second placement setting, which he regarded as very successful. Oliver later made it clear that the second setting offered him a full-time post but, despite enjoying his time there, he did not accept the position. What prevented Oliver from committing to this school was the suggestion of structural changes where all lessons were to be ninety minutes long. Oliver was not convinced by this and could only see it being difficult to manage. Since being a young child, Oliver has maintained his influence on education settings: he continues to do so as a new professional, but is now being brought into an awareness of the impact of this on his professional development.

Lucy

Lucy was working as a teaching assistant, having recently returned from working abroad. She resigned from this post in the first term, and had recently obtained a post in an alternative curriculum centre. She provided little detail about her early experiences of education settings and focused on stories of travelling. Lucy's education biography identified a predisposition towards looking for challenges and that, as a result of these experiences, she would construct an understanding of her life. She can explain eloquently how this drives her.

> But experience is great, I . . . it just sort of clicked in my head, my—one of my greatest desires of life is experience. *Per se.* Point. Because experience is what you know if I have seen a new colour, I mean if I have experienced a new colour in a landscape, if I have seen a mountain top, this is what drives me. If I have talked to somebody you know with a fascinating view on life, take on life, if I have—those experiences are. They just are.

There is passion in Lucy's words and she admits that being part of this research project is associated with her desire to reflect on her life experiences. Lucy discusses this further and makes direct links between experiences and learning and acknowledges that "you have to put yourself out there".

This sense of finding out what will happen is reaffirmed as Lucy's approach to beginning to work as a teaching assistant in a secondary school is discussed, in the light of her eventual decision to resign. Once more, Lucy engages with an experience and waits to see what will happen:

> . . . yeah . . . I wouldn't say it attacked me but I just had to test—I think I had to experience where it took me, um I did get attacked in the end, but that was right at the end and that was really the last straw for me and once all professional . . . um, ability to talk—once all ability to talk professionally had been kicked out the window by senior members of staff who then personally attacked me, it was like, we have reached the bottom . . . goodbye.

When she takes up her teaching assistant role, she admits that she had to push against the boundaries and "just had to test—I think I had to experience where it took me". Lucy begins this by asking to be called by her first name and to wear her everyday rather than "office" clothes. In the formative discussion, when we discuss this, I offer an element of surprise and talk about being able to compromise and be an effective "team player". Lucy abruptly rejects this and is quite defiant that she does not need to compromise her rules and values and that such a response is difficult for her. In fact, she admits that the school's values and structures are not hers, and, I suspect, have never been, hence her teenage style clothing rebellion. She senses this has given her an affinity with those children who are on the edge of exclusion at school and, just as she likes to push the rules, so she also has a respect for those children who do the same.

Lucy claims to have been "freaked out" by deceit, where publicised values, structures, and actions did not match the reality of her school setting. The experience of what she described as the hypocrisy and pretence at the school was such that she could not remain in the workplace. One element of this hypocrisy was the institution's claim to be caring when she felt this was not the case, particularly related to her needs in looking after the difficult group. Even though Lucy ultimately found the role unmanageable and resigned, she was still able to reflect on what the experience had provided her with.

> It's a progression. I think for me life is always a progression and you're only where you are because of what you've done and you only get to where you're going through what you do. So everything is valuable, don't reject—you know I don't reject the experience at Summer Wood, it was incredibly painful, incredibly painful but incredibly valuable as a learning experience . . .

Despite very difficult experiences, Lucy is able to appreciate what she has learnt. What is more, she sees this as pivotal in getting the post she is now in:

> I am very very happy in my position and therefore I would actually . . . I could go to Summer Wood now and be very appreciative of the start I was given, I was given an opportunity and without what I had, the six months at Summer Wood I wouldn't be here . . .

Lucy is enthusiastic about her new post as an assistant on an alternative curriculum programme. It is also important that she is being listened to, that her views are being taken into account, and that she can be called Lucy and can wear her everyday clothes. In this present education setting, Lucy can legitimately push boundaries and engage in the new experiences that provide her with so much meaning.

Conclusion

Previous research was shown to highlight the interaction between personal and professional lives and how professional knowledge was rejected in favour of practical experience. The psychoanalytic interpretation of these findings suggests that educational settings readily evoke unconscious phenomena. The analysis of the case study narratives indicates the importance of the interaction between the past and present. It was also argued that this represented a transference relationship with education where past responses to established education structures and processes were re-enacted during the development of a professional practice. This does not preclude the possibility that such responses might indeed also reflect more intimate familial interactions, but it is argued that formal education settings are more likely to evoke and highlight such responses. What is significant is that when this transference relationship with education was presented to the participants as an "education biography", this led to formative reflexive discussions that enabled the self to be implicated in the development of their professional practice.

The rationale for this research is grounded in the psychoanalytic assumption that the therapeutic encounter facilitates an understanding of the self. This is achieved by identifying transference phenomena and providing an opportunity to bring to awareness the influence of the past on the present. It is suggested that the collection of narratives and identifying an educational biography reflects this process. Importantly, it might enable the new education professional to take part in a reflexive dialogue and to understand how their past affects their developing professional identity. When compared to Anna and Sigmund Freud's suggestion that all new teachers should undergo analysis in order to deal with the transference conflicts that they bring into the classroom, the process of gathering and discussing education biographies has been shown to serve a similar function, while not attempting to be "therapy". Education settings are endowed with the archives of the past and the hopes and desires that serve to motivate actions in the present. They are, therefore, potent arenas for the dynamic unconscious, and to ignore this is to limit our understanding of the professional structures and processes of education settings.

The concluding remarks from this research indicate that tentative movements towards beginning a dialogue between education and psychoanalysis will be beneficial. The application of psychoanalytic theory does not require education to become "therapeutic", but simply to allow a space where the influence of the past on the present can be considered. Neither is it suggested that psychoanalysis offers the only insight into this complex arena. What it does offer, supported by the use of narratives, is the possibility of using a language to discuss professional development that implicates the individual, their values, and emotional responses. This involves a potentially much richer and fruitful process than an overly technical–rational approach: it encourages movement beyond superficiality (Loughran, 2007). It can provide an opportunity for new education professionals to maintain a coherent life narrative that is meaningful and motivating. By considering educational processes and structures from a psychoanalytic perspective, education can look forward to a more human and ethically nuanced future.

Note

1. The term "education professional" is used to denote all those who work with people in an education setting. This will include teachers, teaching assistants, learning mentors, etc.

References

Angus, L., & Hardtke, K. (1994). Narrative processes in psychotherapy. *Canadian Psychology, 35*(2): 190–203.

Angus, L., Levitt, H., & Hardtke, K. (1999). The narrative process coding system: research applications and implications for psychotherapy practice. *Journal of Clinical Psychology, 55*: 1255–1270.

Atkinson, D. (2004). Theorising how student teachers form their identities in initial teacher education. *British Educational Research Journal, 30*(3): 379–394.

Bion, W. R. (1961). *Experiences in Groups.* London: Tavistock.

Britzman, D. P. (1991). *Practice Makes Practice: A Critical Study of Learning to Teach.* Albany, NY: State University of New York Press.

Britzman, D. P. (2000). Teacher education in the confusion of our times. *Journal of Teacher Education, 51*(3): 200–205.

Britzman, D. P. (2003). *After-Education: Anna Freud, Melanie Klein and Psychoanalytic Histories of Learning*. Albany: State University of New York Press.

Britzman, D. P. (2005). Foreword. In: J. Alsup (Ed.), *Teacher Identity Discourses: Negotiating Personal and Professional Spaces* (pp. ix–xii). Mahwah, NJ: Lawrence Erlbaum.

Britzman, D. P., & Pitt, A. J. (1996). Pedagogy and transference: casting the past of learning into the presence of teaching. *Theory into Practice, 35*(2): 117–123.

Cameron, M., & Baker, R. (2004). *Research on Initial Teacher Education in New Zealand: 1993–2004*. Wellington: New Zealand Council for Educational Research.

Connelly, F. M., & Clandinin, D. J. (1988). *Teachers as Curriculum Planners: Narratives of Experience*. New York: Teachers College Press.

Connelly, F. M., & Clandinin, D. J. (1990). Stories of experience and narrative inquiry. *Educational Researcher, 19*(5): 2–14.

Felman, S. (1982). Psychoanalysis and education: teaching terminable and interminable. *Yale French Studies, 63*: 21–44.

Freud, A. (1930). Four lectures on psychoanalysis for teachers and parents. In: *The Writings of Anna Freud, Vol. 1* (pp. 73–136). New York: International University Press.

Freud, S. (1933a). *New Introductory Lectures on Psycho-Analysis. S.E., 22*. London: Hogarth.

Gardner, R. M. (1994). *On Trying To Teach: The Mind in Correspondence*. Hillsdale, NJ: Analytic Press.

Haworth, P. (1998). "Good" teaching and learning: a matter of perception? *set: Research Information for Teachers, 13*: 1–4.

Hollway, W., & Jefferson, T. (2000). *Doing Qualitative Research Differently*. London: Sage.

Huberman, M. (1995). Working with life-history narratives. In: H. McEwan & K. Egan (Eds.), *Narrative in Teaching and Learning Research* (pp. 127–165). New York: Teachers College Press.

Jones, M. (2003). Reconciling personal and professional values and beliefs with the reality of teaching: findings from an evaluative case study of 10 newly qualified teachers during their year of induction. *Teacher Development, 7*(3): 385–401.

Kagan, D. M. (1992). Professional growth among preservice and beginning teachers. *Review of Educational Research, 62*(2): 129–169.

Loughran, J. (2007). Enacting a pedagogy of teacher education. In: T. Russell & J. Loughran (Eds.), *Enacting a Pedagogy of Teacher Education: Values, Relationships and Practices* (pp. 1–15). Oxford: Routledge.

Merrill, B., & West, L. (2009). *Using Biographical Methods in Social Research*. London: Sage.

Moore, A. (2006a). Recognising desire: a psychosocial approach to understanding education policy implementation and effect. *Oxford Review of Education, 32*(4): 487–503.

Moore, A. (2006b). Understanding the social self: the role of reflexivity in schoolteachers' professional learning. In: T. Townsend & R. Bates (Eds.), *Handbook of Teacher Education: Globalization, Standards and Professionalism in Times of Change* (pp. 571–583). Dordrecht: Springer.

Nuthall, G. (2002). The cultural myths and the realities of teaching and learning. *New Zealand Annual Review of Education, 11*: 5–30.

Ovens, A., & Tinning, R. (2009). Reflection as situated practice: a memory-work of lived experience in teacher education. *Teaching and Teacher Education, 25*: 1125–1131.

Pitt, A. J. (1998). Qualifying resistance: some comments on methodological dilemmas. *International Journal in Qualitative Studies in Education, 11*(4): 535–553.

Pitt, A. J., & Britzman, D. P. (2003). Speculations on qualities of difficult knowledge in teaching and learning: an experiment in psychoanalytic research. *International Journal in Qualitative Studies in Education, 16*(6): 755–776.

Schleifer, R. (1987). Lacan's enunciation of the cure of mortality: teaching, transference and desire. *College English, 49*(7): 801–815.

Webster-Wright, A. (2009). Reframing professional development through understanding authentic professional learning. *Review of Educational Research, 79*(2): 702–739.

Weiss, S. (2002a). How teachers' autobiographies influence their responses to children's behaviors. Part I. *Emotional and Behavioural Difficulties, 7*(1): 9–18.

Weiss, S. (2002b). How teachers' autobiographies influence their responses to children's behaviors. Part II. *Emotional and Behavioural Difficulties, 7*(2): 109–127.

Wengraf, T. (2001). *Qualitative Research Interviewing: Biographic Narrative and Semi-Structured Methods*. London: Sage.

West, L. (1996). *Beyond Fragments: Adults, Motivation and Higher Education*. London: Taylor & Francis.

Youell, B. (2006). *The Learning Relationship: Psychoanalytic Thinking in Education*. London: Karnac.

CHAPTER TEN

Border country: using psychodynamic ideas in teaching and research

Celia Hunt and Linden West

Introduction

This chapter arises out of recognition of the importance of psychoanalytic theory in both our approaches to teaching and research. We demonstrate how such ideas—broadly defined as encouraging people to engage more closely with thoughts and feelings that may be hidden from the conscious mind—can be applied in many diverse and radical ways. We also show how such an approach can be problematical for students, teachers, and researchers. In writing this chapter, we take issue with those writers who want to separate therapy from education, insisting as they do that "therapeutic education" involves a "diminished" notion of the subject who sees him- or herself as a victim of circumstances. Instead, we suggest, entering the border country between therapeutic and educational processes and ideas can be deeply rewarding, empowering, but also difficult for teachers, researchers, and learners alike.

Our teaching and research

We have both used a psychodynamic approach to teaching and research in higher and adult education for many years.: "We define 'psychodynamic' broadly as an approach that encourages people to engage more closely with thoughts and feelings that may be hidden from the conscious mind" (Leiper & Maltby, 2004, p. 13). Celia convened a Masters programme on the use of creative writing as a developmental and therapeutic tool at Sussex University for fourteen years. People took this programme to strengthen their creative writing through a deeper engagement with self, to explore life transitions, and/or to acquire skills to work with others in education and health and social care. Part of the work was experiential, involving self-exploration through imagery and metaphor, and rewriting of personal narratives using fiction. While this was not therapy in the strict sense, there was a strong therapeutic dimension to students' studies, but they also developed conceptual understandings of their writing process, drawing on psychodynamic, literary, and cultural theory. So, the learning involved was both emotional and cognitive, often identifying and working through subtle difficulties in learning to write creatively. Linden has used psychodynamic ideas in Masters and Doctoral programmes in developing auto/biographical reflections and research methodology. This includes exploring the role of the researcher, professional guidance worker, or doctor in shaping, sometimes unconsciously, what the "other" might say (e.g., Reid & West, 2010, 2011; West 1996, 2001, 2004, 2009, 2010). In his research, he has explicitly used psychodynamic ideas in interpreting aspects of his own life history as part of interrogating the auto/biographical dimensions of research. Gender, and changing senses of self, in the transitional spaces of education, broadly defined, as well as the interplay of desire and resistance, have similarly emerged as important themes in his work.

Both of us are strongly influenced by object relations theorists.[1] Linden draws on Melanie Klein, Donald Winnicott, and Wilfred Bion, noting their growing influence in social theory and in thinking about transitional processes in learning, as well as the contribution they have made to understanding the deeply contingent, developmental, and often defended nature of subjectivity, in contrast to the one-dimensional, cognitively driven, information processing subject of much conventional social science (Clarke, 2008; Froggett, 2002; Hollway, 2008; Hollway & Jefferson, 2000). He has adopted the term "psychosocial" to describe this psychodynamically informed perspective, which recognises the importance of the socio-cultural in shaping self and subjectivity while not reducing psyche to a simplistic epiphenomenal status. Learning and the subject called the learner are, in this view, both social and psychological at the same time: social, in that subjectivity, including the capacity to learn and to remain open to experience, is forged in our intimate interactions with significant others, which, in turn, are shaped by the structuring forces of class, gender, and ethnicity, for instance, and the discourses of power that pervade them. Social, too, in that our engagement with new social networks or entry into a different habitus, in Bourdieu's language (Bourdieu, 1988), as in higher education, as well as significant experiences of learning more generally, can lead to a questioning of who we are and might want to be, and whether we are able to embrace change (West, 1996). But psyche has its own inner dynamic, grounded in intersubjective life, and cannot be reduced to an epiphenomenal status. Not everyone in similar "objective" situations responds in the same way to oppressive experience. Some, more than others, remain open and creative in the face of difficulties, while others might retreat into defensiveness, paranoia, and even fundamentalism (Frosh, 1991; Giddens, 1999). Moreover, the unconscious is often at work in the relationships that constitute education, or, for that matter, research, given that our engagement with a body of knowledge is always and inevitably mediated through other human beings (Merrill & West, 2009).

Celia draws on Winnicott, too, but also on Christopher Bollas and Marion Milner. Her main influence, though, is the German–American psychoanalyst Karen Horney, whose work explores how we erect psychological defence mechanisms against anxiety and, in the process, lose touch with spontaneous feelings, which Horney identifies as the core of our self-experience (Horney, 1954). Celia has used these theories in her research to understand the effects of such defences on the learning process and how exploring oneself through creative life writing can help to alleviate learning blocks and difficulties (e.g., Hunt, 2000, 2002, 2004, 2010, forthcoming). Horney was deeply concerned with the effects of cultural factors on the development of the personality, but she also believed that the personality could be looked at as having its own dynamic, which can render the individual his or her own worst enemy. Following Horney, Celia believes that there is a value in focusing on the individual psyche when thinking about the learning process, but that it is also important to think about how social, cultural, and historical contexts contribute to individual experience.

For both of us, adult learning occupies a kind of "border country", straddling emotion and cognition, the social and psychological, self and other, education and therapy. Here are examples of our approaches.

Celia: I am currently writing up research into the learning process of students taking the MA Creative Writing and Personal Development. What is striking is how many people report a more open and flexible sense of themselves as a result of this programme. At the start of the study, many of the students taking part identified blocks to, or difficulties with, their creative writing. These typically included difficulties with creating fictional first-person narrators or third-person characters out of themselves; with imbuing their fiction with felt, emotional life; or with finding a writing identity for creative writing, particularly where they already had a strong academic or non-fiction writing identity.

Already, by the end of their first course (an experiential course, within a literary and psychodynamic conceptual framework, and with a large component of collaborative peer learning), many of these students were reporting significant changes and developments in their sense of themselves as writers and learners. Anne, for example, a freelance non-fiction writer, came with a strong professional identity, which seemed to be inhibiting the development of her creative writing. She had high expectations for her creative writing, but, once it was on the page, it made her "cringe"; she did not recognise it as belonging to her, maybe, she suggested, "because I don't want to own it". She also noted a certain perfectionism at work ("There's . . . a part of me that wants to complete all tasks! And precisely!"), combined with premature judgement on the material emerging, which was detrimental to developing a freer, more chaotic process of creative writing.

The combination of emotional, cognitive, and collaborative learning in that first course helped Anne to start uncovering and finding a shape for strongly felt personal material, in particular deep and previously censored feelings about her chronically ill sister. She describes one piece of writing about her sister's destructiveness towards her as "a statement . . . that has taken me my entire life, as her younger sibling, to make". Moving out of the safe boundaries of her non-fiction identity through the use of metaphor and fictional techniques, and through developing a relationship with a small and safe group of peer readers, she began to understand that developing an identity as a creative writer involved embracing a more relational sense of herself, which was quite different from the strongly self-contained person she felt herself to be as a non-fiction writer: "My sense of self and of myself as a writer is linked in to my roles . . . as sister, daughter, aunt, partner, and so on". She was not yet ready to reveal herself fully to an external reader, but felt that she was "learning to allow myself to write both from, and about, me, while trusting myself to read [myself] without critical judgement. This is basic scrub clearing, which I hope will lead to clarity in my writing and a warm willingness to feel freer with the notion of an external reader".

Summing up what she felt she had learnt by the end of the first course, Anne said, "I have finally given myself permission to extend my writing beyond its tight boundaries and what I write is giving myself permission to be me." The psychodynamic approach to teaching that this course involved clearly enabled Anne to expand her sense of herself, beyond the narrow confines of a safe but inhibiting self-identity, and to start using more of herself, particularly her felt, emotional self, in her writing.

Linden: I have been researching, over many years, the experiences of families living in different marginalised communities and the nature of their interactions with a range of family support programmes, such as Sure Start. Joe and Heidi, for instance, and their two children, were part of a "biographical" and longitudinal study of a Sure Start project, which was designed to chronicle and collaboratively interpret experiences through the eyes of families (and staff) on the ground. We wanted to know the extent to which families such as Heidi and Joe's felt supported or threatened, empowered or disempowered, by such projects. Heidi got involved in her local Sure Start project in different ways, such as attending parent support sessions, a playgroup (with the children), adult classes, and also having psychotherapeutic help.

They were understandably cautious about seeing us, as researchers, although they agreed to do so, and were very reticent about talking. They eventually shared experiences, over time, in some depth. Heidi and Joe had known each other since childhood. They had both been abandoned (Heidi at birth), and went into residential homes, followed by periods in foster care. The material poured out as Heidi described being moved from one family to another. She had never been able to talk to anyone about her life history before, she stated. It was hard to explain, and she did "not really understand myself why the things that had happened had happened, and not knowing how or where to start".

She told us that the courses "gave me more confidence to know what to do with my two children". She suffered from mental health problems, she explained, and began to talk about being upset with her children, "when they laugh at me". Sure Start had been very threatening, at first: they were afraid that people might be "checking" on them and "that was going through our heads all the time". They were frightened of their children being put into care, like they were. They filled the fridge with food and bought new clothes for the children whenever a Sure Start worker, or, for that matter, a researcher, came near, despite being unable to afford it. But the relationship to Sure Start shifted, however contingently (as did the research relationship), from suspicion to some trust. Heidi, especially, felt empowered.

Heidi talked about the importance of contact with other mothers and particular workers: "like one big family really". She referred to particular people as "the mums I never had" and felt understood and more legitimate in the eyes of significant others. There was physical relief at getting out of the house, at having a temporal structure to the week, and having access to adult conversations. These processes are not to be judged simply in individualistic terms: time and again, understanding that other parents had difficulties controlling their children, or with their own irritation and anger, provided a sense of relief and helped build self-confidence (Schuller, Preston, Hammond, Brassett-Grundy, & Bynner, 2004). We asked Joe and Heidi about the research and they said it was "good" to be able to share their stories and to weave strands together, in ways they had not done previously, as they linked their own histories of abandonment with intense suspicions of authority at all levels and anxiety that their own children would be taken away from them. But they felt listened to and valued by us, even when talking about disturbing things, in what became, however briefly, a storytelling, meaning-making, and, to an extent, therapeutic research process. Feeling understood can work at a very primitive emotional level, engaging the child in the adult. It can also be cathartic and self-affirming because of feeling understood and seriously listened to.

As these two examples demonstrate, a psychodynamic approach to teaching and research can lead to empowerment and a stronger sense of identity. However, it can also lead us, and those we work with, into a potentially muddled and messy territory. The process of storytelling about a life and reflexively seeking to understand it, and what it feels like to be oneself, can encompass disturbed and disturbing experiences requiring some containment.

Risks of a psychodynamic approach to teaching and research, and their containment

A psychodynamic approach to teaching and research, in short, is not without its risks. Research or teaching does not provide the long-term support available in therapeutic settings once repressed material has surfaced. Educators might not be equipped to handle certain dynamics, such as transference and countertransference, or know what to do when a student encounters disturbing personal material. They are clearly not there as therapists. Working in this "border country" between education and therapy has been challenging for both of us. It has involved taking risks and learning progressively which risks we can take and which we perhaps should not. This has helped us to begin to frame some of the issues more clearly and to explore the relationship between subjectivity and intersubjective processes. It has also helped us to understand better what is involved in creating "containment" (Bion, 1962) or a safe-enough "holding environment" in the transitional spaces of education and research (Merrill & West, 2009; Winnicott, 1971).

In the MA in Creative Writing and Personal Development, containment already began at the interview stage, where Celia, as convener, had to make judgements about who was likely to be able to manage the kinds of learning the programme involved, and to make sure people were aware that reflecting deeply on themselves might give rise to challenging material. Tutors were expected to have therapeutic training, to equip them to deal better with emotional learning. Back-up support mechanisms, provided by student advisers and counselling services, were also crucial for referring students if problems arose.

There were also important methods of containment within the teaching itself, the most important being the use of collaborative peer groups. In the first two courses, people were assigned to such groups for the sharing of creative writing, and these groups remained constant for each course. At their best, these small groups "gelled" in such a way that students built trust, with the members acting as supportive audience to each other's developing writing and sense of self. The creative writing in progress itself provided an element of containment for sometimes difficult personal experience, a way of being simultaneously close to, and distanced from, the material in Winnicott's "potential space" (Winnicott, 1971). Students' emerging conceptual understanding of their writing and learning process, through the study of theory, also framed and, therefore, contained their experience. So, as the MA progressed, they were thinking about themselves and their experience both from inside and outside. Of course, none of these measures can ever be foolproof, but they can reduce the potential for damage.

Linden's psychodynamic approach to research builds on the life history or biographical approach (what is sometimes known, following Stanley (1992), as "auto/biography"), which embraces the idea of relationship and a dynamic co-creation of text or story. This perception of research is, in part, a reaction against methods which can freeze people's experiences into predetermined frames, sometimes provoking intense resentment among those "under investigation", such as in the use of standardised instruments in psychological research (West, 1996). Bruner (1990) says that people narrativise their experience of the world, if given an opportunity to do so, *yet* most conventional interviews expect respondents to answer questions in the categorical form required in formal exchanges rather than the narratives of natural conversation. Using auto/biographical methods, and being sensitive to the emotional content of stories, in a clinical style, allows deeply personal narratives into the research frame and yet it can take the researcher into difficult territory. Sometimes, as noted with Joe and Heidi above, stories might be told, in part for defensive purposes, of fridges being full and new clothes on the children. Furthermore, such people are often unused to being listened to attentively and material can simply pour out (West, 2007). There is a danger, perhaps, of donning the mantle of the therapist (though Linden is indeed a trained psychoanalytic psychotherapist), given the pain that might be being communicated. Research, even of a longitudinal, biographical narrative kind, does not constitute psychotherapy, in the sense of offering a long-term structure of support; maybe, too, there is the danger of researcher narcissism, as we use others' lives for our own professional and or personal ends and boundaries get overly blurred (Josselson, 1996).

In a research context, a holding or containing framework can, to an extent, be provided through the use of ethical codes or ground rules clearly stating the purpose of a particular piece of research, as well as spelling out rights and responsibilities. The building of an alliance is also part of the containing process, analogous to the therapeutic alliance in psychotherapy. This involves establishing trust (partly a consequence of someone feeling understood as well as cared for) alongside clear ground rules (which will include a statement that the process is not psychotherapy, however problematical, in reality, this distinction might be).

The responses and self-understanding of the researcher are also central to containment, including the capacity for distance and understanding, alongside empathic immersion in the story, and to be able to process and feed back what might be difficult issues, in digestible form. The researcher needs to be aware of boundary issues, which, to repeat, can rely on the capacity—central to psychotherapeutic training—to be both absorbed in the other's story and retain some detachment and capacity for thought in the here and now. Decisions need to be made about what might appropriately be dealt with and what is best left alone. In this sense, research, like writing groups, can be seen as a sort of secure, transitional, playful space in which narrative risks can be taken, but in appropriate ways.

Such research can create an environment where new forms of agency, and even selfhood, in Horney's or Winnicott's sense, are created, in processes of storytelling and good enough relationships. Experience can be chronicled and interpreted collaboratively, in new ways, especially when working longitudinally (Merrill & West, 2009; West, 1996, 2001, 2007). But boundary issues do require thought, around where to go as well as where not to. We will all make mistakes, for diverse reasons, and supervision with an experienced critical friend, for instance, can be especially valuable in negotiating the border country. Moreover, anxiety about the process and around the ethics of researching and representing lives, more generally, as Josselson has observed, are essential companions in the territory: "to be uncomfortable with this work, I think, protects us from going too far" (Josselson, 1996, p. 70).

There follow two more examples of what we have learnt about facilitating a psychodynamic approach to teaching and research and managing the anxieties involved.

Celia: What seems to me now to be crucial is deep listening, of the kind that goes on in a therapeutic context proper, paying attention to what is said and the way it is said, as well as to what is not said or only implied. One of my doctoral students, whom I will call Peter, undertook a self-exploratory project, looking at his own experience of creative writing in order to understand better its potential developmental effects. He is a healthcare professional, and well used to reflecting on himself. The first couple of years of our working together involved discussion of Peter's creative writing in progress, work that he was trying to craft into its final form and with which he often felt dissatisfied. Then he brought me a batch of spontaneous personal material in poetic form that he had made no attempt to craft; it was simply in its raw state. This felt like a very important stage in the research relationship. Sufficient trust must have been built up to enable Peter to allow me to see this deeply personal material devoid of the distance that craft provides.

I read the work several times, noticed some recurring themes that seemed significant at a personal level, but was not sure whether I should point them out or whether I should focus on the potential of the writing for further development. I found it quite difficult to know how I should respond, and thought long and hard about it. I wrote myself some notes and decided to wait and see what the next meeting brought. What I remember of our discussion is that we talked primarily about the potential of the material for further development into poems. I think I said what I liked, how it made me feel, but I also remember clearly saying something about the themes I saw emerging, although we did not discuss these. Subsequently, Peter became quite depressed. This lasted for about a month, during which he seemed unable to proceed with the research, but then it lifted. When he started writing crafted poems again, something had definitely changed. There was more self-presence, a deep and often quite subtle focusing-in on a particular feeling or experience.

Subsequently, I asked Peter whether it was my mention of the themes in the material that had triggered the depression and, to my surprise, he said he had no recollection of my doing so; rather, what he remembered was that I had "received" the material with interest, and had discussed it with him from the point of view of its potential for poems. Clearly, something of a therapeutic nature was taking place here, a kind of "cracking-up", to use Bollas's term (Bollas, 1995). Peter was able to let go of his concern with crafting his poems and to risk bringing something new into the open, within a research relationship that provided a "safe-enough" container for this to happen. It reminds me of what Bollas says about developing a "self-analytic attitude", a reflexive stance in relation to oneself, which helps to facilitate the "arrival of news from the self" (Bollas, 1994, pp. 239–241). While Peter was largely engaged in a self-reflective exercise, being able to bring some of this experience out into the open and to share it in a receptive space was beneficial and helped him to move on. My role in this instance was not to interpret what was happening, but to be a receptive audience for Peter's own self-reflective process.

This is an example of emotional learning taking place at a deep level. The fact that it involved an element of depression is not surprising; gaining insight into oneself often entails giving up some of one's cherished beliefs about oneself,[2] but it is obviously important for us, as teachers and supervisors, to be aware of this possible effect when we facilitate such explorations. What this experience teaches me is that therapeutic change can take place in the supervisory relationship with people who are able to manage the potential risks this involves. It also teaches me how important it is to be open to one's own anxieties as a teacher, and to use one's reflexivity to allow difficult feelings, one's own and those of people one is working with, into the potential space of the teaching or research relationship. Of course, one also has to be able to hold that potential space and make it safe enough. A critical friend, as suggested above, would have been ideal in this instance.

Linden: This case study derives from research with a group of young single mothers who live on a run-down, fragmented public housing estate in East London, and who participated in a creative project in the arts. The research sought to chronicle and interpret, dialogically, the lived experience of some of the participants, using in-depth auto/ biographical methods. The example helps us to understand some of the difficulties of researching in border country, but also how artistic and symbolic activity can act as a kind of container, in conjunction with supportive relationships, and good enough research. There can be, in consequence, a cracking up of a hard, defensive edge, and movement into creativity and transformative learning. Or, to put it in other terms, movement from resistance and acting out to risk taking, greater spontaneity, and a stronger sense of self.

Gina is black, lives on her own with her young baby, and has a past riddled with pain, rejection, and hard drugs. I interviewed her early in the project and towards the end, and spent much time with her in the group, over many weeks. Her relationship to the research, rather like the project itself, evolved from suspicion to a more open, committed participation. She told me she felt pressured to participate in education and to get a job, but that a sympathetic Health Visitor had introduced her to the project. She was suffering from depression at the time. At first, she was upset at leaving her daughter in the crèche and resisted involvement. But she changed as a result of the programme, in different ways, she said, including in her relationship with her daughter (Gina talked of learning to play for the first time in her life). Moreover, she became an advocate for young single mothers with a local housing authority over accommodation issues, as well as being involved in peer sex education programmes in schools. There was a time when she would never have imagined herself doing such things, she said, just as she could not tolerate mess, in the home or anywhere else. Everything had to be kept in order, she continued. She had never let her baby play on the floor, in case she got dirty, just as she, Gina, resisted letting herself go in creative ways. She changed, over time, although she resisted the process, often aggressively.

Gina was working on a sculpture when we talked, near the end of the research:

"When I was pregnant and I didn't really get very big. I made myself a little pregnant belly from a washing basket to put your washing in. I used chicken wire and plaster of Paris and painted it up funny colours. They kind of expressed my mood when I was pregnant, bit dark, dull colours, bit cold. Yes . . . I don't know . . . people who are looking at it probably won't get it, but to me it's a hangover for anger."

Her pregnancy had been hard and troubling and she said she felt unreal as she did not look pregnant. She was depressed and "really ill throughout". Her mood was translated into the sculpture. She was trying, she said, "to get across that, the darkness." There was no head on the sculpture, which was deliberate, since she felt disconnected from her bodily experience. Over time, Gina found sculpting to be therapeutic and moved, in effect, from the margins of transitional space into its core, beginning to think of herself as an artist for the first time in her life, as well as an activist. She was perpetually anxious and uncertain, but took risks, mainly because, as she put it, she felt understood and supported by particular youth leaders and tutors. The artistic activity had been a powerful experience and she liked talking to me, too, she said, because I "really listened" and was interested in her and her work, rather than being judgemental.

A young woman like Gina could continue to act out, on her own admission, in highly destructive ways. She could retreat defiantly to the edge of the group. In Klein's depth psychology, there is a never fully resolved struggle between our capacity for love (that is, to give ourselves openly and fully to another or to symbolic activity) and for hate, resistance, and even the destruction of new possibility, alongside the capacity for reparation—to try again—and to make good the damage we do (Froggett, 2002). Art can provide a containing and transitional space, like writing, for reparation. For this to happen, however, people need to feel contained by significant others, such as tutors, as well as by the process itself: people with sufficient psychological resilience, reliability, consistency, and, perhaps, self-understanding, at least at an intuitive level, to cope with learner ambivalence. Such emotionally attuned capabilities might, sometimes, not easily be won and can ask a great deal of educators, including knowledge of self in action as well as an auto/biographical sensitivity to the emotional dimensions of struggles to learn. My auto/biographical research among family doctors, and the role of subjective learning in becoming a more effective practitioner, illustrates much the same point (West, 2001). Such self-understanding is necessary for researchers, too; I have no idea as to how Gina might have reacted to seeing her story in written form, here and in other places; the response might have been mixed, although my representation of her experience is, I hope, sensitive and respectful; neither, for that matter, do I know the longer-term effects of the whole experience, including the research. Anxiety about such matters is a constant, maybe essential, companion to being a researcher.

Questions of defences and interpretations

We have suggested that a psychodynamic approach involves encouraging people to engage more closely with thoughts and feelings that might be hidden from the conscious mind, and the case studies illustrate significant personal change and the overcoming of defences in an educational context. There remains one question about the extent to which, in teaching or research, attention can or should be drawn explicitly to people's defences, by, for instance, reference to what might be happening in creative writing or auto/biographical narrative interviews. Psychoanalytic psychotherapy has identified a whole range of defences that can come into play within and between people, and in relation to symbolic activity. In psychotherapy, often the point of the exercise, in the context of the good enough alliance, is to identify and challenge defences, because they have not worked for people and life might feel empty and meaningless as a result. The therapist digests what might be happening—including attacks on the process itself—and seeks to feed this back in a manageable form, in the context of what is often a long-term relationship.

In research or educational settings, it might simply be inappropriate to challenge defensive mechanisms, such as intellectualisation, denial, or avoidance. On the other hand, there can be some appropriate ways of exploring possible dynamics. A student's reflective essay, for example, that is overly intellectual and distant from feelings, can be discussed in terms of working in a different genre, using poetry or art. This might partly depend on the spirit in which the problem is communicated and the extent to which associated anxieties are contained by the tutor's responses and suggestions. If done well, rich dialogue on the nature of learning itself and how and why we may defend against certain kinds of more imaginative activities can result.

The applicability of these approaches to other
areas of teaching and research

Clearly, the in-depth psychodynamic approaches we adopt in our work are not going to be appropriate to all areas of teaching and research. For example, the psychodynamic approach to teaching adopted in the MA at Sussex was built into the structure and content of the whole programme, and, in some kinds of work, a therapeutic training will be essential. However, attention can be drawn to the emotional dimensions of learning, especially the fundamental role of anxiety and threats to the self, in any context. At a basic level, providing space for people to talk openly at the outset of a course about their fears of embarking on new learning, especially when they are entering higher education for the first time, can be beneficial in helping them to think about learning processes and what might be involved in doing a particular course. It is also possible to introduce a psychodynamic approach into student learning, on the experience and role of self in the learning process, through reflecting and via writing exercises using metaphor and fiction. Such approaches can create a hybrid teaching environment, both seminar and "play space", where students can learn to put more of themselves into their essays and develop their reflexivity as learners (Creme & Hunt, 2002). Making people more aware that there are different dimensions to learning, not only the cognitive, but also the emotional, imaginal, and social, and even the unconscious, can help to create a framework within which the often chaotic experience of learning is rendered more intelligible and safe.

Psychodynamic awareness can also contribute a valuable dimension to understanding what happens between people in research. As Hollway and Jefferson (2000) demonstrated in their study of the fear of crime, and using Kleinian ideas, understanding social phenomena simultaneously from a psychodynamic and social perspective can reveal how internal factors often compound external ones. This can lead to a radically different understanding of how social ills can be addressed: apparently "irrational" fears about crime, for instance, when understood through a psychodynamic and biographical frame, begin to make sense, as individuals might overly idealise a past and demonise a present via processes of splitting. Likewise, in education, anxiety about learning in the present might seem irrational, but can be understood, using psychodynamic insights and auto/biographical research, as part of a lifelong pattern of defensiveness towards any new possibilities, for fear of never being good enough in the eyes of significant others (West, 1996).

Conclusion

We suggest that a psychodynamic approach, carefully and thoughtfully employed in suitable contexts, can help diverse people to work through blocks or difficulties in their learning, enabling movements in and towards less rigid and more reflexive selves, and, thus, becoming more able to embrace the change and development that really significant learning always involves. It can help us as educators and researchers constantly to challenge ourselves and to understand our anxieties, and what we can learn from them, and, thus, to create more awareness of self and other in what we are doing in different roles. In such an imaginative auto/biographical act, perhaps, we will create far more meaning, depth, and connectedness in our educational practice and research.

Notes

1. Object relations theory involves a view of the self as a constructed, contingent phenomenon. One influential account of object relations—the Kleinian, grounded as this is in clinical experience—emphasises how our early experiences with people or parts of people (including the breast) become absorbed as fantasised internal relationships, which, in turn, form some of the building blocks of personality. The existence of self, therefore, becomes contingent on the availability of good enough, stable, and sufficiently supportive conditions (Frosh, 1991).
2. In his research on therapeutic writing, James Pennebaker notes depression as a significant first reaction amongst people he has worked with (see Esterling, L'Abate, Murray, & Pennebaker, 1999).

References

Bion, W. R. (1962). *Learning from Experience.* London: Maresfield.
Bollas, C. (1994). *The Shadow of the Object: Psychoanalysis of the Unthought Known.* London: Free Association Books.
Bollas, C. (1995). *Cracking Up: The Work of Unconscious Experience.* London: Routledge.
Bourdieu, P. (1988). *Homo Academicus.* Stanford, CA: Stanford University Press.
Bruner, J. (1990). *Acts of Meaning.* Cambridge, MA: Harvard University Press.
Clarke, S. (2008). Psycho-social research: relating self, identity, and otherness. In: S. Clarke, H. Hahn, & P. Hoggett (Eds.), *Object Relations and*

Social Relations: The Implications of the Relational Turn in Psychoanalysis (pp. 113–136). London: Karnac.

Creme, P., & Hunt, C. (2002). Creative participation in the essay writing process. *The Arts and Humanities in Higher Education, 1*(2): 145–166.

Esterling, B. A., L'Abate, L., Murray, E. J., & Pennebaker, J. W. (1999). Empirical foundations for writing in prevention and psychotherapy: mental and physical health outcomes. *Clinical Psychology Review, 19*(1): 79–96.

Froggett, L. (2002). *Love, Hate and Welfare*. Bristol: Policy Press.

Frosh, S. (1991). *Identity Crisis: Modernity, Psychoanalysis and the Self*. London: Macmillan.

Giddens, A. (1999). *Runaway World*. London: Profile Books.

Hollway, W. (2008). The importance of relational thinking in the practice of psycho-social research: ontology, epistemology, methodology, and ethics. In: S. Clarke, H. Hahn, & P. Hoggett (Eds.), *Object Relations and Social Relations: The Implications of the Relational Turn in Psychoanalysis* (pp. 137–162). London: Karnac.

Hollway, W., & Jefferson, T. (2000). *Doing Qualitative Research Differently: Free Association, Narrative and the Interview Method*. London: Sage.

Horney, K. (1954). *Neurosis and Human Growth: The Struggle toward Self-realisation*. New York: Norton.

Hunt, C. (2000). *Therapeutic Dimensions of Autobiography in Creative Writing*. London: Jessica Kingsley.

Hunt, C. (2002). Psychological problems of writer identity: towards a Horneyan understanding. In: D. Barford (Ed.), *The Ship of Thought: Essays on Psychoanalysis and Learning* (pp. 175–191). London: Karnac.

Hunt, C. (2004). Writing and reflexivity: training to facilitate writing for personal development. In: F. Sampson (Ed.), *Creative Writing in Health and Social Care* (pp. 154–169). London: Jessica Kingsley.

Hunt, C. (2010). Therapeutic effects of writing fictional autobiography. *Life Writing, 7*(3): 231–244.

Hunt, C. (forthcoming). *Creative Life Writing as a Tool for Transformative Learning*. London: Routledge, in press.

Josselson, R. (1996). On writing other people's lives; self-analytic reflections of a narrative researcher. *Narrative Study of Lives, 4*: 60–71.

Leiper, R., & Maltby, M. (2004). *The Psychodynamic Approach to Therapeutic Change*. London: Sage.

Merrill, B., & West, L. (2009). *Using Biographical Methods in Social Research*. London: Sage.

Reid, H., & West, L. (2010). Telling tales: using narrative in career guidance. *Journal of Vocational Behaviour, 78*(2): 174–183.

Reid, H., & West, L. (2011). Struggles for space: narrative methods and the crisis of professionalism in career guidance in England. *British Journal of Guidance and Counselling, 39*(5): 397–410.

Schuller, T., Preston, J., Hammond, G., Brassett-Grundy, A., & Bynner, J. (2004). *The Benefits of Learning: The Impact of Education on Health, Family Life and Social Capital.* London: RoutledgeFalmer.

Stanley, L. (1992). *The Auto/biographical I.* Manchester: Manchester University Press.

West, L. (1996). *Beyond Fragments: Adults, Motivation and Higher Education.* London: Taylor & Francis.

West, L. (2001). *Doctors on the Edge: General Practitioners, Health and Learning in the Inner-city.* London: Free Association Books.

West, L. (2004). Re-generating our stories: psychoanalytic perspectives, learning and the subject called the learner. In: C. Hunt (Ed.), *Whose Story Now? (Re)generating Research in Adult Learning and Teaching* (pp. 303–310). Exeter: Proceedings of the 34th SCUTREA Conference.

West, L. (2007). The radical challenges of families and their learning. In: L. West, P. Alheit, S. A. Anderson, & B. Merrill (Eds.), *Using Biographical and Life History Approaches in the Study of Adult and Lifelong Learning: European Perspectives* (pp. 221–239). Hamburg: Peter Lang.

West, L. (2009). Really reflexive practice: auto/biographical research and struggles for a critical reflexivity. In: H. Bradbury, N. Frost, S. Kilminster, & M. Zukas (Eds.), *Beyond Reflective Practice: New Approaches to Professional Lifelong Learning* (pp. 66–80). London: Routledge.

West, L. (2010). Apprendre et le sujet apprenant : point de vue psychanalytique dans la recherche auto/biographique. *Cliopsy, Revue électronique, 4:* 21–36.

Winnicott, D. W. (1971). *Playing and Reality.* London: Routledge.

CHAPTER ELEVEN

Training teachers: psychoanalytical issues in the teacher–student relationship

Anna Zurolo

Introduction

This chapter is concerned with training teachers working in difficult educational situations in Southern Italy. It describes a
number of psychoanalytically informed interventions to help
teachers, and reflections on those experiences. Generally speaking, it
is always difficult to promote interventions in very structured organisations; in such contexts, it is important to keep in mind that even
when an intervention is directly requested, various forms of resistance
to any potential change are evident. Following from this general
point, I believe that any intervention should be respectful of the
particular characteristics of each organisation, of its history, and of
relationships between individuals. Any intervention by an external
professional can be perceived as being done by an "external stranger",
whose knowledge and "know how" are, on the one hand, potentially
important instruments to use; and, on the other, might bring in
elements that threaten a pre-existing equilibrium and, as such, are
anxiety provoking. Based on a range of theoretical, largely psychoanalytical insights, as in the work of Bion (1961), Kaës, Anzieu,
Thomas, and Le Guerinel (1979), and Winnicott (1965), I suggest that

any training can be a transformative process which alters the practice of those who take part (Urwand, 2002), but it should be noted that there can be strong resistance, too.

Following on from these ideas, it is worth highlighting the view that any successful training process requires willingness to learn and change. However, such motivation cannot be taken for granted, and needs to be developed as part of the training process itself, including among those working in education. Furthermore, the training process can be viewed as a constant work in progress, rather than leading to a position of mastery. The teaching of knowledge and skills are two aspects of the training, but it is contended that the training is a relational process which challenges trainees and trainers to encounter deeper and more personal feelings. Therefore, the term *formative relationship* (Blandino & Granieri, 1995) is used to describe interactions between two or more people to recognise the part played by individuals' inner worlds and particular emotional experiences. This chapter explores this approach, illustrating a psychological intervention located within the frame of what are termed Operative National Programmes (PON).

Context for the intervention

Before considering the specific intervention, it is important to explain more of the context in which it takes place. The Italian system of schooling has recently been reformed into a tri-partite model, comprising school, job training, and apprenticeship. A student can choose to attend either a high school, focusing on art, humanities, and sciences, or what is termed a professional school. In the latter, the main aim is one of preparation for employment in a range of careers: these schools provide a certificate which enables the student to find a job at the end of the third year, when s/he is about fifteen years old. Alternatively, a student can choose to complete the high school route to obtain the diploma required to undertake university courses, or to find a more specialised job, when s/he is about eighteen years old. There is much concern, in general, about what students actually achieve and the extent to which they engage with, and complete, their courses. In this chapter, the term "school dispersion" is used to cover a range of issues surrounding the achievement and success of students. These include irregularities in attendance, being late for lessons, failing work, and interrupting courses.

The intervention reported here took place in Southern Italy, where schools in certain areas are characterised by difficult work environments, a preponderance of teachers on temporary contracts, and a high rate of student "dispersion" and drop-out. The reasons for the high rate of student dispersion and drop-out are complex, the problem not being confined to areas of economic or social problems, but also affecting areas of relatively high employment. There are, arguably, two key factors involved: the cultural acceptability of an early start to working life, and the availability of jobs not requiring any degree of specialisation. Data from the Italian Education Ministry indicate that the drop-out rate is high in the first year of secondary school, when the student is about twelve–thirteen years old, and is particularly marked in professional schools. The Italian Government, using the framework of the Operative National Programme (PON), with financial support from the European Commission, has sought to address these issues in a number of ways, including through school development programmes (in accordance with the European Union's priority for developing a knowledge-based economy). Specifically, PONs have a range of goals, which include the reduction of school dispersion; improved gender equality awareness; developing teacher training; more integrated links with the world of work. To this end, schools have been allocated resources to develop their own PON.

It is usual for psychologists to be called upon to help with the delivery of such a school development programme, which can include providing alternative training approaches that focus on the particular needs of the institution. It is a fundamental tenet of this work that the psychologist keeps in mind the relationship between the individual teacher and the context in which s/he works, as part of undertaking any "analysis of a request" (Carli & Paniccia, 2003). When responding to a request made by an institution or a group, the psychologist should bear in mind that such a request often corresponds to a break in the equilibrium of the work environment. This equilibrium can be based on a form of collusion derived from the way emotions and feelings are shared or avoided between individuals working in the same context (Carli, Grasso, & Paniccia, 2007). When the collusive processes, which are at the root of relationships, fail, the consequence can be to fracture and disrupt the emotional relationships between individuals and the context. Mindful of this, the psychological intervention aims to improve relationships between individuals and their context, including building more open forms of communication.

The intervention described in the chapter took place following a request for training made to a University in Southern Italy. The training was to include learning facilitation and the management of student–teacher interactions.

An intervention in a "frontier" school

A "frontier school" is an expression used by one of the teachers to describe her own school both as a place where many battles daily take place, and an institution with no strict rules and limits, where students not interested in their formative training decide to go. The intervention was developed for the teachers of students in the first two years of a professional secondary school, located in the Basilicata region. The school was already actively engaged in the development and delivery of training programmes, for both students and teachers. The team used their experience as psychologists, with a range of clinical, educational, and group management backgrounds, to devise a training programme to address specific problems relating to the work and emotional concerns of the teachers. The work was supported by a psychoanalytically orientated observer, and drew on their observations of the training sessions. The intervention took place over ten meetings, during the afternoon, in classrooms at the school: they took place twice a month, for a total of twenty-five hours.

The following techniques were used: circle time, psychodrama activities, narrating one's own experience, and group discussion. In each session, the team reviewed the aims of the training, the activities we would use, and held a discussion to conclude the meeting.

Facing problems, facing opportunities: circle time

Circle time can be regarded as an effective way of improving the level of emotional communication, allowing participants to recognise themselves as well as others (Colasanti & Mastromarino, 1991, Francescato, Putton, & Cudini, 2000). In the first session, we placed everyone in a circle so that they could discuss matters face-to-face. One of the psychologists from our team led the group, and each member was invited to introduce themselves. The rationale for this was to encourage participants to share and think about work and professional identity in a mutually responsive way. This was in contrast to the more formal interactions, typically used by teachers, in discussions on technical matters elsewhere.

The most recurrent themes of the discussion related to professional identity, described as uncertain and precarious, and the problems of working in a "frontier school". As one teacher explained,

> "We work in a difficult frontier school. Many students apply for the hotel management school thinking that the school path will be easier. For example, I teach Italian language and I often teach to only half of the regular number of students . . . and they need to attend only for a few hours!"

In addition, many of these teachers are temporary and are well aware of the short-term nature of their contracts. They are correspondingly disinclined to make too much emotional investment in their work:

> "Some students have severe problems. However, how can we solve them? Often, we are hired for few months and we do not even have enough time to get acquainted with the students and soon we need to leave."

The most distressing of the presented difficulties seemed to relate to the students' lack of motivation. When asked how matters could be improved, the teachers demonstrated a hopeless acceptance of the situation. Everyone defended their own practice, in effect, confining themselves to blaming the students for being uninterested and disinclined to engage with any of the learning on offer. The permanent teachers, from another perspective, described the school as a "temporary parking area" for students who are not really interested in learning:

> "This school has become a parking spot for students thinking they can study less. Our task is teaching, we do what is our duty and we must follow the ministerial curricula."

The discussions revealed deeper concerns, more or less common to all the teachers, to do with the kind of pupils attending a professional school: they were frequently characterised as problematic, coming from socio-economically disadvantaged families, speaking slang and immune to any discipline. We reviewed the problems, and were concerned with various emotional and communication issues that emerged during the circle time discussions. We planned a programme to help the teachers to examine these further.

The teachers appeared despondent about their jobs. Some of them viewed their jobs as a mere collection of duties without any room for thought about themselves, their teaching styles, relationships between teachers and students, or the dynamics between individual students and the class:

> "We are in a school: we have meetings, time schedules, activity planning, the Ministry's requests . . . We have to move with the times . . . we can't even stop or ask "how are you?" We are always in a hurry . . ."

A very restricted perception of the job emerged, one performed in a problematic context and impossible to change. Crucially, the teachers did not believe they could take action and make a contribution to the educational and emotional development of their pupils, limiting themselves solely to the delivery of blocks of information. Having identified these issues in circle time, the purpose of subsequent sessions was to seek to enhance both the recognition and understanding of the problems, and to develop a more complex picture of the teacher's role.

Psychodrama: a typical lesson between playing and reality

The analytical psychodrama technique, frequently used in French training contexts, comprises the dramatisation of significant events: this is followed by a discussion to create some "group breathing space". In other words, the group elaborates on the experiences explored in the psychodrama. Kaës, Missenard, and Nicolle (1999) suggest that three steps contribute to the overall process: the choice of theme, the dramatisation itself, and the ensuing discussion. It is interesting to note that there were mixed reactions to the sessions, with some teachers being sceptical of the scenarios selected, while others enjoyed the opportunities provided by the training. In one session, after an initial whispered discussion to select a topic and decide on roles, there was agreement to perform a "typical" lesson. In this scenario, one member of the group (the only male teacher) took on the role of the teacher, while the rest of the group, comprising female teachers, became part of a mixed gender class, with more males than females.

The group portrayed a highly chaotic scene: the students were disrespectful of any school rules, interrupting the teacher, not respecting any speaking order, throwing papers about, and chatting among themselves. The students were constantly asking to go out, and there were continuous comings and goings. One of our team participated as a female student asking impertinent questions: "How old are you prof? Are you married?" The teacher, presented as inexperienced, struggled to manage or discipline the class. He attempted, with some awkwardness, to apply the teaching rules he had been taught. During the dramatisation an actual student, a female, burst into the classroom and asked one of the "teacher-pupils" taking part to come outside. Initially, the teacher said that she could not do this, but then agreed and left. The dramatisation subsequently resumed.

The "teacher performer" just carried on without reference to the disturbance, and this seemed to reflect what happens in the real classroom, as can be sensed in the following vignette.

> The teacher called by the girl goes outside. The group now seems more anxious to resume the performance . . . There is no time to reflect on what's just happened and what's broken the emotional rhythm. We need to go on . . . to respect the timing . . .

When the teacher-pupil returned after a few minutes, she did not resume her role, but stood back, awaiting the end of the dramatisation.

A breathing space: group discussion

At the end of the dramatisation, the team asked the participants to write down their feelings: all agreed that the psychodrama class felt real and exemplified the behaviours experienced, and often withstood, by the teachers. We then invited the teachers to write down what the teacher did to stimulate the students' learning. The group response was confused, but essentially insisted that the students were deficient in their response to a well-established teaching model. The issue of powerlessness re-emerged. None of them seemed to be aware that a piece of reality had burst in on them: they had carried on, following the established script, obeying the rules. The teacher who left the room said she had had no choice, the dramatisation could not have continued otherwise.

This vignette, the performance, and the interruption, exemplified some of the problems inherent in the student–teacher relationship in this particular context: in particular, the feeling of lack of choice and the failure of the group to respond to the interruption, remaining lifeless and distant from what had happened. Both these dimensions suggest that there is little or no room for thought and considered reflection in the classroom: the task must be finished, above all. We discussed this further and the teachers commented that students are always leaving the classroom, and that the teacher had no choice but to leave the room during the psychodrama at the student's request. The student who interrupted the psychodrama had many problems and came from a needy family, so much so that "It is already saying a lot that she came to school." The discussion continued on the theme of drop-out and the inevitability of some situations, particularly strong feelings of disorientation caused by difficulties in managing similar classrooms.

Narrating one's own experience and the collective narrative

During subsequent meetings, the group was asked to engage in developing a narrative, a device designed to create further breathing and thinking space to consider the student–teacher relationship. The group was invited to compose a collective story, in which each participant could add a narrative fragment to the larger plot. After a short period of disorientation, the most active teacher during the psychodrama activity began the narration, and an overarching story slowly emerged. The first statement offered in the collective narrative was "my job is useless", followed by a tale in which the figure of the helpful teacher takes form. This teacher is described as dedicating his efforts to providing his undisciplined students with suitable learning experiences, although these are ultimately unsuccessful. Then a male pupil was described, screaming and disturbing the regular course of the lessons, arguably trying to get the attention he missed from his family. The pupil had a "good heart" and is not malicious, the story continued, but he also reduces teachers to fury because of his continuous attempts to get attention; he disturbs and causes chaos in the class. For some teachers, the task of dealing with this pupil is described as "a nightmare", a nightmare in which he is an undisciplined, disorderly, pugnacious, and violent boy, and a nightmare to which they are unable to react. In this sense, he can be seen as a figure that attracts the teachers' projections of dissatisfaction and feelings of powerlessness about their jobs. They did not know how to help the disadvantaged pupil(s), who then became the object of such feelings: so they tolerate the truancies, and wait for that time when, inevitably, pupils will drop out.

The narration of the pupil's character becomes more complex, perhaps best expressed in a "good–bad" dichotomy. He is presented as different from the rest of the class, his behaviour does not fit with what is necessary for the class to function, but, at the same time, he deserves more attention, extra mothering perhaps, to understand and, sometimes, to justify his weakness and impetuous behaviour. However, his behaviour is not conducive to working and being with others in purposeful ways. The development of this collective narrative seemed especially important in enabling the teachers to recognise their emotional involvement in the work, and that it was some way from simply being a collection of duties. The narrative also indicated that teaching can cause great discomfort, to which the teachers respond with resignation and emotional withdrawal.

The teacher–school–student triangle: psychoanalytic remarks

Such training experiences enabled us to think about the complexity facing a psychologist organising a training programme for an institution, even when that is specifically requested by the school. They also enabled us to consider the teacher–school–student relationship in more depth. We tried to connect and to enhance the understanding of the teachers, to provide a form of holding that might be transferred into their day-to-day interactions with students. In terms of the institution, the comments of Montesarchio and Marzella (2002) on the

importance of preserving the space–time aspects of the training setting are particularly apposite, not least when training is taking place
within the institution requesting it. In fact, the participation of the
teachers in the programme could be complicated by room changes, by
struggles to find space within the school timetable for the programme,
and then keeping to that time. Frequently, other school meetings,
which the teachers were supposed to attend, were organised at the
time teachers were supposed to come to the training. Arguably, this
reflects a certain ambivalence on the part of the school towards the
training it had requested, embodying a basic tension between the
need for change and fear of it.

In terms of our methodology, the team used a psychodynamic
orientation, planning the training with regard not only to concepts,
but also to focus on individual attitudes, emotions, and the personal
meaning of what it can be to be a teacher (Salzberger-Wittenberg,
Henry-Polacco, & Osborne, 1987). On the one hand, the approach we
took was problematic because it flew in the face of the teachers' expectations of training: that is, being about "how to do". On the other
hand, the process facilitated a more intimate experience. Teachers had
the opportunity to recognise and talk about difficult and potentially
debilitating feelings, some of which they might share with their students, in particular about the social and economic context, or the perceived immutability of the school. The psychologist in this situation is
seen as someone with the responsibility of solving the crisis and
impasse magically, without touching on, or involving, the subjectivity
of the teachers themselves. Furthermore, as an external stranger, the
psychologist can be the repository for a "messianic hope" (Bion, 1961):
s/he is the repository for primitive forms of dependence and need in
the group. Bion has identified such dependence as a function characterising crucial moments in the life of any group: a moment where
there is primitive hope that problems can be solved and desires
realised by a magical other.

However, simply the opportunity for thinking about such things
made the discomfort of working in a so-called frontier school much
clearer. The teachers were able to develop deeper insights into the
anxiety and bewilderment that often feature in a school, in effect,
abandoned by its students. It could be argued that student drop-out
is experienced as a loss by teachers, who feel as if they are losing part
of themselves, or losing a child who abandons the comfortable place

of school/home, despite their best efforts and care. Drop-out is certainly perceived as inevitable by teachers, and contributes to feelings of disinvestment, powerlessness, and resignation.

The training itself sought to create a *facilitating environment* (Winnicott, 1965) in which such feelings could find voice and problems could be viewed from different, and various, perspectives. It was our intention for the training to be experienced as a care-giving relationship, in which significant importance was attached to facilitating the development of individuals. In these terms, a psychodynamically informed training can provide space for teachers to suspend their normal responses, and to activate the capacity for thinking, free from the usual organisational constraints. However, the remarks of Blandino and Granieri (1995) underline the importance of seeing the school as more than a simple social organisation (Rice, 1965): having a major purpose, but also being a complex psychosocial system that can generate defensive mechanisms and resistance to change. In this sense, the school can, on the one hand, engage in a positive rhetoric of change, while, conversely, blocking any moves towards such an end. This seems even more likely when external conditions threaten and evoke anxiety. It is, therefore, important to address issues of anxiety, powerlessness, and resignation in relation to the institution, and to encourage the development of interpersonal relationships, if change is to take place. In conclusion,

> It is not possible for any real change, any real professional cooperation, if the members of an organization (in our case the teachers of the school) do not question the way they use their structure, the meaning that their own professional role has for themselves, (and) the fears and expectation they have in respect to any novelty or change request. (Blandino & Granieri, 1995, p. 93)

We set out to do exactly this by focusing training interventions at the emotional level, taking into account what one of the teachers said in circle time: he had stated that there is no time to think about himself, and himself in the institution. This gets to the heart of the problem, and what needs to be thought about in any search for solutions.

This intervention was carried out in the firm belief that the training process is a relationship, where all individuals involved can react positively, if ambivalently, to the possibility of self-differentiation and growth. A training process, with a potential to evoke conflicting feelings and emotions, is, however, not a simple solution. The willingness to learn involves a willingness to receive what others might give, and, conversely, the willingness to give, in the face of resistance, might also be a site of struggle. It is through the creation of a space to think, for everyone concerned, in which experiences can be processed and then returned in a more digestible form that makes thinking more possible, leading, in turn, to greater personal, but also collective, awareness of what can get in the way.

References

Bion, W. R. (1961). *Experiences in Groups*. London: Tavistock.

Blandino, G., & Granieri, B. (1995). *La disponibilità ad apprendere. Dimensioni emotive nella scuola e formazione degli insegnanti* (Willingness to learn. Emotional issues in training teachers). Milan: Raffaello Cortina.

Carli, R., & Paniccia, R. M. (2003). *Analisi della domanda. Teoria e tecnica dell'intervento in psicologia clinica* (Analysis of a request. Theory and techniques of intervention in clinical psychology). Bologna: Il Mulino.

Carli, R., Grasso, M., & Paniccia, R. M. (2007). *La formazione alla psicologia clinica. Pensare emozioni* (Training in clinical psychology. Emotion-based thinking). Milan: Franco Angeli.

Colasanti, A. R., & Mastromarino, R. (1991). *Ascolto attivo. Elementi teorici ed esercitazioni per la conduzione del colloquio* (Active listening. Theory and practise to interview). Rome: IFREP.

Francescato, D., Putton, A., & Cudini, S. (2000). *Star bene insieme a scuola. Strategie per un'educazione socio-affettiva dalla materna alla media inferiore* (Well-being at school together. Strategies for an emotional training from the nursery school to junior high school). Bologna: Carocci.

Kaës, R., Anzieu, D., Thomas, L. V., & Le Guerinel, N. (1979). *Fantasme et formation* (Phantasm and training). Paris: Dunod.

Kaës, R., Missenard, A., & Nicolle, O. (1999). *Lo psicodramma psicoanalitico di gruppo* (Group psychoanalytic psychodrama). Rome: Borla, 2001.

Montesarchio, G., & Marzella, E. (2002). Narrare la formazione. La costruzione di significati condivisi all'interno dei contesti lavorativi (Giving an account of training. Sharing the construction of meaning in working settings). In: G. Montesarchio (Ed.), *Quattro crediti di colloquio* (pp. 62–94). (Four credits for an exam.) Milan: Franco Angeli.

Rice, A. K. (1965). *Learning for Leadership: Interpersonal and Inter-group Relations*. London: Tavistock.

Salzberger-Wittenberg, I., Henry-Polacco, G., & Osborne, E. (1987). The *Emotional Experience of Learning and Teaching*. London: Routledge & Kegan Paul.

Urwand, S. (2002). Supervision de groupes en groupe. Approche groupale de la formation (Group supervision. Group perspectives on training). *Revue de psychothérapie psychanalytique de groupe, 39*: 29–49.

Winnicott, D. W. (1965). *The Maturational Process and the Facilitating Environment. Studies in the Theory of Emotional Development*. London: Hogarth.

CHAPTER TWELVE

Learning through the emotions: experience-based learning for psychologists

Adele Nunziante Cesàro, Anna Zurolo,
Valentina Boursier, and Allesandra Delli Veneri

Introduction

This chapter reflects on the introduction of an important and distinctive dimension of experience-based training on the Master's programme in Dynamic, Clinical, and Community Psychology at a university in southern Italy. To put this in context, it is important to note the characteristics of this Master's programme and the related training requirements for psychotherapists and psychologists in Italy. A Master's programme is typically an academic training that takes five years. It is usually followed by a one-year apprenticeship, generally in public services, after which students take a further examination to qualify for professional practice and to qualify to become a member of the "Regional Professional Psychologist Society". Overall, this Masters course has a broad remit, training professional psychologists for work with individuals, groups, in industrial settings, and social communities. It aims to develop students who have a theoretical knowledge as well as the technical and methodological skills that will enable them to build and manage relationships with clients and customers. It also aims to promote research and to consider preventative measures. Ultimately, only those students who have undertaken a four-year specialisation in psychotherapy as part of their Master's can practise as psychotherapists.

The training for clinical psychologists and psychotherapists consists of three main aspects: theory, practice, and personal development. The first two are undertaken at university where theoretical aspects tend to prevail. Personal development and self-reflection, with a psychoanalytic focus, usually take place elsewhere, in personal private therapy and/or analytic training. Despite these difficulties, it is very important to promote, and utilise, experience-based learning (Bion, 1962) during the Master's programme, rather than leaving it until the apprenticeship stage. To this end, the Master's programme discussed here introduced short training experiences alongside group discussions.

We believe that emotional, relational, and personal dimensions are all involved in the specific choice of becoming a clinical psychologist, as well as in the training process. We also think that teaching clinical psychology cannot be only a theoretical transfer of abstract knowledge, since it necessarily needs to consider the influence of the self on the other, and this can be achieved through self-reflection. Finally, the clinical work cannot be limited to a "practice", whether supported by theories, methodology, and procedures, because the clinical work is, above all, a working-through of the relationships between client and psychologist and also the psychologist's personal experiences. Therefore, we believe that the university curricula should include an experiential dimension, which, fundamentally, provides experience-based learning (Bion, 1962), thus facilitating and highlighting emotional experience and the opportunity to reflect upon them in order to improve one's own self-reflection and knowledge.

We found that a psychoanalytic perspective enabled us to examine theory and practice and to bring theory and emotional experience alongside each other, so that learning could be viewed from various levels (Blandino & Granieri, 1995; Salzberger-Wittenberg, Henry-Polacco, & Osborne, 1987). We would argue that psychoanalytic theories and methods have a broader application, beyond the specific analytical setting. They have a place in social and educational contexts, as well as in the wider field of experience and behaviour, where, we would suggest, emotional and unconscious aspects play an important part. Psychoanalytic theory, and its clinical application, recognises an inner world and its influence on relationships. We argue that this is highly relevant to our programme and, therefore, see experienced-based learning as an important source of emotional and intellectual growth for our students.

Experience and thinking

The psychoanalytic tradition has emphasised the centrality of conscious, preconscious, and unconscious aspects, in both the personal and professional growth experience (Kaës, Anzieu, Bejarano, Scaglia, & Gori, 1976; Kaës, Anzieu, Thomas, & Le Guerinel, 1979). According to Bion (1962), the child's psychic development is possible through the adult capacity for reverie, where the internal world of the infant is interpreted by the mother. This produces a thoughtful transformational process that supports both thoughts and actions. This concept refers to the mother's role, which consists of accepting and processing elements that the children's psyche cannot represent and process (beta elements) within imaginable emotions (alpha elements). It is through this experience of transformation that the infant psyche slowly becomes capable of developing and thinking, thus emphasising the significant interaction between emotional and cognitive dimensions. We think it is possible, although in a different way, to transfer the mother–infant experience, involving the reverie, to the teacher–student relationship, thereby using the interaction between cognitive and emotional aspects to provide a learning experience, for both students and teachers, that has the potential to transform thinking and actions.

Intellectual functions are, therefore, connected with emotional experience and, as such, there is a profound connection between the emotions and the capacity to think and learn (Blandino, 1997). The focus of psychoanalysis on the appreciation of an emotional dimension has powerful meaning in the daily practice of teaching and training. There are a number of perspectives we would like to highlight here. In particular, we focus on the centrality of self-experience and the transformative process of the learning experience as articulated by Bion. This then leads us on to Winnicott's notion about the mother's function of providing the baby with affective and intellectual nourishment. Here, the possibility of learning is also about being open to experience, the willingness to be in a relationship and of grasping and gathering the "psychic nourishment" coming from the other person involved in the relationship (Kirman, 1982). True learning, in a training context, provides emotional challenges to cognitive aspects of learning. These arise where one's emotions are evoked and tested during the experience of practice, facing up to the competences one has and the competences one wishes one had.

Practising psychology through the emotions

In this chapter, we consider the cyclical nature of the learning process within the Clinical Psychology Master's programme, taking into account the different levels of learning. We introduced experienced-based learning and the practice of identifying one's own emotions in specific "experimental lessons": here, students were exposed to the emotional dimensions of clinical work through a role-play session, derived from socio and psycho-drama (Z. Moreno, 1965; J. Moreno, 1972). The group involved final year students who had some theoretical and limited practical experience of the psychoanalytic methods of infant and child observation. The teaching process involved role-play and includes both theoretical and practical lessons, providing a creative game in a "potential space" (Winnicott, 1965) that moves from a theoretical position and allows the student to confront a range of clinical scenarios within the experimental sessions.

Students proceed to this experiential role-play after they have studied psychoanalytical theory, including gender differences and the maternal role. These teaching sessions are followed by experience-based learning scenarios, structured in two stages.

● A role-play session: this consists of the dramatisation of clinical scenarios, the plot of which is spontaneously decided by students. Each session lasts ten minutes; the group comprises the teacher, the class of students, and a psychoanalytical observer who reports on what happens. The students volunteer to take the role of a psychologist or a client.

● A group discussion session conducted by the teacher, with the observer's contribution, lasting for about twenty minutes after each dramatisation. The work is then developed in various ways, as the following accounts of report observations and material collected during the "experimental lessons" illustrate.

Clinical vignettes

First scenario

The teacher suggests a dramatisation of a psychologist–client relationship after providing theoretical input during a lesson about the maternal role and childhood psycho-sexual development. Two students, a male and a female, offer to participate. The student (male), taking the client's role, talks about his difficulties in studying. He talks of his mother's excessive expectations, which prevent him from pursuing his academic studies. He goes on to say that he is undertaking the degree programme in psychology against his parents' wishes. They want him to be an attorney. He is now about to finish the programme and is having great problems with the examinations. He cannot possibly tell his parents, as he reaches the end of the programme, that he is having such problems with the examinations. The atmosphere is claustrophobic, nobody moves:

> "Since I started the last two years of the Master's Degree Programme in Psychology, I have not done any examination. I do not even want to think of failing and the trouble is that I cannot tell my mother; she would die! I can imagine the criticism I would get for failing to follow my father's career . . ."

The female student, acting as the psychologist, remains silent for a long time, in contrast to the client, who talks of his anxieties, the anguish of feeling incapable/powerless, the fear of abandoning his studies, the dread of a no-way-out situation.

> "What will I do if I do not overcome this situation? I will quit psychology and become a lawyer? I do not want to be a lawyer! My entire life has been controlled by them! I attended a specific high school, as they wanted. I hated my mother for this. I cannot breathe . . . She takes it all! She wants me to become a lawyer, more than my father does, and I have to be her perfect child."

The psychologist invites him to explore the origins of his anxiety, which seem linked to a symbiotic relationship with his mother. The client describes how he experiences his mother as an imposing figure with great powers from which he cannot escape:

"I hate my mother, she takes care of everything and I must be her perfect son, I must be everything, everything she wants."

The psychologist tries to develop the discussion by looking at what the client really wants. This appears mixed in an ambivalent way with his mother's wishes. The dynamics of the relationship result from confusion and fusion with a maternal figure, and leads the client to a constant and complex opposition to his mother. At the end of the dramatisation, the students discuss their reactions.

"It was very difficult. The psychologist and the client performed a clinical vignette but they also talked about most of us!"

One student in particular appears very emotionally involved. She quickly admits to experiencing similar difficulties with her own mother for not succeeding in her examinations. She describes the very real sense of invasion she experienced during the dramatisation as being like an enormous mouth greedily devouring everything and immobilising her.

The dramatisation and the ensuing discussion evoked images and sensations that the students experience and share. They then questioned, "How can we help anybody? How can we act or be psychologists when we, too, experience our patient's problems? What is the limit and what is the distance we have to go before we stop feeling so empty and immobilised?" We think that during this personal development activity—the dramatisation—the students are able to be in contact with their own dilemma, their own sense of powerlessness/immobilisation, those very feelings which are hard to reach in a more academic setting, and which could be the greatest cause of this immobilisation. The students talked further about the negative impact of their emotions on their work as psychologists. They see themselves as psychologists and, at the same time, they also experience their own unconscious processes. They can now understand how these emotions can confuse and obstruct the understanding of others, especially if they are not identified or analysed. This scenario raises questions of "who is the client?" and "who is the psychologist?"

Second scenario

The students' problems are also seen to arise during the dramatisation of a new scenario about separation and loss presented some weeks

later. The student acting as the client initiates the subject of gradua-
tion and the uncertainty relating to the crucial and extremely difficult
task of separating from the family, the university, where, he says, "I
found my second home."

"My Master's is about to finish, I cannot think about this: I will never see
my colleagues again, I will not spend my days with them. I am "at home"
here, perhaps more than at my house. Yet I feel that sooner or later I will
have to go."

The psychologist listens to him in silence and then tries to respond
to his difficulties by evoking an image of a door: "You are on your
doorstep at home and you do not know if you have to, or want to, enter
or to exit". The narration continues by developing the client's request
to be helped in actively doing something, in deciding what to do.

"Yes, but what am I supposed to do? I feel strange, as if I was on the brink
of a precipice and when I think about the end of my studies all that I see
is fog, darkness, emptiness forever. There is something after, but I cannot
see it, I cannot see beyond. The time will come when I must leave everything . . . home and university. That's how I feel."

The client conjures up a sense of the darkness, the empty space of
what will come "after" that is, for them, impossible to imagine. The
psychologist suggests that counselling would provide a potential
space in which to analyse the most pressing elements of his problem,
but this proposal meets scepticism in the client: "*And then what
happens? We will have these talks*, and then?" The psychologist suggests
three or four sessions, but is continually pushed by the client, who
asks insistently, "Three or four sessions? And then what happens?
What will we do?" The dramatisation ends soon after this, while the
psychologist is still trying to open a space for reflection; a space that
seems both insufficient and inadequate. In this situation, the time of
the psychological consultation becomes an undefined space / container
with no limits and shape, reflecting his inner sensations and need to
have a limit and to know exactly what to do.

During the ensuing discussion, the group highlights and analyses
the psychologist's difficulties in managing the client's problems,
which are, in fact, related to a real problem, since the client reveals
that, in reality, he has already asked the university for help from the

student psychological counselling service. The group discussion focuses on the uncertainty and feelings of precariousness that grip all the students as they anticipate the end of the university course. The scenario represented the theme of individual growth for the students, both as young adults and as students on the verge of becoming psychologists. The feeling of precariousness that the psychologist shares with her colleagues pertains to her doubts about herself as a psychologist and how the future will be. The group is virtually silent, almost overwhelmed by thoughts of the future.

Conclusions

As shown above, through this kind of learning the student can encounter the difficulties inherent in the psychologist's position, directly experiencing the role played by subjectivity and intersubjectivity in the clinical sessions. The role-playing seems to create a potential and transitional space (Winnicott, 1971) in which everyday roles have to be suspended and the boundaries between reality and fiction become dissolved and confused. In this case, the experiential dimension allows learning from the experience of one's subjectivity in a guided and protected space. It seems to act as a transitional space by facilitating feelings of new possibility and spontaneity, where everyone can simultaneously act "me and not-me" at the same time. In fact, the creation of a transitional area where the boundary between the subject and the role being impersonated is not so clear allows aspects of the role of the psychologist—that need to be identified and analysed—to be brought into the room. This area then contains both personal and group aspects, which stimulate the need for reflection. This dimension of practical experience evokes processes of group mirroring that sometimes accompany persecutory anxieties: "I felt I was the student that could not take examinations," the student-psychologist says in the first vignette. Another student in the group then adds, "I thought he was speaking about me".

Therefore, the space of dramatisation also becomes a container for original and precocious elements, for anguish and anxieties that are taking place in the others' narration. The possibility for sharing through the group experience allows emotions to be experienced, but also for thinking about less symbolised elements, which demand to be named and given meaning. In fact, the space of dramatisation, as a creative transitional playing zone, also allows, in Bion's terms, the indigestible elements, which need to be digested, to emerge. Finally, psychoanalytic theory is brought alive by the group experience: we can find diverse aspects that need to be integrated through difficult and laborious work, which is both necessary and potentially transformative.

In this situation, the teacher can help the students recognise the emotional dynamics which might beset them in their work as psychologists and interfere with their ability to listen to and understand the other, their client. From this perspective, the educational process that we have described appears to be an experience where it is possible to be in contact with one's subjectivity, which can either enable or disturb listening and comprehension. What the student-psychologist feels in the dramatisation is partially linked to her/his inner world and to what the student-client deposits in him/herself. The concept of projective identification becomes a real notion that is like a mark on the skin for the student: it can be felt and understood through this experience.

Moreover, these role-playing experiences provide evidence of the difficulties associated with the psychology-based practices and professions. The student is able to learn from her/his own experience some of the risks, the anxieties, the issues emerging in clinical work, and the importance of all those aspects that define the internal and external world of psychological settings. Finally, there is an anticipatory dimension: these role-plays enable students to experience, at first hand, some of the tensions and difficulties inherent in the role of a professional psychologist.

References

Bion, W. R. (1962). *Learning from Experience*. London: Heimann.
Blandino, G. (1997). Apprendere gli errori, dall'esperienza. Dimensioni emotive nell'apprendimento (Understanding mistakes through experience). *Rivista del Servizio di Sostegno della scuola media*, 15: 18–32.
Blandino, G., & Granieri, B. (1995). *La disponibilità ad apprendere. Dimensioni emotive nella scuola e formazione degli insegnanti* (Willingness to learn. Emotional issues in training teachers). Milan: Raffaello Cortina.

Kaës, R., Anzieu, D., Bejarano, A., Scaglia, M., & Gori, R. (1976). *Désir de former et formation du savoir* (Wishing to train and origins of desire). Paris: Dunod.

Kaës, R., Anzieu, D., Thomas, L. V., & Le Guerinel, N. (1979). *Fantasme et formation* (Phantasm and training). Paris: Dunod.

Kirman, W. J. (1982). Modern psychoanalysis of learning in the classroom. *Modern Psychoanalysis, 7*: 87–98.

Moreno, J. L. (1972). *Psychodrama* (Vol. I). New York: Beacon House.

Moreno, Z. T. (1965). Psychodramatic rules, techniques, and adjunctive methods. *Group Psychotherapy, IS*: 73–86.

Salzberger-Wittenberg, I., Henry-Polacco, G., & Osborne, E. (1987). *The Emotional Experience of Learning and Teaching*. London: Routledge & Kegan Paul.

Winnicott, D. W. (1965). *The Maturational Process and The Facilitating Environment. Studies in the Theory of Emotional Development*. London: Hogarth.

Winnicott, D. W. (1971). *Playing and Reality*. London: Tavistock.

CHAPTER THIRTEEN

Continua: mentally ill artist students uninterrupted

Olivia Sagan

Introduction

This chapter reports on research with a group of art students, each of whom had a history of mental ill health. The research was funded by the Higher Education Academy and the University of the Arts, London, to explore the experiences of mentally ill students within higher Arts education. Longitudinal, unstructured biographic narrative interviews[1] were used, through which interviewees were encouraged to reflect, in an uninterrupted narrative flow, on their life, their art practice and their illness/health. The research prioritised free associative narrative (Hollway & Jefferson, 2000) to foreground the first-person experience of the interviewee, and allow her/him to shape the content with what felt important to the individual, rather than imposing a set of themes and questions on to the interview setting. This setting was carefully attended to, with priority given to regularity, reliability, and the (same) researcher each time working from within the frame of reference of the interviewee, remembering past details and holding in mind the person's full story. Such a setting evoked a Winnicottian (1971) potential space. In such a space, at best, a trust, once established, allows for the two beings to become other, through dialogue, through co-narrative, through *play*. Seven people were spoken to in total, with each person being interviewed once a term. The shortest connection was for two years, the longest four. Students were recruited through the university counselling service, word of mouth, flyers, the Student Union, a student's mental health support group, and general university advertising. Recruitment was not easy, with both an understandable reluctance to engage in research that was targeted at those experiencing mental ill health, and a high level of protection on the part of counsellors and tutors, who were wary of having individuals in their "care" involved. Several talks were given around the university by the researchers to inform both professionals and students about the research. Eventually, after a high number of enquiries which were not fruitful, several interviews with people who did not, as it turned out, meet the criterion of being diagnosed as having a mental ill health issue, and a number of complaints from around campus that mentioning mental illness in a research flyer was in some way infringing the rights of the mentally ill, a relatively stable sample was obtained. This beginning was a salutary reminder of the sensitivities at play within research that explores the fine lines between mental illness, mental health, self-identification, and the labelling of others through medical diagnosis. Viewing such interruptions and untidiness in the process of research as an integral part of the research and the story it is telling, and being aware of our own emotional responses to these, also offers a deeper insight into the nature of the subject being investigated (Sagan, 2011b).

Narrative: ethics, myths, and approximations

The recorded interviews with these students built an intimate portrait of lives lived and illnesses battled, throwing into relief the different lines of continua these students were negotiating. The extremes of health and illness were narrated, with the painful contrast between "rapid-fire creative production" (Jaques, 1965, p. 229) and the despair of hiatus. Representing students' reflections over a span of years, these narratives show us the importance of the seemingly prosaic decisions and daily minutiae of living with mental illness. But they also command a deeper appreciation of how acts of reparation (Klein, 1998) are made as the psyche strives for integration.

The taking of voice, however, is an act always laden with ethical implications. Beyond immediate and familiar questions of confidentiality lie more tricky dilemmas of power asymmetry in the interviewer–interviewee relationship and the porousness of boundary as that relationship progresses. The process and licence of interpretation, particularly psychoanalytic, is also fraught as a researcher moves into the making of meaning through the acts of presentation and *repre*sentation. By the researcher's hand a person becomes other, perhaps to what s/he feels her/himself to be; that "research participant" is also rendered static by the research and its means of usual dissemination. A case study is frozen in time, despite the growth, change, and/or deterioration of the individual. Such a "case", furthermore, becomes a public object, one which can be the recipient of our curiosities, enchantments, or indifference. While social science grapples with how to embed the uniqueness of an individual in its research and maintain its essence (Froggett & Hollway, 2010), there is still the perennial shortfall of research to do more than offer an approximation.

A further ethical tangle surrounds the use of narrative to explore the experiences of the mentally ill. Despite its undisputed value, this type of research is not immune to criticisms of its gaze, an ideologically weighted system of judgements that define how we come to be seen and known, and its unintentional perpetuation of the mentally ill as Other. An emphasis, too, on the individual in first-person narrative work, while supplying us with valuable fine-grained and nuanced data regarding lives and the complexity of living them, might reinforce images of the "lone madman" and, thus, obscure structural disadvantage. This is particularly pertinent now, when the coalition government in the UK appears to be undermining the very systems of health and welfare that have in the past attempted to offer some support to those with mental illness. This obscuring of structural factors could deter a broader critique of the socio-economic factors at play in contributing to, or exacerbating, mental ill health. An obscuring or overlooking of discursive factors involved in the construction of mental illness, which shifts with society's demands, might also be a consequence of an insistence on the individual narrative.

Work such as this, foregrounding the *artistic activity* of the mentally ill, is, in addition, vulnerable to criticism that it contributes to the maintenance of a still widely held belief in a link between madness and creativity. Such a link, one might argue, as does Sawyer (2006, p. 87) might well be "nothing more than a myth, springing from Romantic era conceptions". Ongoing studies investigating this hypothesised link are, latterly and wisely, circumspect, confining the scope of the investigation to sub-clinical measures of psychopathology such as schizotypy (Nettle, 2006) and hypomania (Furnham, Batey, Anand, & Hanfield, 2008). While it is conceivable that such a link might eventually be confirmed, the area of contention lies in the potential *exploitation* of such a link. If the idea of a link between madness and creativity serves to shore up constructions of the mad, creative, lone/isolated/ feared or revered individual upon whom our fantasies and fears may be projected, then it ensues that understanding of the nature of mental illness could be hampered. Such reinforcing of artist stereotypes also does little to promote newer artistic identities more in line with twenty-first century sensibilities.

Psychosocial research is alive to such questions of voice, representation, power, and its potential abuse. It requires a heightened—some might suggest an almost guilt-laden—sensitivity to the quest for "a different register of knowing" (Hollway, 2011). On a more practical basis, this research sought to gain properly informed consent, with a long lead-in period of one-to-one discussion with potential participants, a regular checking back with them regarding their right to withdraw, updates on the progress of the research, and access to data, final papers, and reports at draft stage. The aim was to make the "space" of research exist as a space where individual stories and trajectories were being held, sensitively, respectfully, in their wholeness. This space included, of course, the interview space in which words, memory, imagination, and auto/biography could be held in a potential for becoming other, a potential for increasing us both. But this is also a tense space; the relationship between researcher and researched is inevitably asymmetrical. Fraught, too, is the arena between us, laden as it might become with difficult psychic traffic: the uncertainty of memory, the risk of fabrication, and the fear of retaliation. Finally, the narrative interview space is fraught because in each narrative lies our own, as details resonate with the researcher's life, bringing one's own memories hurtling into consciousness. Such research, with its multiple approaches and interpretations, finally both suffers from, and is strengthened by, "the theoretical fault lines that traverse it" (Andrews, Squire, & Tamboukou, 2008, p. 3).

Narrative research with mentally ill individuals carries ethical freight, as noted above, but it also acquires a more intense momentum and rationale. First, it seems that "sickness calls forth stories" (Charon, 2004, p. 23), that illness, trauma, and mental illness, in particular, will seek articulation (Frank, 1995; Stone, 2004). Earlier research I have conducted (Sagan, 2007, 2008) has also tracked the almost visceral need to "get it down on paper", and showed how narratives gained a direct importance in the participants' lives. Frank (1995, p. xii) notes, too, that through illness people become storytellers to "recover the voices that illness and its treatment often take away." Yet, we need also to be cautious of assumptions of knowledge based on stories which give us access to so private an experience of mental illness, or madness. Such narratives are sometimes brought from the depths of despair, fragmentation, or bleakness "so overwhelming as to be quite beyond expression" (Styron, 2004, p. 83). Stone (2004, p. 49) also warns that "narrative's tendency toward linearity and resolution" is, perhaps, "inimical to the expression of madness". Narrative is always an approximation, and some authors, in writing about their illness, display a masterful postmodernist allegiance to the twist of identity and of authorial voice. Slater (2000, p. 223), in her "Metaphorical memoir" describes her text as "slippery, playful, impish, exasperating", and Derrida (1987, pp. 54–55) reminds us that the sentence, by its very essence, carries "normality within it" and is, therefore, almost certainly the wrong tool for the job of describing that outside the mainstream.

However approximate as a tool, this research set about to use narrative. The exchanges offered a time and a space in which the participants could talk about their life, their illnesses, and health, their learning and development, and, last but by no means least, their work. That this artistic work existed as a tangible product lent a further corner to a triangle of potential space between the narrator/artist, the listener/viewer, and the artefact. This triangle, evoking an Oedipal joining (Britton, 1989) with the artefact/narrative as the creation, the child, evokes the family unit, with all its good, or, in this case, more often bad, memories of the power of this unit and its role in our auto/biography.

Continua of health, continua of artistic practice

The role of continua in the narratives appeared to perform an important function that was intrinsically linked to the experience of mental ill health. Such ill health had ravaged careers, relationships and identities. Arguably, such ruptured narratives had a coherence of their own, but one that was less acknowledged by our linear thinking, as "it is the implicit or explicit assumption of continuity that underlies the experience of disruption as one of the traumatic aspects of illness" (Rimmon-Kenan, 2002, p. 12).

This pull towards continuity might indeed have made the continua in these narratives a deliberate, if unconscious, attempt at "wellness" associated with coherence. Lines of continua were embedded across the interview data, and used to represent the journey from illness through to beyond. In these journeys from powerlessness to empowerment, from actual or symbolic "homelessness" to a being in the world, a picture emerges of fast-flowing traffic along multiple lanes. There were hold-ups, pile-ups, times of cruising, breakdown, and gridlock. The overwhelming sense now, after interviewing this most engaging of participant groups, is one of the sheer *hard work* that was going on, along these lanes and lines. This chapter focuses on two intimately interconnected continua: those of health and of artistic practice, and the attempts made by each student to locate her or himself therein.

Continua of health

These narratives of health and histories of illness, were broadly in line with what Frank (1995, p. 115) referred to as "quest narratives", those which "meet suffering head on; they accept illness and seek to use it". There was no sign, among this group of highly articulate, motivated individuals, of Frank's other categories. First, there was no "restitution narrative", where the individual's story of being well and becoming ill holds an implicit or explicit reference to an assumption that s/he will again be well. All participants in this research had sophisticated narratives in which they considered their illness to be a part of themselves, albeit one that they needed to "manage". It was a part that would, from time to time, be given reprieve, through a lessening of symptoms and greater insight ushering in more manageability. These were narratives of journeying, which indicated that "for some people a key aspect of learning to live with chronic incurable illness is not to transcend the illness but to find ways to incorporate it into daily living" (Jackson, 2006, p. 52).

There was no sign, either, of Frank's other category in his useful topography, that of the chaos narrative, where "stories are chaotic in their absence of narrative order" (Frank, 1995, p. 97). That said, when I have discussed this with participants, there were comments which indicated this type of narrative chimed with their *past* experience. Eva, for example, quipped, "That would've been me, three years ago!" (laughs).

In the "quest narratives" of this group of people, there was a starting point:

"By the end of 2003 my mind started to unravel and that was the start of psychosis" (Lottie).

After that, the deterioration and sometimes destitution and desperation were spoken of:

"Eventually—I was homeless—I had to stay here and there—I'd end up in half-way house things." (Lottie)

Culmination was in the "arrival", physically, mentally, socioeconomically, at the position of being an art student:

"I saw the course I wanted to do, and at that stage I still had quite a bit of agoraphobia so I think over that summer of 2006 I basically got myself on a bus everyday going a little bit further each day, greater exposure. After about a month of doing that I finally got to the college intact, so I thought, ok now I can go ahead and chase one of my dreams, really." (Dan)

There were numerous references to the "fuelling" effect of this attainment being able to motor a more integrated and optimistic future. In this future, illness would play a part, but not one that would again overpower the person. Arrival at the university, thus, represented a huge achievement and the height of a continuum whose starting point, narratively, did sometimes *change* as our relationship developed. Students sometimes spoke, for example, in an almost nonchalant, flat delivery about an initial breakdown, or hospitalisation, yet, as the narratives and trust developed, "thicker" stories emerged, more heavily laden with affect which detailed early years' stories of trauma, abandonment, and, in some cases, abuse. For almost all of the participants, fears were triggered regarding their mental health in their teens, often after a culmination of difficult, sometimes tragic, experience. But for Dan and one other student, a psychiatric history began much earlier:

> "It started when I was nine, actually . . . That was anxiety and an eating disorder. I saw a psychiatrist once a week for about half a year when I was nine to ten. Then I was fine until age sixteen. I think I had normal kind of teenage problems from about twelve, thirteen, fourteen. Things started going wrong when I was sixteen. Then I was ok for a bit. The schizophrenia really started when I was eighteen."

The continuum of health, with the huge, neon-lit landmark of arriving at university, did not stop there. One of the most poignant details of the narratives was the hyper-vigilance of health and ill-health on a continuum which now threatened to jeopardise the dearly won achievement of becoming an arts student. Such narratives were quite explicit in demonstrating the "sliding scale of well-ness" like a barometer, which each individual held in her or his head, and against which s/he anxiously measured creative production and potential:

> "I get on a high and I can't stop I can't stop talking and working and talking and I go on and on and I know, I can feel that they're all thinking . . . well . . . I just go on and on, but it's good but I know that it'll end and they'll be thinking 'what was that?!' So I try and watch myself, for when that phase comes . . . comes . . . back . . . watch myself . . ." (Eva)

As Eva demonstrates, this barometer, however, was a deceptive measurer of identity and creativity, revealing the difficult decisions, choices, and compromises made. It was clear that sometimes a choice for health, and being able to, as Ginny put it, "fly beneath the radar" meant negating or even fearing periods of creative intensity, desirable though they were to Eva. Such hypomania has been explored in the literature, for its value.

> Hypomania is important for creative output for three reasons: 1) it facilitates the speed and range of imagination 2) it provides the energy to push through on an activity, and 3) the depression element

provides a more pessimistic assessment of what can be achieved. (St John Burch, Pavelis, Hemsley, & Corr, 2006, p. 178)

The splitting off of one's hypomania, or depression, or other outward signs of an illness seemed also to endorse a negating of an aspect of self, as though the "less desirable" could be split off from one. Rimmon-Kenan (2002, p. 14) cites Murphy in talking about his illness, which, although of a very different kind, is also viewed in a particular way by the "well" (1987, p. 92):

> Murphy poignantly analyzes the price the disabled have to pay for normal social relations: 'they must comfort others about their own condition. They cannot show fear, sorrow, depression, sexuality, or anger, for this disturbs the able-bodied'.

This attempt at conformity did not always come easily or even "naturally". In talking about ways of thinking and managing social relations as a schizophrenic, Dan, for example, mentions losing something "that was really me", while Lottie, with her history of failure and illness, sadly had to hide her effervescence and joy at her achievement of arrival at her university because such explosions of emotion and hypomania were, for her, "symptomatic" and on a continuum of "acceptable" to "non-acceptable" outward signs of mental illness. She felt under pressure to hide behaviour that other students could display without eliciting comment:

> "You know when you want to start singing and dancing and you can't . . . I've got to sort of keep a lid on it because some people might not get it."

This care-taking of social relations led to a particular role and function for the continuum. Some individuals were to speak passionately, particularly in later interviews, about having arrived at a point where their acceptance of themselves, that represented self in the artistic practice, and an acceptance of how they were viewed by others *as artists*, had reached a more integrated and comfortable place. The vigilance and caution, over the span of the research, appeared to lessen. This sometimes led to a period of "in your face" coming out, through displaying a particular work:

> "I certainly remember watching their reactions to it . . . with fear and dread and an absolute sense of 'other'-ness." (Ginny)

Ginny, much later, commented how

"Eventually the purge is over. Then you can get on and be bigger than a single label."

This movement evokes an observation of Polkinghorne (1996) that many narratives of illness emerge and recede between perceived agentic and victimic poles. Enmeshed in why, perhaps, many of the narratives in this study became increasingly agentic is the role of artistic practice, and that practice was continually beleaguered by the stark reality of being on, sometimes heavy, medication. For the individuals with whom I talked, the subject of medication was forefront in their minds in a way that it is difficult for anyone not bound to medication to appreciate. Within what was overwhelmingly seen as a dependency, there were, again, continua of options and standpoints, along which individuals positioned themselves, sometimes warily, sometimes defiantly:

"And sometimes you have to be a bit . . . [bangs on the table] . . . because otherwise they want to prescribe you medication and I don't want to go back on that crap." (Lottie)

Narrative data where individuals spoke about the decisions and choices or, in some cases, lack of choices regarding their medication is stark in its portrayal of a daily battle alien to those outside the world of mental illness. Each individual spoke of a personal experiment, either long or short term, that they were involved in to lessen, or change, their medication and their contact with mental health support. The continuum from medication dependent to medication free was littered with serious hurdles. These included the impact on one's creativity and art practice of coming off medication or, as more commonly the choice, lessening or changing it:

"Another [option] is going to hospital and coming off my clozapine, going on something different. That's an option, but I'm sure I'll be persuaded not to do that. Unless I can come up with a really good argument. It really is affecting my creativity." (Dan)

Included, too, was the real possibility of serious relapse and the return of extreme symptoms and suicidal tendencies. Individuals expressed a fear of jeopardising that for which they had worked so hard, the relative stability and validation of being an art student and having the hope of a more creative, integrated future.

> "... so what do I do? I carry on like this and learn to manage it. I keep getting pushed towards going on these drugs and I really don't want to. I've been thinking about it months, but I'm still sticking to my guns. There's all the weight gain and everything. If I lose this, the art, then what have I got?" (Eva)

For all, the history of medication was one which began in a difficult, sometimes traumatic, time of their lives.

> "So I was like, ok I will go in, but I had no idea what they were going to do to me in there. I had no idea they were gonna ask me to take medication, and I had no idea that the doors would be locked either. They didn't tell me that. So I had one bag, and when I found out that the doors were going to be locked and that I was just locked in, there was no ... I just waited by the door trying to, like, escape. Whenever anyone came in I was waiting there with my bag just trying to get out, and um, then they came into my room at night and said, will you take this medication? She said, if you don't take it, then you won't be allowed out. That's what she said. That was that. I was there for twenty-eight days." (Tracy)

Since such a time, these individuals had moved along the continuum, through therapy, friends, support networks, altered and more sympathetic medication regimes, and, overwhelmingly mentioned, an involvement with college and art practice. They had arrived, for now, at a place of relative autonomy and hope. Each was acutely aware, however, of the ease with which they could slide back down the continuum; holidays, for example, from the routine of study and practice were often challenging, and breaks were often planned for carefully, with the inclusion of extra support, activities, and social contact. Eva was not alone in her sentiment that she was somehow more herself at university:

> "Sometimes I wish I didn't have to come home from uni ... not because I don't love my family but because I know that when I get home I will probably come down from hypomania ... and don't want to."

Yet, such splitting between home (non-art engagement) and university (art engagement) meant that sometimes there was a sense of idealisation of the latter, and consequent denigration of the former. Home, and a world of non-, or lesser, art engagement, represented a rupture from the milieu so long fantasised and now attained. It was also the place that symbolised a point earlier along the continuum, which was undesirable.

With the passing of time and researcher–researched engagement, I became, unsurprisingly, involved in these continua and where these students were on them at any given point. But there was a historic continuum that was to remain outside of the bounds of this study; I raise it here as it emerged in the narratives, and offers another glimpse into the efforts involved in making life changes. This continuum was the transgenerational—involving parents or grandparents with histories of mental illness:

> "My mum was diagnosed about ten years ago with a paranoid schizoid disorder. It seems that my personality disorder is linked to the abuse I suffered from her from when I was a baby. My first hospital admission is when I was two when she broke my arm. I've had other broken bones from her since then." (Ginny)

> ". . . my mum suffers from manic depression, bipolar disorder, so growing up was quite difficult living with her and her mental illness. I've just got normal depression . . . My mum's one happens every year. She gets sectioned into the mental home." (Eliza)

If not mental illness, there were transgenerational histories of abuse or drug or alcohol addiction:

> "My Dad's er . . . I haven't spoken to him for about fifteen years and yes he used to beat us up and stuff and shout a lot . . . A lot . . . And it left me a bit . . . erm . . . under-confident . . ." (Ayden)

And there were some acute worries that this lineage would stretch on into the future, and on into the next generation. Eva, whose little girl has serious irritable bowel syndrome at the age of four, is saddened by the impacts her own mental illness has on her family:

> "I had the breakdown when I was pregnant with her . . . I love her to bits, but I haven't got the bond with her that I have with my first son. I've had difficulty bonding with her. Perhaps I blame her a little bit for the breakdown."

Defiantly, again, there was a sense of responsibility articulated, that in some way the buck had to stop here, through *this* individual gaining insight, control, expression, and working to halt any slippage back down the line to dark times and states. Here is Ginny, talking about her meeting her abusive mother after having no contact with her:

> "I mean the first time I met my mum, which was just over a year ago prob-
> ably ... physically being in her presence and her crying ... all of the
> power that she had, she lost when she appeared as this old woman with
> a walking stick and grey hair who was fat, and crying. So, it shows me
> that when you feel the fear, do it anyway ... you get a reward."

Ginny had been edging towards this point in therapy for years, moving from a position of terror and loathing to one of far more control and empowerment. Once again, implicated in this, as compass point of desideratum, was one's precious, difficult, painful, but necessary artistic practice.

Continua of artistic practice

Prominent in interviews was the narrative of striving to locate a developing artistic practice, felt variously as therapy, autobiographic catharsis, or pristine content, breaking with the stultifying bonds of history, pathology, and class. For the most part, this group of students did not utilise a discourse of learning frequently adopted by students in higher education. Instead, the learning was *intrinsically* meshed with a developing insight into identity and into their art. The artistic discipline was expressed as being a part of oneself and vice versa, in a way that, speculatively, one would not find among students of another academic discipline. Artistic practice appeared to hold the other continua, and function as the point at which they could either converge, or, frustratingly, throw into relief the schisms and chasms of self, illness, and development. This is *not* to suggest that the work undertaken was "therapy", although art production emerged as instrumental in wellbeing. In demanding a rigorous intellectual appraisal of one's creative endeavour, along with an immersion in the affect and embodied experience of art production, artistic engagement was providing a unique process of bringing together internal and external worlds. Indeed, across the data, the particular line of continuum regarding artistic practice was repeatedly described. It began at a point where art activity had acted as therapy, commonly as part of a mental health rehabilitation programme, but the continuum offered a journey away from this:

> "I had art therapy. Everything I made was autobiographical. In the same way as talking therapy, to start with you have to stick everything up." (Ginny)

This point of departure was heralded as important. It was the point at which one moved from patient to artist, from one having therapy to one deliberately using an art form to create, to transcend, and to become other, as artist, with her/his practice breaking through the context of therapy in content and in process. Individuals positioned themselves carefully along this continuum, but all were aware, with more or less anxiety and articulation, of the real possibility of ghettoisation. As Love (2005, p. 161) argues:

> ... it's one thing to encourage someone to find their 'own voice' and make work about their 'own experience,' but what if such an appeal to this so-called unerring veracity only serves to keep that person in their 'own place;' to fix or reify that voice or experience as essentially and irrevocably marginal and different?

Particularly because of the stigma and stereotypes surrounding the mentally ill, paradoxically, an identity excavation which was encouraged in other students was felt to be less intrepidly welcomed by this group, who frequently described a hastening to move on from this.

Over time, these narratives displayed the increasing sophistication with which individuals moved along this continuum, and negotiated some of the "high art"/art therapy/community art schisms. Ginny, at one point, mused that her work either directly challenged her illness by putting herself in situations which she would normally find very difficult, or it actively explored her illness by using auto/biographic content. She went on, in the interview reflections, to ask,

> "Is it possible that my theoretical interests sit in between and bridge these two elements of my practice, and if so, does this in turn mean that these three elements together can combine to form a more cohesive whole self?"

Much later on in the research, she had moved again, significantly, although still grappling with a private/public face and the challenges of conscious over unconscious process. Her objective, however, remained a cohesive self, where the two ends of the continuum, worked through, and struggled with, merged to provide an experience of integration which went beyond the linear.

The content of the artefacts themselves was reflected upon and woven back into the narratives. But content was frequently less of a focal point than process, what an individual was trying to achieve, and how the methods of working *were* the creative act, the act of bringing together parts of oneself from different points along the continua. So, for Ginny, whose BPD (borderline personality disorder) had earlier encased her in a spatial isolation as well as an isolation from social relatedness, the act of filmmaking, involving crew, participants, team working, location, mobility, and communication, became the way in which she addressed these difficult aspects of herself. For Stella, a history of self-harm was examined, initially, through "embroidery with suture thread". Her delicate works suggest an intensely private exploration of pain and self-harm within a context of being held together, sewn up, secured. Such sewn artworks reworked herself as made new through a stitched image of completion, rather than a thing fraying or falling apart.

There is no doubt that *staying with* such projects was often difficult: they caused turbulence, and identities formed shot up and down the continua—integrating, disintegrating, and regrouping. But not only did individuals grapple with the task of gauging their position on the continuum of mental stability, or on the continuum of positioning one's self as an artist, they were also facing the task of being an art student within a high-octane atmosphere of an elite arts university, where measurement against a raft of factors was a constant.

Within all this, the capacity to tolerate not knowing was vital. This capacity, to stay in contact with the creative work while not knowing where it might lead or what risks lie ahead, to be able to "make accidental happenings in the work itself" (Safan-Gerard, 2002) is, perhaps, the creative and educative project. Such not knowing was difficult, however, while the self-policing around illness, symptoms, and medication, mentioned earlier, was so prevalent.

Continuing psychoanalytically

Psychoanalytic theory attends well to the nature of extremes and drives towards integration of these. Some of the thoughts in its literature help with considering the continuum as leitmotif in this data, and what such a leitmotif might suggest about its purpose and function.

Continua, first, are both time and space constructs. The "once upon a time" of stories sets up a temporal anticipation of what is to come, of how it will end. But we also envisage a continuum and move through it, sometimes physically, spatially, sometimes in a very concrete way, as imaging oneself moving through the continuum or sometimes being stuck in a rut, in limbo. While collapsing the time and space aspects of continua is a necessity of the brevity of this chapter, and the ways in which continua as a metaphorical device is used by the people in this research is idiographic, it is still well worth considering the continuum as a construct in time and space.

Freud (1920g, p. 299) remarked that time and space are "necessary forms of thought", and later (Freud, 1933a) that the id, chaotic and unbridled was alone a timeless domain. So important is an ability to think through time, and have a dimensional mode of thinking, that Noel-Smith (2002, p. 390) lays down as *prerogatives* of a healthy ego "temporal and spatial ways of thinking". Manoeuvrability, between stages, standpoints, and mental states, is very different to the psychotic black and white immediacy which brooks no margin for change, self reflection, or tolerance of shades of grey. It is also different to the experience of chaos, where "time and space, as necessary organising principles of the mind, cannot operate" (ibid., p. 396). The symbol of continuum, I suggest, fulfils a function, and that function is to aid healing and repair, the very ability to "think" a continuum indicating a movement of thought, a move indeed towards more creative thought. A narrative that moves through time allows room for the agentic—literally, a rewriting of our narrative, a remaking of who and what we are, where, and how.

Klein's theory of splitting (1946) also offers an insight into what the psyche is trying to *do* through keeping things separate or bringing them together, as, for example, through a cohesive narrative, a continuum. Her topography of paranoid–schizoid (PS) and depressive positions, and our oscillation between the two, suggests that while in the

PS position, there is an impeded ability to think in spatial or tempo-ral terms. In later work, Grotstein (1978, p. 57) refers to the narcissism of the "zero dimension" where there is "no space for manoeuvring of thought". He describes this psychological state as one in which there is "no differentiation", the main victim being thought. It is in the Kleinian depressive position where one moves towards the capacity for symbol formation and toleration of a sense of integration, bringing together part objects and aspects of one's self previously kept apart. It is these capabilities that suggest a move towards health and life.

An interest in exploring the impulse to bring things together, or keep them apart, was also explored by Bion, who suggested the crea-tive individual is one who has "negative capability" (Bion, 1970, after Keats, 1970), or, one able to hold paradox without resolving it through a "flight to split-off intellectual functioning" (Winnicott, 1971, p. xii). The bringing together, integrating, and tolerating the risk to one's schemata involves difficult, creative work (Ehrenzweig, 1967). Indeed, the PS position, uncreative and negating as it is, still performs the key role of keeping out the intolerable and defending against the toil and loneliness of moving to the depressive position. This latter position heralds the beginning of the work of mourning, and of reparation—an acceptance of things gone and a sense of courage in the face of that to come.

It is when this movement in time and space cannot occur that "toxic stories" (Roberts, 2000, p. 435) hold individuals hostage (Sagan, 2011a). This chronicity, observed by Kleinman, arises "in part by telling dead or static stories, situating the individual in a wasteland" (Kleinman, 1988, p. 438). The stories in this research displayed little of this chronicity and one could point to the role of learning and art prac-tice in this health. While it might be that such stagnant stages had been worked through before arriving at university and the arts, art practice itself, and the *possibility imagined in its encounter*, appears to offer healing in some fundamental, unconscious way.

Learning, and its inherent place in artistic practice, which is live with self-reflection and iterative addressing of themes and symbols resonant to the individual, is traditionally rich with metaphors of movement and journey. Freud's reality and pleasure principles (1920g), and the individual's struggles to move from the realm of instinctual pleasure to an acceptance of reality, itself offers an under-standing of much of the difficult work of learning. Education, as

Freud claimed, is "an incitement to the conquest of the pleasure principle, and to its replacement by the reality principle" (Freud, 1911b, p. 224). This move was embedded in narratives which told of, for example, artwork being produced to meet the demands of the reality principle when a looser, perhaps more passionate and risky approach was yearned for. Lifestyles were spoken of as compromised as individuals bowed to the limitations imposed by an illness that required surveillance. While it is true that the forces of civilisation impose such decrees on us all, the "high stakes game" meant that such reining in by the ego was particularly active. There was the looming threat of a return to fragmentation, increased medication, and hospitalisation, not to mention financial disaster, perceived family or peer shame, and a re-entrenchment into cycles of poverty, non-attainment, and illness. Such fears and realities were more than enough to police a sober approach to one's work, to some extent sacrificing, ironically, spontaneity and artistic risk.

For these students, there was, in fact, little distinction in the narratives of learning with those of artistic production; a natural oscillation between learning and artistic practice was a common feature to all participants. Thus, the continuum of learning, that of artistic positioning, *and* that of becoming other to a "mentally ill person" all involved the image of leaving behind exuviae of oneself. In this drama of becoming new, the continuum served as the stage. But the real "trick" involved avoiding a clear disavowal of who one was, or is. Benau (2009, p. 84), in writing about Janusian thinking, the ability to look both forward and back, describes the importance of maintaining "the sustained interest toward and ultimately successful processing and integration of previously denied and irreconcilable aspects of self, other, and relationship".

Indeed, as the interviews in this research progressed, an old self was often tentatively *reclaimed* as an integral part of one's autobiography. This was a crucial point on the continuum.

In these narratives, the symbol of continuum, unsurprising as it is in life narratives, was particularly pronounced. One simple reason for this might be that the beginnings of illness "stamped" a before and a hopeful after on to a life narrative, and this was seized by minds determined to repair. Within this, the metaphor of continuum offers a "road-map" of hope that is more tightly clung to by these students than by those of us less blown by the winds of mental unrest.

The student artists in this research[2] gave generously of their lives in their narratives and art works, and dispel any residual prejudice of "deficit", still heard, that mentally ill students represent a risk we cannot afford. I hope to have offered a glimpse, in this chapter, of the hard work and elegance of their developing a *beyondness* through their reflections, learning, and artistic engagement.

Notes

1. This form of biographic narrative traces its allegiances to the politicisation of the personal, in the work of feminist writers and researchers (see, *inter alia*, Reinharz (1992)) who first explored the empowering potential of autobiographic practices and the role of first-person narrative in counteracting culturally sanctioned narratives.
2. Some of these students are practising artists and participants in a later audiovisual, participatory research project, headed by the same researchers, and funded by the Arts Council England, and South London and Maudsley Charitable Trust. For more information see "Thou Art" (www.thouart.org/).

References

Andrews, M., Squire, C., & Tamboukou, M. (Eds.) (2008). *Doing Narrative Research*. London: Sage.

Benau, K. S. (2009). Contrasts, symbol formation and creative transformation in art and life. *Psychoanalytic Review, 96*(1): 83–112.

Bion, W. R. (1970). *Attention and interpretation*. London: Tavistock.

Britton, R. (1989). The missing link: parental sexuality in the Oedipus complex. In: J. Steiner (Ed.), *The Oedipus Complex Today* (pp. 83–101). London: Karnac.

Charon, R. (2004). The ethicality of narrative medicine. In: B. Hurwitz, T. Greenhalgh, & V. Skultans (Eds.), *Narrative Research in Health and Illness* (pp. 23–37). Oxford: Blackwell.

Derrida, J. (1987). *The Post Card: From Socrates to Freud and Beyond*. London: University of Chicago Press.

Ehrenzweig, A. (1967). *The Hidden Order of Art*. Berkeley, CA: University of California Press.

Frank, A. W. (1995). *The Wounded Storyteller: Body, Illness and Ethic*. Chicago, IL: University of Chicago Press.

Freud, S. (1911b). Formulations on the two principles of mental functioning. *S.E.*, *12*: 213–226. London: Hogarth.

Freud, S. (1920g). *Beyond the Pleasure Principle*. *S.E.*, *18*: 1–64. London: Hogarth.

Freud, S. (1933a). *New Introductory Lectures on Psychoanalysis*. *S.E.*, *12*: 1–182. London: Hogarth.

Froggett, L., & Hollway, W. (2010). Psychosocial research analysis and scenic understanding. *Psychoanalysis, Culture and Society*, *15*(3): 281–301.

Furnham, A., Batey, M., Anand, K., & Manfield, J. (2008). Personality, hypomania, intelligence and creativity. *Personality and Individual Differences*, *44*: 115–121.

Grotstein, J. (1978). Inner space: its dimensions and its coordinates. *International Journal of Psychoanalysis*, *59*: 55–61.

Hollway, W. (2011). Psychosocial writing from data: Editorial. *Journal of Psycho-social Studies*, *4*(2): 3–10. http://hls.uwe.ac.uk/research/Data/Sites/1/journalpsychosocialstudies/jan2011/whollwaypsychosocialwritingfromdata.pdf (accessed May 2011).

Hollway, W., & Jefferson, T. (2000). *Doing Qualitative Research Differently: Free Association, Narrative and the Interview Method*. London: Sage.

Jackson, S. (2006). Learning to live: the relationship between lifelong learning and lifelong illness. *International Journal of Lifelong Education*, *25*(1): 51–73.

Jaques, E. (1965). Death and the mid-life crisis. In: E. B. Spillius (Ed.), *Melanie Klein Today, Volume 2: Mainly Practice*. London: Routledge, 1990.

Keats, J. (1970). *The Letters of John Keats: A Selection*, R. Gittings (Ed.). Oxford: Oxford University Press.

Klein, M. (1946). Notes on some schizoid mechanisms. *International Journal of Psychoanalysis*, *27*(2): 99–110.

Klein, M. (1998). *Love, Guilt and Reparation and Other Works 1921–1945*. London: Vintage.

Kleinman, A. (1988). *The Illness Narratives: Suffering, Healing and the Human Condition*. New York: Basic Books.

Love, K. (2005). The experience of art as a living through of language. In: G. Butt (Ed.), *After Criticism, New Responses to Art and Performance* (pp. 156–176). Oxford: Blackwell.

Nettle, D. (2006). Schizotypy and mental health amongst poets, visual artists, and mathematicians. *Journal of Research in Personality, 40*: 876–890.

Noel-Smith, K. (2002). Time and space as 'necessary forms of thought'. *Free Associations*, 9(51): 394–442.

Murphy, R. F. (1987). *The Body Silent*. London: J. M. Dent and Sons.

Polkinghorne, D. (1996). Transformative narratives: from victimic to agentic life plots. *American Journal of Occupational Therapy*, 50(4): 299–305.

Reinharz, S. (1992). *Feminist Methods in Social Resesarch*. New York: Oxford University Press.

Rimmon-Kenan, S. (2002). The story of "I": illness and narrative identity. *Narrative*, 10(1): 9–27.

Roberts, G. A. (2000). Narrative and severe mental illness: what place do stories have in an evidence-based world? *Advances in Psychiatric Treatment*, 6: 432–441.

Safan-Gerard, D. (2002). On not knowing: discerning the mental and emotional requirements of creative work. Paper presented to Bion Conference, Los Angeles, California, February.

Sagan, O. (2007). An interplay of learning, creativity and narrative biography in a mental health setting: Bertie's story. In: P. Chamberlayne (Ed.), *Art, Creativity and Imagination in Social Work Practice* (pp. 311–321). London: Routledge.

Sagan, O. (2008). The loneliness of the long-anxious learner: mental illness, narrative biography and learning to write. *Psychodynamic Practice*, 14(1): 43–58.

Sagan, O. (2011a). Interminable knots: hostages to toxic stories. *Pedagogy, Culture & Society*, 19(1): 97–118

Sagan, O. (2011b). Thou art: the multiple gaze of audio-visual, community-based participatory research. *Journal of Applied Arts and Health*, 2(2): 125–136.

Sawyer, R. K. (2006). *Explaining Creativity: The Science of Human Innovation*. Oxford: Oxford University Press.

Slater, L. (2000). *Lying: A Metaphorical Memoir*. New York: Random House.

St John Burch, G., Pavelis, C., Hemsley, D. R., & Corr, P. (2006). Schizotypy and creativity in visual artists. *British Journal of Psychology*, 97: 177–190.

Stone, B. (2004). Towards a writing without power: notes on the narration of madness. *Auto/Biography*, 12(1): 16–33.

Styron, W. (2004). *Darkness Visible,* London: Vintage.

Winnicott, D. W. (1971). *Playing and Reality*. London: Tavistock/Routledge.

CHAPTER FOURTEEN

Transformative learning: a passage through the liminal zone

Larry Green

Introduction

This chapter will explore the role and contribution of trauma theory and praxis to the understanding of transformative learning (TL). TL distinguishes itself from previous educational models, such as the banking and transmission models (Freire, 1993). These models were critiqued for their assumption that students were passive containers into which the teacher deposited content (ibid.). Transformative learning acknowledges that the container changes shape—the person reconfigures over their lifetime. It is not just a matter of adding or reorganising content (concepts) into an already formed container (self). Rather, the self can and often does change its shape. If we think of the self as delineated by the boundary that separates the "me" from the "not-me", or the self from the other, then, as various psychoanalytically orientated theorists (e.g., Fairbairn, 1952; Guntrip, 1968; Kegan, 1982; Winnicott, 1965) have pointed out, that defining boundary is renegotiated over time. According to Kegan (1982), each developmental stage involves a reformulation of what is self and what is other (or object). It begins with the realisation, "mummy and I are not one person". As this occurs, what was once experienced as an aspect of self—the mother—

moves over to the object pole of the relationship. Separation anxiety could be more accurately described as not anxiety as a result of separation from the mother, but, rather, a separation from the self that one formerly was (ibid.). Kegan claimed that at each stage of development, a similar separation occurs, where what was once experienced as subject is moved over to the object side. For example, a tired child "sees" frustrating adults at every turn; later, she will objectify her "tiredness" and factor that compensating knowledge into her perceptions. Her tiredness no longer unconsciously conditions her perceptions, but, rather, becomes an object of her perception. In this movement, the psyche has undergone structural change.

Transformational learning theorists also make a case for structural change in the psyche. Originally, they gave a predominately cognitive account of this process. Mezirow (1991), the founder of that school, claimed that the fundamental premises on which a person constructs a self are revised by that person during a transformative learning episode. Kegan corrected this predominately cognitive approach with his claim that transformation always involves anxiety and depression. That is, as the person realises that her way of framing the world is inadequate, she experiences anxiety about the possibility of losing herself. Depression, on the other hand, might be triggered by the recognition that one's familiar self is already lost. Grieving is a necessary part of the transformational process. Thus, transformation is simultaneously a cognitive and affective process—existential through and through. This chapter makes use of psychoanalytic and psychological theory to address the pedagogical implications of transformative learning. To accomplish this purpose, I articulate the micro-processes involved in TL. My hope is that such mapping will aid educators to understand and facilitate self-transformation. I draw support for this investigation from trauma theory.

Both trauma and TL engage the core of selfhood. This is a self not shielded by assumptions or defensive structures, but, rather, directly engaged—a self existentially aware of its own precarious freedom. I will make use of two theoretical foci for this enquiry: first, the processes involved in meaning breaking and meaning making (Kegan, 1982) and second, the emotional aspects associated with each. The emotions of anxiety and depression accompany the very difficult process of dis-integration, re-constitution, and re-integration that is transformational learning. (I hyphenate these words because I want to emphasise the denotative meaning of disintegration rather than its connotation of complete destruction. It is not destruction, but, rather, a loosening of the associations between elements of the psychic structure.) My knowledge of the micro-processes involved is based on my forty years' experience as a psychotherapist.

Lacan (1966) is the psychoanalyst whose work most influences my own. I prefer his emphasis on cultural and linguistic determinates to Freud's (1905d) biological emphasis on drives. I see humans as primarily meaning making creatures: language and culture provide the material from which we construct our personal meanings. On the other hand, these meanings can be energised or flat, vital or dead. Freud's concept of "libido" and Lacan's of "desire" speak to this energy that animates some meanings and not others. Nobel prize winning novelist Coetzee (2003) said something similar when he claimed that belief was like a battery that we plug into ideas to make them work. Something more than formal concepts is at work in self transformation. As this chapter will demonstrate, metaphor is the linguistic tool that I find most useful in meaning making. When working with patients, I register metaphors that are meaningful or vital *vs.* metaphors that are emptied and clichéd. That is, desire fills in some meanings and vacates others. By tracking that combination of meaning and vital energy, I am able to detect how patients compose themselves and where that composure is disturbed. That disturbance is a potential entry point into a transformative experience. In this chapter, I make use of my clinical experience to elucidate the abstractions of transformative learning theory in the context of the therapeutic encounter. It was through these encounters that I began to map the micro-processes involved in transformation. Later in my career, these understandings informed my pedagogical approach while teaching counselling theory at a number of community colleges in Canada. I will suggest that both TL and trauma theory, while most often applied to individuals, can also inform a rapidly transforming culture—a culture where everything that once was solid "melts in the air".

Shape shifting or identity change

Fundamental change is difficult because it involves a radical shift in identity. "Fundamental", "structural", and "radical" are terms that highlight different aspects of TL. These terms focus on the synchronic, the snapshot in time, whereas "transformation" highlights the dia-chronic—change over time—aspect. An apt metaphor for transforma-tional change is the caterpillar's metamorphosis into a butterfly—not a difference of degree, but, rather, one of kind; not superficial, but, rather, structural in nature. When we move from the biologic meta-phor to the psychologic of TL, the structures implicated are those of identity rather than those of anatomy. The ground of assumptions upon which we construct our identities is remade during transforma-tional learning. The term "structure" often implies a solid, static thing; however, I prefer to think of mental structures as repeating patterns. The metaphor of a whirlpool, or eddy, might be helpful here. The material constituent of the whirlpool, water, is constantly changing, yet the pattern persists. Kegan (1982) has a wonderful way of captur-ing this notion of continual but patterned flux:

> What we know of the way our client holds himself and his world together can help us understand what his experience means to him . . . We are especially helped by our awareness of the fact that *the way he composes himself* is at once a kind of achievement and a constraint. (p. 3, my italics)

Indeed, we are not solid, inert things; our constancy requires continual construction. We "compose" ourselves. We hold ourselves and our world together. This suggests both the notions of agency and of limitedness. With regard to agency, the composition of our identity is an "achievement". At the same time, this composition imposes a "constraint". The deep structures or fundamental premises form a platform upon which the conscious mind plays. This platform neces-sarily limits the range of the conscious mind. One's conscious self is not as autonomous as one might think. Certain master meanings are anchored in the psyche, for example: "Adults often hurt you, so be careful"; "If I want it, I should have it"; "Is there a money-making opportunity here?"; "What would Jesus do?"; and "Knowing that death is approaching, how do I want to spend what remains of my time?", and so on. These master meanings are often preconscious con-ceptions that structure or condition a person's conscious experience (Epstein, 1983). They are the touchstones, the basic premises, from which derivative meanings are generated. They produce the repeating patterns that compose identity and are the means for orientating to one's circumstances. When in doubt, when a decision is required, when the stakes are high, we turn to our basic premises for guidance. It does not take much extrapolation to see how each of these reference points would generate quite different identities. Our hypothetical subject who orientates to money will develop a nuanced financial vocabulary, whereas his relationship vocabulary might be impoverished. Lacan (1966) makes a useful contribution to my understanding of the process of TL with his concept of a master signifier. A master signifier, or primary reference point, is the *anchor* that guarantees all other derivative meanings their worth and stability. For example, if my master signifier is "environmentalism", then the derivative values of recycling, solar and wind power, and vegetarianism are generated by it. My master signifier must, therefore, be anchored, or else I will begin to feel that I am "going to pieces". That is, the derivative meanings, which once were systematic and coherent, become increasingly fragmented. This is a daunting prospect. Consequently, many people prefer to reassert their previous master meanings in an attempt to retrieve their coherency. In order to minimise this unfortunate outcome, TL theory needs to acknowledge that as we shift from one set of basic premises to another, we are indeed flirting with the danger of relativising all meaning. This is the particular danger of liminality— the transitional zone between two ways of being. In traditional cultures, rites of passage provided an external structure or container that enabled the individual to dis-integrate one internal structure in preparation for the next to emerge. As one moves through a liminal experience, one can lose the boundary between subject and object—the "me" from the "not me". One realises how fraught such an experience can be when one understands that this boundary is the fundamental structure by which we hope to distinguish objective reality from our "mere" subjectivity.

Transformative learning as structural change

Transformative learning implies structural change, a morphing of one's identity, a reconfiguration of one's psychological shape. As Guntrip (1971) put it, "The problem of having an unquestioned possession or else a lack of a sense of personal reality and selfhood, the identity problem, is the biggest single issue that can be raised about human existence" (p. 119).

Guntrip is conflating "personal reality" and "selfhood" with "identity". Likewise, I use the terms "self" and "identity" as interchangeable. In addition, I would like to add the term "ipseity" (Latin for "self"). Sass (1992) describes schizophrenia as a self disorder or ipseity disturbance. According to his reading, a schizophrenic has lost her self—no longer inhabiting, and living from a self, but, rather, viewing their self as one would view an object. This is not the goal of transformative learning, but it is a risk of which the learner is often aware. "What if I turn into someone I don't even know?" Kegan and Lahey (2009) name the consequence of this fear "immunity to change" (p. 48). That is, the rigidity of behaviour is generated by the person's "anxiety management system" (p. 48). Accordingly, we are immune or resistant to change because transformation might involve dismantling a part or all of our anxiety management system.

Anxiety: the fluidisation of all that once was stable

When that system is operating effectively, we are unaware of its presence. However, when we intend to change our behaviour and are unable to do so, we have the opportunity to become aware of its constraining nature. If one persists with the intention to change, the anxiety that has been bound and contained by one's former identity will be loosened until more comprehensive premises are developed and a new identity established. Retroactively, one can realise that one's anxiety management system contributes significantly to one's characteristic shape—our dynamic identity. It is a major factor in how we go about composing ourselves. It is as if the subject observes, "I only go so far in any direction before I reach a limit, beyond which I begin to experience intolerable anxiety. Those limits, over time, become my identifying boundary." We might, for example, be limited by a punitive superego. That is, our vital energy, or libido, instead of seeking pleasure and satisfaction, will be repressed in order to prevent anxiety and guilt. I have a colleague who will only allow himself to work and play squash because, for him, those are the only conflict-free zones.

The micro-processes of TL

The organisation of the remainder of this chapter has a three-part focus. First, I claim that identity is formed via an investment in, and attachment to, foundational premises. These foundational premises are not explicitly formulated or stated in a propositional form. Rather, they are embodied meanings—the "unthought known" is how Bollas (1987) put it. For example, an individual comes to the realisation that his past three partners had high foreheads, like his mother's. Apparently this "unthought" criteria—high foreheads coincide with nurturing—was operating without his conscious awareness. In the majority of cases, one's investment and attachment to such a premise occurs spontaneously through pre-reflective engagement (Deikman, 1966; Loy, 1988). One's identity is built on this bedrock. This process of psychologic development is distinct from the process of "identification", which psychoanalytic theory uses to refer to the process of internalising a role model—that is, attempting to become like someone else (Guntrip, 1971). One of my patients described himself as a caricature of a man—not authentic, but, rather, imitative. Both pre-reflective engagement and identification contribute to the elaboration of the psychic structure. After this exploration of these premises, I turn my attention to the crisis or trauma experience where one realises that one's foundational assumptions are broken (Janoff-Bulman, 1992). Last, I describe how the therapeutic encounter provides a holding environment as the person revisits her founding premises, examines them for their continued viability, and begins the process of constructing a more adequate platform from which to live. My hope is that this description will provide some insight into the facilitation of transformative learning in other contexts.

Self formation: identification and pre-reflective engagement

If we understand those processes of identification, we could be much more skilful in "midwifing" someone through a transformative learning experience. The psychoanalytic term, introjection, extends or refines what is occurring with identification. An identification occurs when something external to the person is imported, or introjected, and becomes part of the self. I will start at the back end, with the person's recognition that some of her behaviours are generated by something other than her will; that sometimes she acts in ways that are contrary to her self interest. Then I will retrace the steps or processes that installed that perceptual-action protocol that the person now finds so distressing. How does one know that they have been "colonised" by an agency other than their own? The following aphorism makes it clear: "Reactive patterns are like little self sustaining engines. The only question is, who is going to lead your life: you, or your reactive patterns?" (Feldmar, personal communication, May 1981).

Feldmar was psychoanalytically trained and his genius resides in his ability to generate metaphors that make intrapsychic realities intelligible to the lay person, the quote above being an example. The patient, on hearing that metaphor, is shown how to distinguish her personal identity or self from introjections. The phrase, "little, *self sustaining* engines" reveals that they run without one's conscious volition, and, therefore, are not "owned" by the self. When a certain stimulus occurs, the same response runs its course every time. For example, when someone disagrees with Jack's opinion, he becomes defensive, as if they were attacking him personally. One could say that Jack has become identified with his opinions or meanings. A therapist might reframe Jack's defensiveness as a "reactive pattern" in order to begin the process of dis-identification. If the intervention is successful, Jack might say, "I no longer *am* my opinions; now, I *have* opinions." The process moves from investing in, or committing to, a meaning, to withdrawing or divesting from that meaning. Instead of being a subject of one's opinions, they become objects of consciousness that one can notice and critique. This is the outcome of a therapeutic intervention or transformative learning experience. I've started at the back end of the process, the working through or deconstruction of one's identifications. Now I would like to turn my attention to the beginning: when identification was formed.

Precisely what occurs when the self *invests* in a meaning? Deikman (1966) offers some clues. Participants in his study were to look at a blue vase for half an hour over ten trials. He instructed them to attend to (perceive) the blue vase without lapsing into thinking (cognition). Subject A reported the following:

> One of the points that I remember most vividly is when I really began to feel, you know, almost as though the blue and I were perhaps

merging, or that vase and I were. I almost get scared to the point where I found myself bringing myself back in some way from it . . . It was though everything was sort of merging and I was somehow *losing my sense of consciousness* almost. At one point it felt . . . as though the vase were *in my head* rather than out there: I know it was out there but it seemed as though it were *almost a part of me*. (p. 83, my italics)

I want to suggest that this experiment artificially produced the same qualitative experience as that of childhood. That is, it encouraged pre-reflective *engagement* in contrast with the critical or reflective *distance* that adults typically employ. With the former, we fuse with our surroundings, whether those surroundings include one's mother or a blue vase. It is only in reflection, and then only retroactively, that we are able to separate subject from object, our person from the blue vase. Returning to the quotation above, we see that the subject was losing her defining boundary, and merging with that to which she was attending. That is, she was *investing* herself in the vase. In psychoanalytic language, she was introjecting the blue vase—"it seemed as though it were almost a part of me". With this merging, she felt as if she was losing her sense of consciousness, the substrate of her identity. No wonder she attempted to "bring herself back from it". Not only did she wish to reaffirm her separate identity, but also she wanted to consolidate it on a familiar existential plane. Her process exemplifies, in a simplified form, the emotional vicissitudes undergone in transformational learning.

A child, in contrast to the adult subject above, experiences less self-conscious identity. They may talk *to* themselves, but seldom *about* themselves. The latter requires a developed self-concept. Instead of being a clearly demarcated self, the child tends to *merge* with their circumstances. It is via this process that a pre-reflective self is being built, layer upon layer. At a later stage of development, this pre-reflective self resists the intentions of the conscious, reflective mind. It resists because to co-operate would bring about its own dismantling. Yet, what is one to do with the reflexive realisation that one has merged with a neurotic mother? What if, on the basis of that foundational experience, one established the premise that anxious attachment was the only one possible? One could predict a complete life style evolving from that basic premise. Metaphorically, the child would assume a concave shape to merge with mother's convex one. That concave impression would persist after mother had left the scene. And it would provide a snug fit for the next convex person that entered this person's life. How does one transcend that pre-reflexive conditioning?

Spurs to change: internal and external

A person who anxiously attached to a neurotic mother might later resolve that their next relationship would enact healthy attachment. After repeated failures, she is forced to acknowledge her inability to do so. Such an experience would reveal that her conscious mind was not the only player in the game. Some *other* intentionality exercised more power. That other intentionality emanated from her pre-reflective self. As a result, the person is conflicted: one part strives for a healthy attachment; another is attracted to the "wrong" person. This internal conflict is disturbing, and, therefore, can be utilised as the motive for transformational learning. When working with clients who are divided in this way, I ask them to look for a "good reason" for being so constrained. I do this because my client typically identifies with their conscious goals and, therefore, is not aware of the subjectivity that generates the resistance to change. When I attribute a "good reason" to this resistance, I am inviting them to reinhabit the existential plane where those premises were originally laid down—in the pre-reflective self. Fink (1995), a Lacanian therapist, refers to this process as "subjectivization, a process of making 'one's own' what was formerly alien" (p. xii). This is the means to retrieve missing agency. I have a friend who values the experience of emotional crisis. "Why?" I wondered. He replied, "Because these emotions give me conscious access to the motives that are generating my behaviour. When I'm well defended I am being controlled by them without any awareness of being so." He is retrieving the subjectivity that designed his reactive patterns. Or, stated differently, he is re-subjectivising his reactive patterns. This retrieval is not the only mobilising condition for transformational learning. Crisis and trauma destabilise the self and the imperative to regain one's balance is a profound motivator. Both can be understood as environmental challenges to the person's way of being in the world. The crisis event reveals that one's taken for granted protocols will not address the crisis adequately (Mezirow,

1991). The cocoon of mediating assumptions that were supposed to vouchsafe one's existence has been breached. Janoff-Bulman (1992), the trauma theorist, quotes Epstein (1983) as follows: "A personal theory of reality does not exist in conscious awareness, but is a preconscious conceptual system that automatically structures a person's experiences" (p. 5).

The traumatic breach in the preconscious conceptual system allows the event to impinge directly on the self. In Lacanian terms, the Real has pierced the barrier of symbolic representation (Žižek, 2000). The symbolic system, which acted as a stand-in for reality, has been torn and one finds one's self in the throes of an existential crisis. Previous to the trauma, one lived primarily within an internal world of reified representations rather than with the things themselves, or, stated less dramatically, one's experience was mediated rather than immediate. Trauma is similar to, but more distressing than, subject A's experience. In both cases, there is a sense of losing one's familiar self.

Transformation: a liminal phenomenon

The relative certainties of one's previous conceptual system dissolve as one moves into a liminal zone. The *Oxford English Dictionary* (2007) defines liminality as "being on the 'threshold' of or between two different existential planes". The subject is situated between alternate realities: the known but inadequate, and the unknown and possibly adequate. "Which one will I commit to?" As stated earlier, rites of passage are designed to contain or structure difficult experiences. A therapeutic alliance also provides the structure to safely transition from one plane to another.

Feldmar (personal communication, April 1988) developed the following metaphor for conveying this existential challenge. "When the sperm fertilizes the egg and together become a zygote, we see the first kind of growth—the cells divide and multiply, *each cell exactly like all the others*". The illuminating aspect of this metaphor is the zygote's "free floating" status. Only after the zygote *implants* do the cells begin to develop uniquely. "You could imagine", Feldmar continued, "that as the zygote floats down toward the uterine wall, it would oscillate between two existential planes: 'I'm going to be trapped' versus 'I'm just putting down roots'." I suggest that something like this happens with transformative learning: one realises that one is being offered an alternate way of being in the world. That offer does not come with a guarantee that it will be superior to one's former way—only further experience can reveal that. Examples drawn from my therapeutic practice include the following: a woman, whose husband left her and remarried, is afraid to sell the family house in case her ex-husband changes his mind and wants to reconcile. She realises the absurdity of her wish and knows that she must push off into a new life or stagnate. A stepson refuses to bond with his mother's new mate because to do so would betray his loyalty to his biological father. A part of his self remains on hold, refusing to adapt to his new circumstances. Trouble and conflict ensue. An immigrant fantasises her eventual return to the "old country" and so feels little need to commit to her new one. However, her children are merging with their new circumstances. Trouble and conflict ensue. In order for her to maintain her connection to her children, she must open to their new circumstance. In each of these examples the person is entering the "in between"—the liminal zone between two ways of being. Ortega y Gasset (1985) eloquently describes the defensive manoeuvres that one employs to avoid the liminal experience.

> Take stock of those around you and you will . . . hear them talk in precise terms about themselves and their surroundings, which would seem to point to them having ideas on the matter. But start to analyze those ideas and you will find that they hardly reflect in any way the reality in which they appear to refer, and if you go deeper you will discover that there is not even an attempt to adjust the ideas to this reality. [T]hrough these notions the individual is trying to cut off any personal vision of reality, of his own very life. For life is at the start a chaos in which one is lost. The individual suspects this, but he is frightened at finding himself face to face with this terrible reality, and tries to cover it over with a curtain of fantasy, where everything is clear. It does not worry him that his 'ideas' are true, he uses them as trenches for the defense of his existence, as scarecrows to frighten away reality. (p. 75, my italics)

This powerful description depicts a person who is desperately clinging to their reflective mind's conceptions and blocking any emergent news of their circumstances.

From individual to collective change

The concept of liminality has much to offer—understandings that suggest the possible connections between individual and collective transformation. For example, Turner (1969) stated that if liminality is regarded as a time and place of withdrawal from normal modes of social action, it can be seen as potentially a "period of scrutiny for the central values and axioms of the culture in which it occurs—one where normal limits to thought, self-understanding, and behaviour are undone" (p. 156).

Here, one can see that identity is a psycho*social* phenomenon. During a liminal experience, the hold of social convention is revealed as arbitrary and, therefore, potentially revisable. Whereas Turner (1969) places the emphasis on the individual's experience, Horvath, Thomassen, and Wydra (2009) highlight the cultural consequences. They use the concept of liminality to discuss cultures in transition that are characterised by a dislocation of established structures, institutions in crisis, and uncertainty regarding the continuity of tradition and future outcomes. During a crisis, traditional ways of making sense are bypassed (Giddens, 1991). The recent global economic meltdown was paradigmatic in that respect. While listening to the pundits, I sensed that they were attempting to explain the never-before-seen with an old, yet reassuringly familiar vocabulary. At times, their explanations seemed more like invocations—an invocation to summon forth the old reality by chanting its many names. I suggest that, in both individual and collective crises, there is first a dimly perceived threat to one's way of being, followed by a response that invokes and reinforce old meanings as a means of foreclosing that threat. Only later, as one perceives that the crisis is growing in spite of one's invocations, does one realise that what is called for is a creative, existential response. Turner (1969), as cited by Thomassen (2009), was aware that liminality involved "the sudden foregrounding of agency, and the sometimes dramatic tying together of thought and experience" (p. 14). During crisis, one moves from being a "subject" to being an "agent". One realises that "following the rules" will not do it; one must respond with action or behaviour that addresses the crisis. Only later will one be able to systematically work out the new meanings that were implicit in that existential move.

The role of emotions in transformative learning

Crisis and trauma make enormous existential demands and, therefore, engage core emotions. As Žižek (2009) points out, this does not automatically lead to a transformative learning experience:

> While crises do shake people out of their complacency, forcing them to question the fundamentals of their lives, the most spontaneous first reaction is panic which leads to the return to 'the basics': the basic premises of the ruling ideology, far from put into doubt, are even more violently reasserted. (p. 18)

Why would this be so? Kegan (1982) claims that anxiety and depression are the affective concomitants of transformation. That is, a person retreats into a familiar shell of their former premises because they sense the anxiety attendant on moving forward. Kegan (1982) redescribes an infant's separation anxiety in a manner that reveals its prototypical nature—the original transformative experience. Because the infant is fused with mother, she experiences her mother as an aspect of self. When mother leaves the room, the infant is no longer the same self. It is the loss of self, rather than the loss of mother, that is causing distress. The child has become a stranger to her self—one who is "homesick" for her old self/world. I see the same dynamic at work in culture shock. The person has not only lost "the old country" but also their old self. Anxiety is the recognition that this is about to happen, while depression is the recognition that it has happened. The familiar cocoon of meaning no longer provides the shelter that it once did.

Therapeutic assisted reintegration

In order to overcome the inherently conservative impulse "to get back to my old self", the therapeutic relationship is utilised as a "holding" environment. For the therapeutic hour, I attempt to join, rather than challenge, the client's reality. I want to understand their dilemma from the inside. I have no concern that by doing so the client will feel that their fundamental premises are validated. An event has occurred that reveals their inadequacy. Being held in relationship, my clients have less need to cling to old meanings. Instead, they can afford to turn their attention inward and scrutinise their meaning-making premises. Discovering the limits to these premises, the client can make the existential choice to adopt new, more encompassing ones. That is, they can exercise agency through making the choice to live their life rather than defaulting to the reactive patterns of their little self-sustaining engines.

Educational implications

These same processes get played out (often covertly) in educational settings. Perry (1970) developed a model of the epistemological stages that college students experience during their undergraduate years. The developmental poles ranged from the most dualistic and abso-lutist to the most relativist and contingent. Somewhere along this developmental path, the student comes to realise that there is no "right answer" because all knowledge is relativist and contextual. "It depends" prefaces an answer that acknowledges contingency. The way forward, therefore, is not launched from a platform of irrefutable knowledge. Rather, it is based on making a commitment. Loevinger (1976) summarises this stage as follows: "The student makes a commitment . . . accepting its origin in his own experience or choice, and deciding *how much he will seek continuity with his past values and how much he will break away from them*" (p. 130, my italics).

In the emphasised phrase, I see an existential choice: "Do I make the leap of faith or stay with what has served me up to this point?" Perry (1970) gives a nuanced articulation of the emotions that accom-pany this journey. "At every step, the movement required the students to "face up" to limits, uncertainties, and the dissolution of established beliefs, while simultaneously it demanded new decisions and the undertaking of new forms of responsibility" (p. 52).

This is the same liminal zone that was discussed earlier. Perry (1970) recognises that there are countervailing forces that work against further development. He identifies the same conservative impulse to which Žižek (2009) pointed. Among these is the desire to maintain community with one's previous friends and family. The most important of these countervailing forces is the

wish to maintain a self one has felt oneself to be. Pervading all . . . motives of conservation lay the apprehension that one change might lead to another in a rapidity which might result in catastrophic disorganization. (p. 52)

That perilous journey will be undertaken more frequently if there are mentors and teachers who understand and appreciate the affective component of transformation. Anxiety and depression (as well as excitement and courage) are legitimate aspects of the journey and should be seen as that rather than as signs of pathology.

The times in which we live seem to require a fundamental change in the way that we think of education. It seems archaic to think that knowledge and goodness are accumulated bit by bit through obedience and hard work, as the banking and transmission models of education assume (Freire, 1993). On the contrary, individuals who are in a liminal process are often not able to act rationally "because the structure on which 'objective' rationality was based has disappeared" (Szakolczai, 2009, p. 154). The banking and transmission models rested on the assumption that that structure was immutable. Transformational learning theory recognised that that was not always the case. There are, indeed, times when one must reflect on, and even replace, one's basic premises in order to attune with one's emergent environment. Moreover, by mapping the processes involved, TL provides the necessary, perhaps temporary, reference points for navigating this fluid zone. Both the educator and student would be empowered by the knowledge of those reference points. In traditional cultures, rites of passage provide a framework for negotiating difficult transitions. These rites communicate: "Others have been here before you and others will follow". Moreover, there is a communal aspect to those rites that reassure the transforming individual that their community continues to support them and will recognise and affirm their new way of being. With these supports, the individual is more likely to experience the confidence to exercise their agency and see the process all the way through. Finally, TL showed up at a historical moment when the capacity to make structural change has become an urgent requirement. The accelerating pace of social change seems to require the ability to self transcend more than once in a lifetime. Perhaps the role for today's educator is to model that process and midwife it in her students. This is line with the aphorism that we teach what we are. This places more emphasis on the educator's style and behaviour over and above the transmission of content. Behaviour expresses fundamental premises. Over time, one's behaviour also expresses one's willingness to reflect on and transcend those premises. Actions speak louder than words. I am aware that the majority of this chapter articulates the processes leading up to and occurring within transformational learning. It offers virtually no description of what comes out on the other end. This may leave the reader feeling as if they are experiencing a meaning vacuum. Yet, I cannot help but feel that it is a necessary vacuum. What is the shape of the emerging self? It depends on the person's context and the courage that they bring to it. It is a creative moment that cannot be predicted beforehand.

References

Bollas, C. (1987). *The Shadow of the Object: Psychoanalysis of the Unthought Known*. New York: Columbia University Press.

Coetzee, J. M. (2003). *Elizabeth Costello*. New York: Viking Press.

Deikman, A. J. (1966). Implications of experimentally induced contemplative meditation. *Journal of Nervous and Mental Diseases, 142*(2): 101–116.

Epstein, S. (1983). The unconscious, the preconscious and the self-concept. In: J. Suls & A. Greenwald (Eds.), *Psychological Perspectives on the Self* (pp. 219–247). Hillsdale, NJ: Lawrence Erlbaum.

Fairbairn, W. R. D. (1952). *Psychoanalytic Studies of the Personality*. London: Tavistock.

Feldmar, A. (1981). Personal communication.

Feldmar, A. (1988). Personal communication.

Fink, B. (1995). *The Lacanian Subject: Between Language and Jouissance*. Princeton, NJ: Princeton University Press.

Freire, P. (1993). *Pedagogy of the Oppressed*, M. Bergman Ramos (Trans.). New York: Continuum.

Freud, S. (1905d). *Three Essays on the Theory of Sexuality. S.E., 7*: 125–145. London: Hogarth.

Giddens, A. (1991). *Modernity and Self-identity: Self and Society in the Late Modern Age*. Cambridge: Polity Press.

Guntrip, H. (1968). *Schizoid Phenomena, Object Relations and the Self*. New York: International Universities Press.

Guntrip, H. (1971). *Psychoanalytic Theory, Therapy and the Self*. New York: Basic Books.

Horvath, A., Thomassen, B., & Wydra, H. (2009). Introduction: liminality and cultures of change. *International Political Anthropology*, 2(1): 3–4.

Janoff-Bulman, R. (1992). *Shattered Assumptions*. New York: Free Press.

Kegan, R. (1982). *The Evolving Self: Problem and Process in Human Development*. Cambridge, MA: Harvard University Press.

Kegan, R., & Lahey, L. L. (2009). *Immunity to Change*. Boston, MA: Harvard Business Press.

Lacan, J. (1966). *Écrits: A Selection*, A. Sheridan (Trans.). New York: Norton.

Loevinger, J. (1976). *Ego Development*. San Francisco, CA: Jossey-Bass.

Loy, D. (1988). *Nonduality: A Study in Comparative Philosophy*. New York: Humanities Books.

Mezirow, J. (1991). *Transformative Dimensions of Adult Learning*. San Francisco, CA: Jossey-Bass.

Ortega y Gasset, J. (1985). *The Revolt of the Masses*. Notre Dame, IN: University of Notre Dame Press.

Oxford English Dictionary (2007). 2nd edn, J. A. Simpson & E .S. C. Weiner (Eds.). Oxford: Clarendon Press, 1989. OED Online Oxford University Press. Accessed 23 June 2011.

Perry, W. G. (1970). *Forms of Intellectual and Ethical Development in the College Years*. New York: Holt, Rinehart and Winston.

Sass, L. A. (1992). *Madness and Modernism: Insanity in the Light of Modern Art, Literature, and Thought*. New York: Basic Books.

Szakolczai, A. (2009). Liminality and experience: structuring transitory situations and transformative events. *International Political Anthropology*, 2(1): 141–172.

Thomassen, B. (2009). The uses and meanings of liminality. *International Political Anthropology*, 2(1): 5–27.

Turner, V. W. (1969). *The Ritual Process: Structure and Anti-structure*. Chicago, IL: Aldine.

Winnicott, D. W. (1965). *The Maturational Processes and the Facilitating Environment*. New York: International Universities Press.

Žižek, S. (2000). *The Fragile Absolute*. London: Verso.

Žižek, S. (2009). *First As Tragedy Then As Farce*. London: Verso.

CHAPTER FIFTEEN

The dynamics of student identity: the threats from neo-liberal models and the benefits of a relational pedagogy

Tony Brown and Mark Murphy

Introduction: the consequences of neo-liberalism and how integration of psychoanalytic theory and Honneth's critical philosophy provides a healthier alternative

The decision to make the UK student population financially responsible for their own university education has major implications for the future of higher education (HE) provision. Chief among these will undoubtedly be a much stronger emphasis on the student experience, though this emphasis will not be confined to teaching and learning. Given the increasing influence of consumerism, the distinct possibility exists that opening HE to commercial markets will raise the importance of the non-academic aspects of university experience above that of the academic, thus changing forever the way we see and define student identity and students' experiences of higher education.

If the American university experience is a guide to possible UK behaviour, then the shift to student as consumer will bring increased attention to the social and leisure aspects of the student experience (no bad thing in an absolute sense) together with a shift in emphasis away from academic standards, intellectual achievement, and student learning. Students who have bought a degree are less likely to sign up to tackle difficult learning and more likely to expect higher costs to be reflected in higher grades. Grade inflation (clearly the bottom line in *value for money* in a "student as consumer" world) is an inevitable outcome of a consumerist model since the value of the degree will increasingly be determined by grade comparisons between students, and between the different degree programmes that students have bought. Less attractive by far will be the option to struggle with difficult conceptual knowledge, with its attendant risk of lower grades on the lower slopes of understanding. Less attractive, too, when student unemployment is increasing, will be the idea that education can be intellectually and culturally transformative, and that it is for the public good. It is an appropriate time to explore the impact of consumerism and the dangerous shift in what "student experience" could come to mean: a shift that inevitably reframes accountability in terms of economic exchange.

In this chapter, we explain the dangers of the consumerist model and then go on to develop alternative possibilities for describing student identity by arguing for a new pedagogy for HE, a pedagogy based on relational dynamics and derived from a synthesis of critical theory and psychoanalysis. By emphasising the intersubjective nature of learning and teaching and the role of emotions in this regard, we argue that a relationally focused approach takes seriously questions of trust, recognition, and respect which lie at the heart of the students' experience of higher education, while also making space for doubt, confusion, and relational anxiety—agendas that are highly appropriate for students in higher education. We argue against the unreliable and sometimes false information that has been used to present the marketisation of UK higher education as an opportunity for raising academic standards, and we develop an argument for promoting an alternative pedagogy of higher education based on psychoanalytic and critical theory. We explore their intersections and the implications for theories of learning in the HE setting.

Both psychoanalytic and critical theory have a long history of application to education and pedagogy, while also exerting a strong intellectual pull toward one another. This productive, if sometimes fraught, historical association has recently coalesced around the work of Axel Honneth (1995) and his critical theory of recognition. We explore the potential of utilising his theoretical apparatus in the context of developing an alternative relational pedagogy, one that takes seriously the personal needs and desires of students, while situating these needs at the centre of the struggle for a more democratic higher education.

Marketisation of higher education: a disaster unfolds

Although successive governments have argued that widening participation has been driven by a desire to increase equality of opportunity, openness, and transparency, much of the political engagement with universities has been anti-democratic, accompanied by an erosion of civic values. One strategy allied to this erosion has been the steady imposition of the language of commerce and consumerism, suggesting that students no longer study: they invest in courses, and have become customers who buy their education rather than engage in intellectual development through the acquisition of difficult and dangerous knowledge.

Although the pretence of this business model is to expedite democratic openness and increase choice, the reality is the opposite. The effects of marketisation on universities tend to be a heightening of institutional competition and a concomitant narrowing of focus, with courses targeted in order to satisfy students' (predicted) desire for courses geared to employment. As a result, student choice, diversity, and the liberal concept of education as pursuit of knowledge for personal development tend to be sidelined in favour of education for training, with increasingly prescriptive controls of university course provision by the forced competition for funding.

In the highly competitive commercial sector, product standardisation means cheaper production costs. The constant invention of new (short-lived and disposable) products and packaging is intended to create and maintain consumer excitement and demand. Reduction from a broad to a narrow range of product and the shift from local to regional, national, and global production sites are all key to commercialisation and exploitation. This same process applied to universities could lead to the effect of reducing a student's range of options, not increasing them. It can also increase the cost, where students are expected to pay for a public service which is being re-presented as a private commodity, and where universities are forced to spend large sums on marketising (and marketing) their courses and demonstrating that their study programmes meet the arbitrary (and frequently changing) criteria invented by government policy.

The business model that neoliberal[1] policies seek to impose on education and elsewhere attacks local means of production and local ownership. It seeks to sidestep discussions of ethics in a drive to transfer power and decision-making about production and location away from local sites of production to the strongest national and international business enterprises. Large global industries seek to destroy local means of production for local consumers (e.g., coffee, bananas, flowers, car production . . .) and instead deliberately switch production methods and products so as to damage not only competitors and consumer choice, but also product diversity and niche product design. They promote a narrow range of brands conducive to their own survival and profitability. Having globalised, they no longer have intimate contact with local consumers. Advertising and marketing become increasingly important because consumer and producer occupy different spaces.

Applied to universities, this model will push institutions away from continuing with a local specialist role, such as providing courses for the unemployed in areas of urban or rural deprivation. Instead, clusters of universities will need to combine and then later turn against each other within their cluster to increase local market share, before competing with other clusters and attacking them. This process narrows choice and threatens the knowledge economy in local areas where currently local knowledge of employers and universities presents them with opportunities to collaborate on improving local employment conditions.

All this competitive activity in a quasi market demands an increasing proportion of resource, which has to be diverted from the original provision: student education. Some institutions will disappear en route, leaving areas of the country without local provision and local knowledge of student need. Regional and national institutions, at increased distances from local students, will need to produce more homogenised courses that reject idiosyncratic and specialist programmes in favour of blandness that can appeal to the mass recruitment of faceless students. The significant increase in trans-national education provision from UK HEIs further reinforces this point. This is not a model for ensuring quality, or for driving down costs, despite neo-liberal arguments to the contrary and, most especially, when used in relation to quality in education. The damage will take decades to be repaired, or, indeed, might be irreparable in the medium term.

This attempt to transfer a set of values from one sector to another could never expect to avoid resistance, and there is an increasing challenge to the business model of the university as a centrally controlled extension of market activity. Observers are increasingly concerned about the erosion of the traditional values of university study, which include students' engagement with a subject discipline. Increasingly, researchers challenge the cost analysis of neo-liberal claims, with, for example, van Vught (2007, p. 13) arguing that the application of market forces to universities "has resulted in a huge increase in the costs of higher education with serious consequences for students and for universities".

There are real dangers identified by Hotson (2011) who shows that the student experience for many American students at elite US universities has now become defined not so much by learning, but increasingly by customer attitudes to "accommodation, a rich programme of social events, and state of the art athletic facilities". Hotson quotes Jonathan Cole, writing in *The Huffington Post* in 2010 as former Provost and Dean of Faculties at Columbia. Cole writes about the huge shift in university budgets away from providing education into social and leisure services, forced on universities by student choice in a "customer is always right' environment:

> Money is well spent on psychological counselling, but the number of offices that focus on student activities, athletics, and athletic facilities, summer job placement and out-sourced dining services . . . dormitory rooms and suites that only the Four Seasons can match, leads to an expansion of administrators and increased cost of administration. (Cole, quoted in Hotson, 2011, p. 21)

Hotson points out that consumerist forces in HE will not focus on the quality of educational provision, the quality of teaching, or academic success. It will not focus on the significance of questions of accountability and democracy. These areas risk being left behind in a consumerist drive for better social, leisure, and athletic experiences. This situation has already occurred for many American students. In order to attract students, universities have to redirect an increasing percentage of the student fee away from educational provision and on to social and leisure facilities.

The economic arguments as they are applied to Higher Education in the Browne Report (2010) in the UK are not sound. They appear to be based on narrow and selective evidence that found what ministers wanted rather than what pertained.

> The Browne Report was a shoddy, ill-argued and under-researched document which attracted a firestorm of criticism . . . One reason the Commons' vote on 9 December 2010 to remove public funding from teaching and to triple undergraduate fees was a scandal is that such a measure hadn't been in the election manifesto of any party – indeed, the Liberal Democrats had made a commitment to abolish fees. (Collini, 2011, p. 10)

There is clear evidence that higher education quality will decline and costs will soar as a consequence of the introduction of market forces to education. Much of the available evidence was ignored or massaged to provide the answers required by government. Research evidence was selectively used for the purposes of political expediency.

Even now, in mid 2011, with the proposals in their infancy, coalition ministers have been "taken by surprise" by the large number of institutions which have opted for the maximum allowable £9,000 fee for students. The knock-on effect on the student loan budget will create a black hole sucking in as much student debt financing as the treasury can make available at a time when public sector jobs are disappearing in their thousands and inflation is beginning to head beyond 5%. One option—actively being considered—is to limit student numbers so as to contain the future debt burden. Already this "economic" model for higher education has been compromised by spiralling costs, and student access to education eroded by cost analysis based on a market model that claimed it would support an expansion of student numbers.

There are few reliable and robust global comparisons of universities and fewer still that do not focus on (nebulous conceptions of) research excellence. Despite the lack of comparative data about teaching quality and student learning, it is worth looking at the information on excellence provided by tables such as the *THE World University Rankings*[2] to explore the argument that private universities out-perform public sector institutions. That argument appears to be the one appropriated by UK government ministers. The top twenty universities in the annual *THE* tables regularly include thirteen American and four British. Of these thirteen US institutions, twelve are privately funded and charge high student fees.

Unsurprisingly, we find that UK universities and their staff are criticised for not performing as well as these top private American institutions. To be totally simplistic, which is where many government arguments about education start and finish, the "top twenty" data table has been used to argue that private institutions out-perform publicly funded ones.

Suppose we look at per capita results. Britain's population is around sixty-two million compared with a USA population of around 310 million. The number of universities in the top twenty per capita then reads approximately as: the UK, one per fifteen million of population, the USA, one per twenty-four million. Britain scores handsomely by that comparison.

What about student ambition? If you want to study at an internationally renowned top twenty university, are your chances better in the UK or the USA? The 2009–2010 HESA data show the total student population to be 2,490,000 at UK universities.[3] The four UK universities in the *THE* rankings averaged just under 20,000 students each. So, about 80,000 students out of a total population of around 2.5 million can achieve this ambition. That's one in thirty. In the USA[4] there is only a one in seventy-seven chance of being in a top institution, with thirteen universities in that particular international top twenty and a total university enrolment of twenty million.[5]

Of course, in terms of value for money, the UK must be terrible, otherwise why push for marketisation of higher education? The USA's GDP for 2010 was estimated by the IMF[6] as $14,657 trillion, while the estimate for the UK was $2,247 trillion. The US spends around 3.1 per cent of its GDP on tertiary education, while in the UK the figure is about 1.3 per cent. This means the total cost of higher education in the USA is around $455 trillion, while for the UK it is about $29 trillion. That money buys (among other things) thirteen places in the top twenty for the USA and four for the UK, or $35 trillion per institution compared with the UK figure of $7.25 trillion. So, the USA has to spend *five times* as much to achieve the institutional recognition that the UK enjoys. Far from being terrible value for money, the UK does very well on this measure of international recognition. So, why all this pressure from the UK coalition government to marketise the British university sector? If it is not student ambition, or financial cost, it must be ideological: "whatever the cost, we *must* privatise". It is this ideological driver that has led to a disaster in the making.

One financial cost not mentioned so far is that of attending the top US Ivy League institutions. Current costs for a student attending Harvard are running at around $50,000 per annum. Of course, the riposte is that hardly anyone pays that amount. If Harvard wants you they will get you to attend—even if you do not pay. While this could conceivably be an option for the best endowed Oxford and Cambridge colleges, it is a joke in very poor taste to suggest that a cash starved ex-polytechnic or a Russell Group university offering internationally renowned research and teaching while also struggling with millions of pounds of debt following removal of the teaching grant is going to pay its students to attend. This is not an option. The race to attach the highest price to a university degree in the UK has started and universities have only stopped at £9,000 because they have been prevented from going higher. No university can afford to be seen as a low fee (implying a low quality) institution.

For the poorest students in the UK the consequence of this neoliberal ideology will be exclusion by price. Only in October 1920 were women deemed eligible for admission as full members of Oxford University and given the right to take degrees. In the USA in the 1950s and 1960s, black student admission to university was strongly resisted and often prevented through threats and violence. Fortunately, both these forms of discrimination are now illegal, even if the effects have not been eradicated entirely. Discrimination by cost is something that the very rich have always practised, but, up to now, they have not been able to practise this with the UK higher education system as a whole; sadly, they now have that opportunity. For a long time, mature and part-time students and those with caring responsibilities—many of whom are women—have faced what many regard as a form of gendered exclusion. The current proposals extend this discrimination by cost to all those on low incomes. In his detailed analysis of the claims that private sector competition improves academic standards, Hotson (2011) finds no supporting evidence, but he does find that

There is clear evidence that market competition drives up prices, since academic excellence apparently costs much more in the US than in the UK ... Wherever a small and strictly limited supply of a highly desirable commodity – such as places at Harvard – is introduced into a genuinely open market, the wealthiest cohort in society will drive its price up to levels only they can afford. (Hotson, 2011, p. 20)

Hotson shows that tuition fees for American students at top universities have "been rising at double, triple and even quadruple the rate of cost-of-living inflation, first at the most exclusive universities, and then throughout the private sector" (ibid.), leading to a situation where more than a hundred private institutions are now charging "at least $50,000 annually for fees, room and board" (ibid.). The UK faces a situation where exclusion through cost could drive down participation rates among the poorest students and divert increasing proportions of university budgets away from teaching and learning.

Relational pedagogy: an opportunity for reconceptualising student identity

Disciplinary engagement in higher education necessitates study of the impact of the discipline on society in ways that have the potential to turn "the abstract concept of social citizenship into a practical reality" (Bauman, 2007, p. 9). This is a direct challenge to managerialist approaches that have emerged as a result of neo-liberal policies seeking to position higher education primarily as preparation for employment rather than the pursuit of knowledge for the benefit of personal and social development (Giroux, 2009, p. 253).

This erosion of higher education as a space for intellectual development of critical faculties is in evidence, for example, in professional education programmes. In a psychoanalytically informed paper on Initial (pre-service) Teacher Education, Hanley (2007) draws attention to the consequences of the UK government's education policy for England in terms of contradictory fantasies. According to Hanley, students are recruited using a "fantasy of aspiration". Their training, however, is based on conformist and highly regulatory approaches developed out of a "fantasy of efficiency" (Hanley, 2007, p. 254). The fantasy of efficiency is based on the hope that instructing teacher behaviour will result in efficient school student learning:

The teacher demonstrates, using a physical model such as bricks and a number line. The teacher says, then the children repeat, 'three and one make four'. The teacher points at each part – the children watch and listen. (DfEE, 1999, p. 80)

The construction of the subject (student teachers) takes place against a background of tensions between these two contrasting desires. One desire expressed by parents, school students, and the media is for education as *personal care*, "something individual and special" (ibid., p. 254), while the desire for a conforming, controllable other squeezes out opportunities to think critically about one's development or to prepare professionally for a role that calls for caring attitudes and approaches, and rich personal relationships. The tensions created by these opposing fantasies have seen governments try to incorporate the charismatic and personal within its codified statements of teaching, a process that risks increasingly rigid prescriptions by codifying subtle and spontaneous human interaction. This not only further endangers the status of teaching as a caring profession, but also leaves students and teachers struggling to integrate the competing fantasies within a coherent and stable professional identity.

Many academics and students—not only those in Education Departments—reject the current move towards a market model as an anti-democratic process that leads to narrowing of choice, erosion of quality, and loss of local autonomy for institutions, academics, and students. Ironically, it is the "public information" argument—the provision of data that should usefully inform students' and parents' choices of institution and programme—that is being used as a smokescreen for ideological subversion of the HE system. An approach to higher education is needed that recognises that learning comes from interrelational experiences which address academic, intellectual, and social agendas, where values are explicitly articulated as part of the student experience. These can be part of a programme aligned with business interests and employability, but the constant risk is that neoliberal agendas will marginalise desires for critical thinking, equality, justice, and social change, leaving only a market morality to guide thinking and behaviour.

The present moment, when neo-liberal values and behaviours are being rejected ever more vociferously, offers an important opportunity for educators to debate the kind of education that matters to a participatory democracy. Public higher education is important because of the contribution it makes to public life as well as its contribution to economic prosperity. Asserting the democratic function of higher education requires a commitment from educators to engage with the re-establishment of higher education policies, values and social practices that promote commitment to a more equal and just society. The aim of education in general, and higher education in particular, should be to demonstrate success and to "teach young people how to participate in and shape public life and exercise critical judgment, and provide the pedagogical conditions that enable them to" (Giroux, 2009, p. 250).

The role of learning in higher education includes how to cultivate the civic values that university staff and students can exercise in order for universities to play a full role in local interpretations of citizenship as well as providing skilled and employable graduates. From this perspective, learning in higher education requires new paradigms for reconceptualising models of learning. This reconceptualisation is also required because learning is not the predominantly intellectual, cognitive process implied by individualistic cognitive psychologies. Rather, it is one where there is "ever-present affectivity" (Tahta, 1995). Learning is embedded in the emotional life of learners, a relational experience that gives rise to identifications with peers, tutors, and the subject discipline (Hodkinson, 2005). While the identifications are not always wholly positive, unified, coherent, or beneficial, learning is always the result of a relational activity from which the subject is continually being recreated through intersubjective processes that shape identification through a process of self–other recognition. Higher education pedagogy should, therefore, allow for "exploration, expression and acceptance of emotions and feelings of self and others in ways that contribute to learning" (Beard, Clegg, & Smith, 2007, p. 240).

Attempting to understand the learning process from this perspective is inevitably fraught with challenges, not least the potential to slide into therapeutic compensatory forms of education stripped of intellectual and personal challenge (Ecclestone & Hayes, 2008; Furedi, 2003). There is also the danger that the student learning experience can be abstracted out of its political and economic contexts, something that consumerism, for all its faults, cannot be accused of. Taken together, psychoanalytic and critical theory can alleviate some of these concerns, offering an innovative approach that engages with the affective domain in the context of values such as equality, justice, and social responsibility. Combined, they offer the possibility of a psychoanalytically informed pedagogy that transcends the limitations of current dominant models of learning, while also placing educational experiences within a more appropriate *relational* context. This relational context is explored in more detail below, beginning with an overview of psychoanalytic principles and their relevance to learning in higher education.

Psychoanalysis and learning in higher education

Although psychoanalytic theory originated as primarily a product of European thinking, its take-up in the UK and mainland European education systems has been noticeably different. For example, as noted in Chapter One, Section 13 of the German Society for Education includes psychoanalysis and education, unlike the British Education Research Association, which offers no explicit space for groups to meet to explore psychoanalytic theory and research. The British educational research community's lack of involvement with psychoanalytic pedagogy contrasts with the German view expressed on the DGfE website that sees "psychoanalytic pedagogy ultimately as an indispensable aspect of a truly 'general education'".[7]

Psychoanalytic approaches to education fell out of favour in the UK around the middle of the twentieth century, at a time when individualistic psychologies and the cult of the individual were becoming significant features of the UK educational landscape and were beginning to enter educational theory. That aside, psychoanalytic theory has a long association with education. A conference on "Psychoanalysis and Pedagogy" in 1908, in Salzburg, was used by Sándor Ferenczi, a disciple of Freud, to strongly question the educational practices of the time. The work of several of Freud's early associates and followers (Pfister, Adler, Aichhorn, Stekel, Zulliger) was directed towards finding pedagogical connections between education and psychoanalysis for the benefit of individuals and society. However, Freud saw education as inherently problematic, something that is essentially disturbing and not necessarily able to contribute directly to psychological harmony: a view echoed by current writers. "Something about education makes us nervous" (Britzman, 2003, p. 1). Education, both in terms of schooling and in the wider sense that Freud employed—education as upbringing—is inherently troublesome. Freud's famous observation was that education, alongside analysis and government, was one those "impossible professions in which one can be sure beforehand of achieving unsatisfying results" (Freud 1933c, p. 248).

Psychoanalytically, much of this dissatisfaction arises from trouble that surfaces via the learning process, a process to which the unconscious is central, and which is a condensation of fragments of experience that return to us in the present when we least expect it, often with surprising results. Freud's view was that education inevitably produces discontents which can be worked on later and changed in some way, by recognising repetitions in thinking and behaviour and finding ways to avoid acting out by working through challenges. All education is, therefore, "[a] play between present and past, between presence and absence, and then, by that strange return that Sigmund Freud (1914) describes as deferred: it is registered and revised by remembering, repeating, and working through" (Britzman, 2003, p. 1).

This notion of education as deferred can apply equally to post-compulsory higher education and compulsory schooling. A student's education continuously unfolds and is reworked in the present: a turbulence of unanticipated conjunctions of affect, reworkings of old learning, and unexpected responses to current life experiences. Every education is born out of a mixture of highly memorable experiences that were never intended as education, and which exist in stark contrast to those experiences that were intended as education, many of which failed to make the impact intended. Working within a psychoanalytic pedagogy means working within this flux of past and present, where sensitivities to self and others emerge in ways that provoke the reworking of previous experience into what Freud calls an after-education. According to Britzman, this after-education "refers us back to an original flaw made from education: something within its very nature has led it to fail. But it also refers to the work yet to be accomplished, directing us toward new constructions" (Britzman, 2003, p. 4).

Alongside an emphasis on the unconscious and experience, Freud's writing about analysis can also be reworked to offer a more psychoanalytically informed view of learning. In Freud's (1914g) view, the role of the psychoanalyst is to offer an after-education that reworks the damage that upbringing inflicts. The confluence of past and present, and the psychological processes of resistance and defence, make the work of analysis and, indeed, education achievable only in a space–time which is outside that of formal schooling. The challenge faced by a psychoanalytically informed pedagogy is to make the necessary theoretical transformation from analyst to teacher, from therapy to education, and from education to after-education, so that it is possible to make a study of student learning free from notions of therapeutic intervention: "tough love", in the current jargon.

What are the qualities of higher education that create the opportunities for learners to rework previous educational experiences? Much of the reworking in which we engage as learners is a corrective to interior processes in relation to the experience of past events, to the teacher/educator and to self–other relations. The possibility of idealising peers, educators, and educational experiences can give rise to a powerful superego that reflects back the love, hate, guilt, and authority encountered in education. Our past idealisations are habit forming. They can shape our unconscious responses to present educational opportunity. After-education (meant as the reworking of our earlier interior responses to experience) becomes productive when learners respond to the new opportunities of university learning by exploring the connections they make between present and past educational experiences: where they link the affective responses to studying their chosen discipline with their self–other relating, and their previous education (in the broadest sense of "that which has gone before").

Building on theories of the unconscious, troublesome knowledge and the role of analysis/analyst are significant in the development of a psychoanalytic pedagogy. In moving towards a more relational pedagogy, however, one aspect of classic psychoanalytic theory that needs to be avoided is its tendency to think in terms of *deficiency*. In classic psychoanalysis, failures in learning and teaching are identified as either the result of the teacher's inability to make relationships or the student's destructive inner world and psychic shortcomings. Failure to achieve good grades, failure to manage the relationship between tutor and student, poor attendance, and drop-out, are conceived on a "deficit" model. The tutor lacks knowledge, skills, training, or an appropriate disposition. The student lacks motivation, language or study skills, or confidence. The work of learning and teaching then becomes focused on simply making up the deficit. This is unhelpful and potentially corrosive to learning and student identity.

In contrast, a relational psychoanalytic pedagogy seeks to avoid pathologies defined by failing individuals, preferring to read the difficulties of learning (and teaching) as properties of relationships and their cultural dimensions, such as Oedipal struggles, dependency, or the desire (that can easily emerge from neo-liberal policies) to be able to buy a qualification without being disturbed or transformed by the experience of education. Post-Freudian psychoanalytical thinkers such as Klein (1946) and Winnicott (1971) paved the way for such a relational view, arguing that the psychological work needed to achieve self-realisation by necessity occurs within a relational context (Klein, 1946; Winnicott, 1971).[8]

While much of Klein's and Winnicott's work explored mother–infant dyadic relations, there is much to be gained from adapting their ideas in the context of a relational pedagogy. The way in which infants gain self-recognition through the gaze of the other, in particular, can be applied in the context of the teacher–learner relationship in HE without infantilising or patronising the student or the teacher:

> Mothers' psychic work involves a response that unites the elements generally understood as passive – taking in – and active – giving back or putting out. The processing of other's psychic material, and its integration in intersubjective expression – recognition – constitutes the active–passive reconciliation in the work of the maternal subject. (Benjamin, 1998, p. 29)

This formative link between child and parent can be applied to the university context, a context within which students, too, are vulnerable to a "crisis of rapprochement", a feature of childhood identified by Mahler (1972), which can be replayed as part of the process of accommodating to university living. In childhood, a crisis emerges when children are caught between opposing desires: they want their mothers, but when they get what they want, they are left feeling unsatisfied and reject the mother. For the student, a similar crisis of rapprochement can arise when building relationships with tutors, peers, and the subject they are studying. Like the child in its first rapprochement crisis, it can be difficult to find a comfortable fit between closeness and distance in new relations at university and, importantly, also in those long-term relations with friends and family established prior to arrival at university. The emotion commonly experienced in childhood is anger, but for students a range of feelings can lead to disruption of learning. Just as in infancy, student learning can be disturbed when, for example, a student feels the need for closer attachment to the object they are now angry with, be that a close relation with a critical tutor, a deeper understanding of complex issues associated with their subject discipline, or anxiety experienced when closer friendship with peers seems to be possible only through destructive games associated with alcohol. Benjamin (1995, p. 36) succinctly captures the relational ambivalence in the crisis of rapprochement:

> In trying to establish itself as an independent entity, the self must yet recognize the other as a subject like itself in order to be recognized by the other. This immediately compromises the self's absoluteness and poses the problem that the other could be equally absolute and independent. Each self wants to be recognized and yet to maintain its absolute identity: the self says, I want to affect you, but I want nothing you do or say to affect me; I am who I am. In its encounter with the other, the self wishes to affirm its absolute independence, even though its need for the other and the other's similar wish undercut that affirmation.

Learning is shaped and developed by these powerful and disruptive forces. University study offers an opportunity for the individual to rework previously unsatisfying relational dynamics in new but fairly formal and regulated surroundings. Students might feel isolated in the relatively impersonal contexts that are part of university life, but the opportunity exists to achieve ego stability through intersubjective recognition in new settings with new friends and new circumstances. Rather than offering a pathology of student learning, or failure of tutor skills and techniques, a relational pedagogy locates failures, crises, and difficulties within the relationships that the student establishes with tutors, peers, the institution (as a disembodied other), and the discipline under study (economics, medicine, design . . .). In a psychoanalytically informed pedagogy, student learning is seen as embedded and embodied within subject-to-subject relational dynamics.

The move to a post-Freudian psychoanalytic approach has the main benefit of situating personal issues within a relational paradigm of sorts. What it is not intended to do, however, is to place this form of research within a broader social context, one in which a more appropriate theory of learning and teaching can be situated. The developing critical theory of Honneth, with its emphasis on the importance of intersubjective recognition in society, offers a feasible platform from which to extend the reach of relational pedagogy.

Psychoanalysis, critical theory, and learning

Axel Honneth has developed critical theory by building on the work of the Frankfurt School and by drawing on psychoanalytic theory, in particular the work of Klein and Winnicott in the object relations school of psychoanalysis. He argues that an understanding of social relations is predicated on an understanding of the intersubjective relationships of recognition. Honneth includes both non- and mis-recognition in his theory of social relations. Accordingly, the dynamic interplay of recognition, non- and mis-recognition determine interpersonal and social rapport and conflict. Honneth extends his theory beyond intimate social groupings to include, for instance, grievances regarding the distribution of material goods in society, which are ultimately struggles for recognition.

The intersubjective dimension is central to Honneth's theory of self-formation. As Anderson puts it in the introduction to Honneth's *The Struggle for Recognition* (1995, p. xii),

[O]ne's relationship to oneself ... is not a matter of a solitary ego appraising itself, but an *intersubjective* process, in which one's attitude towards oneself emerges in one's encounter with an other's attitude toward oneself.

In summary, there are three types of relation to self within Honneth's theoretical model, all of which are integral to the development of identity and self-realisation: self-confidence, self-respect, and self-esteem. This tripartite definition of self-relation was developed in the context of Hegel's early work (Huttunen, 2007, p. 424), "where the person begins at the first level and gradually moves on to the higher levels". In relation to the first level of recognition, an individual's self-confidence is established within the relations of friendship and love.

Key to the first level is the need for recognition of one's own existence, that is, that one has the right to exist. Honneth uses Winnicott's object-relations theory (1971), which places strong emphasis on interpersonal relations, to support the notion that the first form of self-relation, in which a balance is achieved between ego-dissolution and ego-demarcation (a key stage in successful identity formation), provides the "enduring, intersubjectively reproduced basis for relationships of love and friendship with peers" (Anderson, 1995, p. xiv).

While the different levels of recognition are important in themselves, especially given the fact that Honneth's broader political theory of recognition strongly depends on this "psychology of recognition" (Thompson, 2006, p. 20),[9] the key issue for Honneth is that distortion to any of these forms of recognition leads to three forms of *disrespect*, the term "disrespect" signifying the "denial of recognition" for Honneth (1995, p. 131). Just as important in the current context is the fact that Honneth takes seriously the affective domain as both a core component of relational life and a worthy point of enquiry for social theory. According to Honneth, the emotional domain acts as the "missing psychological link" (1995, p. 135) between experience of disrespect and the struggle for recognition. According to him, the motivational function

> can be performed by negative emotional reactions, such as being ashamed and enraged, feeling hurt or indignant. These comprise the psychological symptoms on the basis of which one can realise that one is being illegitimately denied social recognition. (ibid., p. 136)

By acknowledging the affective domain and its significance to a relational analysis of social processes, Honneth legitimises existing strands of research that take the intersubjective domain as their starting point. Honneth's emphasis on recognition specifically places relationships at the centre of social enquiry, to some extent shifting what were previously considered "private" (or, at least, individual) matters into a public arena. Most importantly, Honneth's work suggests that interpersonal relationships, theoretically speaking, are a force to be reckoned with, and the intersubjective domain should not be underestimated or reduced to questions of class or other "objective" relations.

This psychoanalytically inclined version of critical theory has major potential implications for higher education. Because it situates recognition as a social and political issue as much as a personal one, critical theory allows for this relational dynamic in higher education to assume its position as a democratic imperative, one that cannot be restricted to purely consumerist or utilitarian concerns. A critical theory reading of relational pedagogy allows teaching and learning in HE to traverse the division between private and public, and suggests that the interpersonal, no more so than in the intimate relationship between academic and student, is political. While any kind of "politicisation" of teaching and learning might be problematic for academics, it is difficult to conclude otherwise if HE pedagogy is viewed through a relational paradigm. The desire for respect and recognition is never far away from the learning process, and, in fact, could be argued to be embedded in this process—consumption as a rationale comes a poor second to the demands placed on learning from the perspective of recognition.

The shift to an intersubjective frame of reference, if accepted, offers something of a challenge to the prevailing pedagogical model, particularly given its reliance on a philosophy of consciousness. A theory of recognition of the type Honneth proposes could potentially allow for a move away from current concerns over the significance or otherwise of teaching *vis-à-vis* individual learners (incorporating concerns to facilitative approaches to pedagogy) to an approach that sidelines the teacher–learner paradigm in favour of an intersubjective paradigm. Such a shift offers an alternative to the current long-standing focus on concepts such as learning styles and motivational typologies. A move towards a recognition approach could potentially allow for a new set of ideas and "techniques" that could offer a way forward to a more effective approach to learning.

Understanding student–academic interaction as an intersubjective process has the potential, then, to reshape the way learning in higher education is imagined. It can help reaffirm the purpose of higher education as an intellectual activity intended to advance knowledge, skills, and values in a chosen subject discipline while recognising that the complexity of learning includes self-referential engagement and the existence of unconscious mental processes. Education is, in essence, an experiential process of self–other recognition, of "coming to know" oneself as constructed through self–other recognition. Higher education offers a valuable repetition of education from its position as a formal set of structures and activities (lecture, seminar, tutorial, workshop, private study, assessed work) within a socially loose framework that offers a curious variety of opportunities for intimacy, independence, distance, collaboration, and isolation.

Psychoanalytic and critical theory allow student learning to be explored in terms of a relational dynamic where the ego stability is maintained by intersubjective recognition. Engagement, non-engagement, success, failure, collaboration with tutors, group work with peers, work placements, independent study, work avoidance, collusion, plagiarism; all engagements with learning have the potential to threaten ego stability.

Students often feel that once they struggle to know something, they can never be quite the same again. And, as if this struggle were not enough, the process continually returns, refusing to offer consolation for very long. Egos are not formed, neither are desires done away with once and for all. The ego is never finished, but always incomplete (Todd, 2001, p. 433).

Alongside this dynamic lies the significance of disciplinarity. Ogden (1994) identifies a "third subject" which shapes and controls the relationship between therapist and analysand in therapeutic settings. Within the context of student learning, this insight allows for exploration of the third subject as the *subject discipline*, an intellectual space that tutor and student share, in terms of knowledge, skills, and values. The student has to engage in work in the form of essays, research, seminar papers, tutorial notes, and by demonstrating a growing ability to function effectively within and through the appropriate discourse associated with the discipline.

Ogden observes that the third subject can be subjugating, creating a tyrannical control over subject–subject relations. Tutor and student might well find that their opportunities for thinking, feeling, and acting become limited, with neither one able to experience self or other outside of a very narrow range. This can promote feelings of belonging to a high status and privileged group—an exclusive society defined by its access to knowledge. However, relations with the third subject can be dysfunctional, a situation implied by the work of Meyer and Land (2006) on threshold concepts and troublesome knowledge. In this case, the narrow range of thoughts and feelings can be predominantly irrational or can lock the relating pair into a "compulsively repeated perverse scenario", leading to feelings of being excluded, disregarded, attacked, or dehumanised. Ogden's contribution is useful in reminding us that the student's work (to engage with and demonstrate understanding of a body of knowledge *as the student of a tutor*) includes a component that connects directly to unconscious processes.

Such understandings of teaching and learning undoubtedly provide an awkward fit with current dominant understandings of academic practice. With the adoption of a consumerist approach to teaching and learning, it is difficult to envisage how, if at all, such complex dynamics between disciplinarity and relationality can be understood and engaged with. The benefits of a relational pedagogy are such that both unconscious and intersubjective processes are taken seriously as impacting on the educational process while, at the same time, situating these processes within broader relations of power. When placed alongside the struggle for recognition and respect, the struggle to understand academic knowledge becomes less of an economic/strategic imperative and more of a communicative/political one.

Conclusion

The seemingly unstoppable march towards a market vision for UK higher education surely means that institutions cannot hide from direct forms of accountability, and it would be unsurprising if certain developments took place as a result: more contact hours, more visible employment links, a diversion of university funding away from current preoccupations towards meeting consumer demands, etc. Simplistic and superficial notions of quality have been clearly exposed by the research and analysis of Gibbs (2010) in this regard. The decision to move to such a system can be debated forever, but the implications of its introduction for service delivery cannot be denied. Certainly, what are not deniable are its effects on academic–student relationships. It has been shown elsewhere that market-driven forms of accountability can have negative unintended consequences, not least those that involve damage to the accountability mechanism itself (Papadopoulos, 2010). While it is correct to state that academics should be accountable in some form to their students, as a form of institutionalised public, it is less than correct to state that this should be based on the mechanisms of a market exchange model.

The value of a relational approach to HE pedagogy is that, while it takes the accountability agenda seriously, it also seeks to preserve and illuminate the core relationship that, in the end, accountability is supposed to ensure. By seeking to understand the complex interpersonal dynamics of this relationship, a relational pedagogy seeks, in the current jargon of management-speak, to truly enhance the quality agenda at the heart of higher education. The consumerist model now evident in UK higher education does not seek to promote values, ethics, or human interrelatedness *per se*, but claims their growth will be a natural consequence in what is falsely argued as a largely benign process of "fair competition". We firmly reject this as smoke and mirrors—an invidious neo-liberal ideology. We cannot emphasise too strongly the corrosive and destructive effect that a consumerist model will have on the *quality* of learning if applied to higher education.

Notes

1. In this chapter, neoliberalism is used to relate to policy and practice that encourages market-driven approaches to economic and social activity. It emphasises trade, makes claims for the efficiency of private enterprise over all other forms of wealth creation and the public services, and seeks to impose private sector solutions when considering all political and economic priorities of state. It seeks to impose the language of enterprise and markets on the broadest range of human activity and to move risk away from governments and corporations on to individuals. It works to deregulate markets, to increase the exploitation of labour, and to neutralise labour groups and unions. It does not recognise, or adhere to, ethics and values that seek to reduce environmental degradation.

2. http://www.timeshighereducation.co.uk/world-university-rankings/2010-2011/top-200.html (accessed 4 July 2011).

3. http://www.hesa.ac.uk/index.php?option=com_content&task=view&id=1897&Itemid=239 (accessed 4 July 2011).

4. "The Almanac of Higher Education". *The Chronicle of Higher Education*, *LVI*(1): 5 (28 August 2009).

5. http://nces.ed.gov/pubsearch/pubsinfo.asp?pubid=2011015 (Chapter Three: post secondary education, accessed 5 July 2011).

6. http://www.imf.org/external/pubs/ft/weo/2011/01/weodata/index.aspx (accessed 5 July 2011).

7. http://www.dgfe.de/ueber/sektionen/folder.2004-09-09.8994874332/

folder.2005-03-13.6143335249/tagungen/fruehjahr2009 (accessed 28 December 2009).

8. In his paper, "The capacity to be alone" (1958), Winnicott sets out the stages, beginning with dependence, leading to being alone together, and on towards self-realisation and autonomy. Klein's (1946) contribution to psychoanalytic theory was to draw on Freud's work with adults and apply it to the analysis of very young children as well as adults, giving her an enormous breadth of experience, which led her to identify the paranoid–schizoid and depressive positions from which we relate to others. This work allowed Klein to demonstrate that powerful developmental infantile processes remain present throughout adulthood.

9. The development of this elementary form of self-relation is the bedrock of his theory of recognition: without it, there could be no development of more advanced self-relations: self-respect, and self-esteem. As Thompson puts it (2006, p. 20), without love, "respect and esteem are impossible". Importantly, Honneth recognises that, while the first form of recognition is vital to human existence, the second and third forms of self-relation are products of historically changing relations. As Anderson (1995, p. xiv) states, the "ways in which both respect and esteem are accorded have undergone a significant historical transformation". It is also important to consider the environments and situations within which the achievements of these various levels of self-relation take place, which are family (love), civil society (rights), and the state (solidarity) (Huttunen, 2007, p. 424).

   The second level of recognition relates to the striving by the individual for self-respect, the experience of which enables an individual to view him or herself as a "subject with dignity and with moral autonomy" (Stojanov, 2007, p. 78). According to Thompson (2006, p. 76), Honneth's understanding of the third level of recognition, self-esteem, is that individuals have the opportunity to earn esteem if "their particular traits and abilities are in tune with the values of their society". The allocation of social esteem enables a person to "articulate those personal features and capabilities" through which they can make a valuable contribution to social life, which in turn provides the basis upon which they can become worthy members of society (Stojanov, 2007, p. 78).

References

Anderson, J. (1995). Introduction. In: A. Honneth, *The Struggle for Recognition: The Moral Grammar of Social Conflicts* (pp. x–xxi). Cambridge: Polity Press.

Bauman, Z. (2007). Has the future a left? *Soundings, 35*: 1–6.

Beard, C., Clegg, S., & Smith, K. (2007). Acknowledging the affective in higher education. *British Educational Research Journal, 33*(2): 235–252.

Benjamin, J. (1995). *Like Subjects, Love Objects: Essays on Recognition and Sexual Difference*. New Haven, CT: Yale University Press.

Benjamin, J. (1998). The primal leap of psychoanalysis, from body to speech. In: *Shadow of the Other: Intersubjectivity and Gender in Psycho-analysis* (pp. 1–34). London: Routledge.

Britzman, D. (2003). *After-education: Anna Freud, Melanie Klein, and Psycho-analytic Histories of Learning*. New York: State University of New York Press.

Browne, J., Barber, M., Coyle, D., Eastwood, D., King, J., Naik, R., & Sands, P. (2010). *Securing A Sustainable Future for Higher Education: An Indepen-dent Review of Higher Education Funding & Student Finance*. October, 2010. Available at: www.independent.gov.uk/browne-report.

Collini, S. (2011). From Robbins to McKinsey. *London Review of Books, 33*(16): 9–14.

Department for Education and Employment (DfEE) (1999). *The National Numeracy Strategy*. Cambridge: DfEE/QCA.

Ecclestone, K., & Hayes, D. (2008). *The Dangerous Rise of Therapeutic Education*. London: Routledge.

Freud, S. (1914g). Remembering, repeating and working-through. *S.E., 12*: 145–156. London: Hogarth.

Freud, S. (1933c). Analysis terminable and interminable. *S.E., 23*: 209–253. London: Hogarth.

Furedi, F. (2003). *Therapy Culture: Cultivating Vulnerability in an Uncertain Age*. London: Routledge.

Gibbs, G. (2010). *Dimensions of Quality*. York: Higher Education Academy.

Giroux, H. (2009). Obama's dilemma: postpartisan politics and the crisis of American education. *Harvard Education Review, 79*(2): 250–266.

Hanley, U. (2007). Fantasies of teaching: handling the paradoxes inherent in models of practice. *British Educational Research Journal, 33*(2): 253–271.

Hodkinson, P. (2005). Learning as cultural and relational: moving past some troubling dualisms. *Cambridge Journal of Education, 35*(1): 107–119.

Honneth, A. (1995). *The Struggle for Recognition: The Moral Grammar of Social Conflicts*. Cambridge: Polity Press.

Hotson, H. (2011). Don't look to the Ivy League. *London Review of Books, 3*(10): 20–22.

Huttunen, R. (2007). Critical adult education and the political–philosoph-ical debate between Nancy Fraser and Axel Honneth. *Educational Theory, 57*(4): 423–433.

Klein, M. (1946). Notes on some schizoid mechanisms. In: J. Mitchell (Ed.), *The Selected Melanie Klein* (pp. 176–200). Harmondsworth: Penguin.

Mahler, M. S. (1972). Rapprochement subphase of the separation-individ-uation process. *Psychoanalytic Quarterly, 41*: 487–506.

Meyer, J. H. F., & Land, R. (Eds.) (2006). *Overcoming Barriers to Student Understanding: Threshold Concepts and Troublesome Knowledge*. London: RoutledgeFalmer.

Ogden, T. H. (1994). The analytic third: working with intersubjective clin-ical facts. *International Journal of Psychoanalysis, 75*: 3–19.

Papadopoulos, Y. (2010). Accountability and multi-level governance: more accountability, less democracy? *West European Politics, 33*(5): 1030–1049.

Stojanov, K. (2007). Intersubjective recognition and the development of propositional thinking. *Journal of Philosophy of Education, 41*(1), 75–93.

Tahta, D. (1995). Ever present affectivity. *Chreods, 9*: 3–9.

Thompson, S. (2006). *The Political Theory of Recognition: A Critical Intro-duction*. Cambridge: Polity Press.

Todd, S. (2001). Bringing more than I contain: ethics, curriculum, and the pedagogical demand for altered egos. *Journal of Curriculum Studies, 33*(4): 431–450.

Van Vught, F. (2007). Diversity and differentiation in higher education systems. Paper presented to CHET anniversary conference, Cape Town.

Winnicott, D. W. (1958). The capacity to be alone. *International Journal of Psychoanalysis, 39*: 416–420.

Winnicott, D. W. (1971). *Playing and Reality*. London: Routledge, 1991.

CHAPTER SIXTEEN

Bridging gaps

Linden West and Alan Bainbridge

In the final chapter, we summarise some core themes presented in the proceeding chapters and recognise the difficult, yet potentially rich, border country that exists between psychoanalysis and education. We also sketch out certain ways in which psychoanalytic ideas can contribute to a renewed relationship with education, at a practical level as well as in research. Our fundamental premise is that psychoanalytic ideas and practices allow "what happens in the particular" to be focused on building a more fulsome understanding of processes of meaning making in specific educational settings, yet one that also works to compose more general understandings of being human, of learning and change processes. Such understanding is grounded in careful and sustained chronicling of human experience.

Modern psychoanalysis, predicated on relational dynamics, considers the ebb and flow of the individual, the other(s), and a wider cultural world (Clarke, Hahn, & Hoggett, 2008). It highlights the influence that the dynamic unconscious often has in our interactions with others, and in their responses to us, in ways conventionally only barely comprehended. It offers a view of human experience and struggles for selfhood that is responsive to physiological, neurological, psychological, social, and cultural dimensions, while foregrounding the experiencing self. In addition, the clinical practice of psychoanalysis provides a relational lens through which experience and anxiety in the interplay of the known and unknown is better understood. This, we argue, is mirrored in biographical narrative research or observational studies. Just as the clinic provides a safe, containing space for thinking, so, too, can research, although the two processes are not simple equivalents and should not be considered so. However, the psychoanalytic interpretative repertoire, uniquely, engages with understanding the process of "a particular becoming" and can be used in education and research, as well as clinical settings, to provide richer interpretation of learners and their stories.

We should make clear, as does each author, more or less explicitly, that psychoanalysis relates to normal people in everyday life in apparently unexceptional encounters, rather than simply in pathological states or extreme situations. Its conceptual and interpretative grasp is of ubiquitous relevance. There is a direct thread linking diagnosis and normality, aetiology and personality development, in psychoanalysis (Honneth, 2009). Therefore, psychoanalytic thought, of whatever school, addresses and revises our view of human subjectivity as a whole: everyone has to address inner texts riddled with displacements, anxieties, and omissions, forged in our early, absolute dependence on others, and how these play out across a life. The self of psychoanalysis might be interpreted slightly differently across its various schools (Mollon, 1993), but, in general, this is a self perceived to be deeply contingent in its dependence on others. Anxiety—to greater or lesser extents—is inevitably what we are all heir to. However, being anxious can be the spur to deeper forms of learning, since discontents can be worked on and we recognise repetitions in thinking and behaviour and how we might act out in relation to new possibility, for fear of being exposed as deficient. What is significant about the processes of education chronicled across the chapters is how individuals and organisations react to anxiety and the range of defences that can come into play; also, how difficulties can be resolved, in good enough contexts. The very process of thinking itself creates anxiety and thoughts might be a nuisance, and, as such, can be unwanted. It might be difficult, as Lene Auestad (Chapter Two) contends, to think outside the restrictive socially and culturally constructed parameters, as well as the relationships, in which we are embedded, and which often serve to constrain us. But it is possible, and education can represent a potential source of relative creativity and freedom.

Gaps and why they matter

We have used the metaphor of the gap—in both general and highly specific ways—to encapsulate the problematic relationship between psychoanalysis and education. The sense of growing distance, and a need to bridge this, explains, in fact, the dynamic behind our book. There are different dimensions to the gap: in the gulf of comprehension, for instance, in some of the educational literature, as to what psychoanalysis is; in the growing gap between present trends in education and a more psychoanalytic sensibility towards what is required: in higher education, for instance, students who have bought a degree might be discouraged from tackling difficult learning and more likely to expect higher costs to be reflected in higher grades and what is of more obvious utility in labour markets. There is a fear that grade inflation, as Brown and Murphy argued, might be an outcome of a more consumerist model, because the value of what is studied might be determined by grade comparisons between students, and between the different degree programmes that students have bought. It could become less attractive to struggle with difficult conceptual knowledge, "with its attendant risk of lower grades on the lower slopes of understanding. Less attractive, too, when student unemployment is increasing, will be the idea that education can be intellectually and culturally transformative, and that it is for the public good".

There are also gaps between the important insights generated in clinical settings (around the interplay of desire and resistance, for instance) and the understanding of experience in the world of everyday educational life. There are continuing gaps in comprehending the relationship between cognition and emotion, mind and body, outer and inner worlds, self and other, rationality and the dynamic unconscious. There can be a yawning chasm between the lived experience of people as learners, when chronicled in in-depth biographical and observational research (whether of children, young people or adults whose stories enliven our chapters), and what is conventionally reported. All these gaps, and what happens in-between learning and non-learning, matter if we want to understand Larry Green's (Chapter Fourteen) notion of transformative possibilities in liminal spaces and experiences of becoming; and, therefore, create a more experientially based, holistic, dynamic, as well as interdisciplinary, understanding of education.

We have noted how resistance to using psychoanalytic ideas in education or to considering education across the lifespan partly stems from the continuing influence of cognitivist approaches in mapping and theorising learning in the earlier stages of the lifespan and in building typologies. Piaget's cognitive stages, it should be noted, were mainly derived from studies of, and applied to, children. His notion of a final mature adult stage of formal operational thought—in which thinking hypothetically and, thus, abstractly about the "possible" finds expression—has been criticised for freezing adult development into a single, over-rigid frame. This fails to respect adulthood as a time of development in its own right, in which a capacity for reflexivity as well as more dialectical forms of engagement with personal and social worlds can be cultivated (Allman, 1985; Tennant, 1997). The problem here might be partly the absence of in-depth studies of adults and their learning in building models of cognitive functioning alongside the neglect of the affect. The dominance of cognition can apply to theorising the human more generally: the notion of a cognitively driven, information processing, overly rational subject can hold discursive sway, as can the idea of a subject whose cognition and intelligence is simply innate and fixed, disconnected from the relationships in which s/he is embedded and the cultures shaping and infusing these.

The obvious and pernicious

We have also identified how psychoanalytic ideas can be considered dangerous, threatening, irrelevant, and/or unscientific; but also, paradoxically, matters of everyday, if often banal, truth. The Freudian slip and acting out are part of the professional lexicon, while notions of the defence mechanism and psycho-sexual stages have entered our language. Colleagues will often talk about "the ego", "repression", and even "projection", for instance, in initial teacher education, although the discussion can be superficial. However, modern psychoanalytic thought, especially in its object relational, socio-culturally aware guises, remains largely absent from academic and professional discourse. Even more worryingly, critics of "therapeutic education" claim to know this territory well, and its language, but this is accompanied by significant misunderstanding of what psychoanalysis is and its elision with quite different conceptual frames such as emotional intelligence. The accusations of "anti-intellectualism" made by the critics of "therapeutic education", and of therapy having to do with simply making people feel better about themselves, can have a ring of truth in some educational and even "therapeutic" contexts, yet it remains deeply ill-informed about psychoanalysis and its interpretation of education's purpose.

Our book represents a very different interpretation to that of Ecclestone and Hayes (2009) of what may be the crisis of contemporary education. Anastasios Gaitanidis, in Chapter Three, talked of a half-education, in which integration and conformity to an established order become the central focus. Students might be offered a set of presumptions which filter their actual existence, providing them with a way of dealing with anxiety by smoothing over contradictions and tensions generated in thoughtless adaptation to a given social and economic order. Students can become convinced that the existing social order will never change, while this provides stimulation for a potentially tedious and powerless existence as consumers. At an extreme end of a spectrum, Lene Auestad, drawing on Hannah Arendt, reminded us of how totalitarian regimes may close down thinking and communication altogether, or any building of connections between events, when a neighbour mysteriously goes missing. Fear and anxiety might stalk a community: however, if this is an extreme situation, it can be considered as but part of a spectrum, in which a half or even anti-education spirit can easily develop, as difficult ideas are avoided, including in universities.

We have tried to understand how more transformative levels of educational experience can be realised by concentrating, in the words of Tara Fenwick, a Professor of Professional Education, "less on reported meanings and motivations" and more on what is happening "under the surface of human encounters", including "the desire for and resistance to different objects and relationships" (Fenwick, 2003, p. 131). Each author has engaged, if in differing ways, "under the surface", yet working from some shared assumptions, such as the idea, as Honneth (2009) has framed it, drawing on Freud, of the human as always and inevitably a divided, inwardly ruptured being. For example, Britzman (2009) and Klein (1975) have reminded us that the child first experiences the self and mother as one, but it is then, as a result of maturation, that the infant begins to explore the world beyond this unique and dependent dyad. Such a wider exploration gradually and inevitably leads to a separation from the mother, away from states of absolute dependence, which are accompanied by powerful fears of being alone and abandoned, fears that can continue to overwhelm if an initial rupture was too painful, perhaps because of the other's emotionally unavailability. Loss and rupture exist from the outset, registered, as Klein put it, in embodied ways, via memory in feeling.

Inevitably, it is necessary to negotiate such inner turmoil if we are to maintain a coherent and meaningful relationship between inner and outer worlds. And greater inner freedom is possible, born in the attentiveness, concern, commitment, and attunement of the other—love, put simply, of a non-narcissistic kind—where one can seek, with the help of (m)others, to transcend some of the rupturedness. Such life affirming moments can find diverse expression: in a relationship with a primary school teacher or even a university lecturer, where s/he can help to give some words and meaning to the dread of not knowing or of never being good enough, laying groundwork for a more vital openness towards experience. Thus, Britzman concludes that engaging in education, (like psychoanalysis), evokes archives of past anxieties that are continually (re)experienced within the dynamic unconscious in and between individuals, yet these can be contained and transcended via good enough relationships.

From earliest times, but also in later ones, significant others can help or hinder children, young people, and adults in educational settings to understand feelings of loneliness, togetherness, hunger, love, hate, and desire. Apparently small things might matter, psychically, as a nursery teacher holds a child's frustration while they struggle to tie shoelaces; a secondary teacher allows an adolescent to think fanciful and creative thoughts; the child enables the parent to understand the role technology can play in their life; and the group in the pub offer support to encourage a colleague to return to formal education and to keep on keeping on. A teacher in adult education facilitates imaginative play and, in the process, contains a student's anxiety that they can never be good enough; an artist-tutor facilitates projections into a third, containing space of expressive art, and a continuum is created of thinking, rather than disjointed thoughts.

Why Jack hit Jill: why and what Gina learnt

A starting point of the book was Stephen Frosh's work (Frosh, 1989) on the gap between mainstream psychology and psychoanalysis. Frosh posed a deceptively simple question in developing his concern at the gulf between syntactical and semantic levels of understanding in psychology. "Why did Jack hit Jill?", he asked, in an effort to explore the contributions of different types of psychology and why there can be a fundamental problem in the psychological mainstream's comprehension of people and processes. He suggested that biology or neuroscience can make a contribution, but cannot provide the breadth of the epistemological imagination required. As in certain physiologically focused studies of depression, there can be a failure to comprehend the actual lived experience of depressives (which, we could imagine, includes Jack). Crucial areas of human functioning and, thus, potential for understanding are omitted in a physiological framing alone. Central to Frosh's question lies the need to distinguish between research processes of gathering numbers, words, images, symbols, and observing acts—to build a grammar of human behaviour—and an empathic attempt to create contextual, semantic understanding of what is happening, and has happened, within a person and his/her relationships. And if contemporary neuroscience, with its influential place in contemporary psychology, can powerfully chronicle and illuminate structural changes in the brain (Carroll, 2003)—when Jack gets angry, for example—we still flounder for an answer to the question of why he actually *hit* Jill.

Neuroscience can indicate that the aggressive act could be accounted for by reference to electrical and chemical activity in the brain, and even structural deficiencies, which can be electronically scanned and interpreted in comparison with the brains of more obviously empathic individuals. The movement of the arm might be imagined, as suggested in Chapter One, to be an outcome of neurones firing in particular ways, or the absence of certain structures and neurone connections that seem essential to empathic behaviour. However, at a different, more subjective, level, we could say that Jack was filled with rage and really wanted to hurt Jill. We begin to enter, here, as Frosh sees it, the worlds of intention and psychological states. Movement from the physiological/neurological level to the psychological, however, is far from straightforward or linear in causal terms. Structures in the brain might be products of our relationships, as well as vice versa: the word or experience made flesh in profoundly non-linear or non-determinist ways (Carroll, 2003), but we are still struggling to answer that question as to *why* Jack hit her.

Psychoanalysis can provide a fuller understanding: it could revolve around the difficulty, perhaps, men like Jack face in expressing rage alongside, maybe, an unconscious desire to hit women. We might also, psychosocially, connect Jack's actions with misogyny in a patriarchal culture, one that feeds into individual acts and rationalisations. And if Jack was to enter analysis, or be the subject of in-depth biographical narrative research in a clinical style, we could factor in his representations of lived experience and understanding of his relationship with Jill, and other women, and think about them together. We might even (and this is our imaginative suggestion rather than Frosh's), for the sake of the argument, become more aware of his history, maybe involving an emotionally withdrawn mother unable to give Jack good enough experiences of containment or love. There might also be the literal and or emotional absence of a father, someone who could offer support to both and provide a means for engagement with a wider world in psychologically healthy ways. Helplessness, desperation, and rage, and their irresolution, might have been forged, for someone called Jack, in these early and subsequent relationships. Ultimately, Frosh's question is only satisfactorily answerable by reference to knowledge of the dynamic individual living within a particular intimate, cultural, and discursive order. And, to repeat our claim, we see modern psychoanalytic thought as being able to provide both the ideas and skills to pursue such a project.

So, what could be an equivalent question for education? Each author, in every chapter, is asking questions of a related kind to Frosh's: why someone learns, or not, and of how learning itself can be theorised. Linden's work on learner motivation among adults and young people helps us to frame a relevant question with reference to the young black mother called Gina, referred to in Chapter Ten and a subject of extensive writing elsewhere (West, 2007, 2009a, 2010). We could ask, "Why and what did Gina learn?" She was a young single parent, as observed, participating in a community arts project, and Linden's biographical research has chronicled her encounters with the project, understood in the context of a difficult life history and pregnancy. Her relationship to the arts programme, as well as to the research, evolved from intense suspicion to more open, committed participation. She eventually talked of herself as being an artist for the first time in her life as she completed, described in Chapter Ten, a sculpture of her pregnancy, and of being able to play more whole-heartedly with her baby. Furthermore, she told stories of becoming a political activist and advocate for those in similar situations to herself.

We might begin, like Frosh, to answer our question by reference to changes in the brain, which could have been, if we can imagine this for the sake of an argument, mapped from the outset in relation to Gina and her significant others: the brain, as noted, is now conceived as dynamic and non-linear, a complex hierarchy of systems and sub-systems. Interest is increasingly focused on neurochemistry in the dynamic equation of psychological functions. We understand more of how a child's experience in attachment relationships is internalised as structural changes in the brain, in the form of increasing complexity and connectivity, or not. In contemporary systems theory, which some neuroscientists draw on, systems develop by coupling with other systems through ongoing feedback as recurrent interactions trigger mutual structural changes (Carroll, 2003). We can comprehend, in the case of Gina, difficult patterns in her early attachments, but also that change and new qualities of attachment become possible. But, like Jack, there remains a missing dimension. Gina made, we recall, "a pregnant belly from a washing basket to put your washing in". She used chicken wire and plaster of Paris and painted this with "funny colours". She told a story of being pregnant, of darkness, anger, but also of movement on, as she connected past, present, and future in a continuum.

We might still, of course, satisfy ourselves in the relatively straightforward territory of pedagogic theory alone, such as, "Gina's understanding of herself as a learner developed, thanks to tutors providing, in their strategies, supportive scaffolding to enable her to move to completing a sculpture of her pregnancy". The scaffolding moments might have initiated the interest and reduced the complexity of the original task, followed by careful monitoring and guidance as the sculpture took shape. Importantly, the tutor worked to manage anxiety and to praise Gina's sculpturing efforts. A Vygotskian understanding of Gina's progress would implicate how interpersonal communication, mediated through culture and history via the language and symbols of significant others, served to help her make sense of experience. Gina was, therefore, able to interact with and progress in her external world with a richer repertoire. We might also use sociological motivation theory of how learners might be marginalised people, caught between and negotiating different social worlds and possibilities (West, 1996). In Gina's case, between the worlds of a run down, distressed estate and personal isolation, as well as depression, and the potentially different quality of the world offered by the group, her tutors, and a future at college. Seen through the frame of marginality, being caught betwixt and between has to find a resolution, either in retreat and avoidance or self-expression and entry into new social affiliations. Maybe, in what transpired, we could also factor in, at a more cognitive level, changes in the categorisation of Gina's functioning, with movement towards more abstract, systematic, but also reflexive, ways of knowing. Yet, such answers are still insufficient.

Focusing on Gina, and thinking with her about the meaning of what was happening, begins to address some of the gap in answering the question of how she found sculpting to be therapeutic and moved, in effect, from the edge of a community of practice into beginning to think of herself as an artist for the first time in her life. Also, of how she was perpetually anxious and uncertain but took risks, mainly because she felt understood and supported by particular youth leaders and tutors. It was like being part "of one big family really". A more psychoanalytical, as well as socio-culturally aware, explanation, grounded in her rich narrative material and in thinking collaboratively about it, begins to make more sense of why and what she learnt. The answer may now be formulated as follows: "from a history of family abuse, but also isolation in a distressed community, Gina, via loving attentiveness at crucial stages, and because of feeling seen by significant others and legitimate in their eyes, was able to transcend some of her anxiety. She moved towards more heartfelt engagement, sculpting, among other things, aspects of her life. The sculpture itself acted as a narrative container into which disturbed feelings were projected, worked on, and, to an extent, transformed, in symbolic play redolent with selfhood. We can also perceive changing object relations at work, as new characters, such as tutors, entered her storytelling and, by implication, over time, shifted some of the dynamics of her inner world. So, to conclude, why did Gina learn? Because she felt valued, contained yet challenged in a liminal or transitional zone of self-negotiation and meaning making. What did she learn? Well, a capacity to sculpt and tell stories, but also to play, creatively, with less inhibition, and to experience stronger feelings of selfhood, and of agentic potential in the process. She felt good enough, transformed even, in the eyes of significant others and in a particular community of practice".

Biographical and observational research of a clinical style and the analytic setting

There is clearly a parallel to be drawn between the clinical world of psychoanalysis and observational studies or conducting biographical narrative research of a clinical style in educational settings. The analytical setting provides a space where relationships can be developed and stories thought about, not least around what is difficult to say. Stories are often messy as well as partial, and the role of the analyst is to provide a safe environment where anxieties can be contained and difficult experiences given some narrative expression. Similarly, the biographical narrative researcher, particularly when working longitudinally, offers space, time, and encouragement for lives to be narrated and thought about in a relationship. Interviews are conducted in ways that encourage openness and exploration of emotionally charged material and inconsistencies. The stance of the researcher is important here: the fact of her interest in the life of the other, and how she, the researcher, responds to difficult experiences and her reflexivity will affect the other, in ways analogous to patient–analyst dynamics. Mimetic processes can be at work, involving bodily gestures, for instance, as well as in the fact of someone taking a meaningful interest in a life, and treating it respectfully and seriously: the subject can begin to take her own experience more seriously as a result (Mollon, 1993). In using recordings and transcripts, for example, and in sharing these as a basis for subsequent sessions, a subject's relationship to a life might begin to change, because a valued other is treating them and their material respectfully. Olivia Sagan, in Chapter

Thirteen, also describes how she works in a largely unstructured way, encouraging free associations in a manner analogous to the analytic hour (also see Frosh, Phoenix, & Pattman, 2005; Hollway & Jefferson, 2000).

We can argue, therefore, that the process of biographically orientated research, although not analytic therapy, mirrors the analytic setting, in such terms, having the potential to build rich, contextual insight into individual experience. Furthermore, attention can be given to the quality of the research relationship, and to processes of auto/biography, or what we can term the countertransference. There are, of course, problematic issues in research of this kind (as there are in clinical work) around whose story is being generated, and the conventional genre distinctions between self and other, immediacy and memory, one life and another are always brought into question. In Linden's work, use is made of an analytic proforma, which enables collaborative analysis of themes but also allows attention to be given to the research process, including the feelings and even fantasies of the researcher in the countertransference. The research process, in its entirety, is subject to critical interrogation by colleagues, which reinforces reflexivity in relation to all its dimensions (Merrill & West, 2009).

Notwithstanding, biographical narrative research is not the same as clinical analytic work, even if there are strong parallels. Clinical settings are carefully designed to provide a safe holding environment where a patient's anxieties are brought to awareness, contained by an empathic other, and better understood within a therapeutic alliance. The analyst's room, practices, and responses are all managed to increase the intensity of the relationship with the patient and to provoke transference interactions. Psychoanalytic psychotherapists spend many years in training and in their own therapy. This intensive work is required not least because the ability to be aware of transference and countertransference phenomena between patient and analyst is always deeply problematic: there is, inevitably, difficulty in identifying what feelings properly belong to the patient and what to the analyst, or, for that matter, what might just belong to both. The analytic situation provides a unique opportunity for an intense, reflexive relationship between people, focusing on feelings and diverse associations, often over many years, whereas in biographical narrative research, relationships and processes are more fleeting, and, thus, less susceptible to sustained enquiry. Moreover, the analytic setting is designed, in the final resort, to address and challenge defensive formations in the relationships of the other (established ways of relating and avoidant patterns that might have evoked feelings of meaninglessness), which simply might not be appropriate or ethical to address directly in research. In the border country of research of a clinical style, the use of free association might also need to proceed with caution: the researcher requires some awareness of where not to go, in the absence of a sufficient and long-term containing relationship (Merrill & West, 2009).

None the less, we have numerous examples in the book of how research—biographical and observational, combined with intense, supportive group reflection—can generate thick and rich description of, and insight into, neglected dimensions of education. We can better understand what facilitates imaginative play or evokes potent anxiety between a teacher and a pupil at a particular juncture in the classroom; or comprehend the struggle to write in freer, less self-conscious ways, or the interplay of a teacher trainee's educational and personal biography with those of her students. We can imaginatively engage with attempts to build a narrative continuum and to create some relative freedom in lives bedevilled by mental illness. We can, quite fundamentally, witness the redemptive power of education in lives like Gina's: such moments provide the core testimony of our book, fuelling our concern at the neglect of such levels and quality of evidence in the educational mainstream.

Work to be done

Psychoanalysis, as explained, does not offer an exclusive understanding of the human condition, but we argue that it is essential in illuminating its subjective, semantic dimensions, including in educational settings. We do not reject other theories of education, linked to cognitive perception and development, for instance, or those that give attention to the design of programmes and how scaffolds can be constructed to enable learners to progress in more and better ways, or theories that emphasise the social, cultural, and community-embedded nature of learning: how learning is often to do with membership of communities, with ambivalent movement from peripheries towards centres, or from one set of affiliations to another. Our intention, rather, is to bridge some of the gap—arguably fundamental—in the conceptual imagination required for everyday understanding of what is really going on in classrooms and more informal settings. We need to place more of the experiencing subject at the centre of our deliberations.

We have also sought to build better dialogue with those many educators, we suspect, who might be increasingly disenchanted with dominant contemporary trends in education, at many levels. One example is in the penetration of the language of the market into institutions and relationships between teachers and learners, in which learning is presented as equivalent to processes of buying and selling. There is growing anxiety, we believe, at what has been termed in our book "half-education", which might be experienced by teachers and students as ultimately a soulless and dispiriting condition. There is neglect of relationships in current trends and of the importance of professional creativity and flexibility in a frenetic world of over-prescribing what is taught, and how, and in the ubiquitous testing of what teachers and students do by government and its agencies in the name of ensuring "standards" or economic efficiency. But, like us, there could be many who are sceptical of nostalgic longing for some lost world, because the Enlightenment project has, in part, been found wanting: under its gaze, the role of education was to create "autonomous" individuals who could overcome their racial, gender, and social situations and also their "natural" inclinations and desires so as to formulate more rational and moral judgements. The inner subjective and emotional world came to be treated with suspicion, something to be transcended rather than to be engaged with and learnt from. At the heart of the liberal idea was a notion of culture and education that separated the rational and moral from the natural and overly privileged a disembodied reason. Nature needed to be mastered and was conceived to be an extrinsic object to be manipulated and controlled. Objects and understanding were to be engaged with at a calculated distance. In a sense, we needed, as Gaintanidis argued, so as to control it more, to learn how to renounce what we shared with nature and to reject the embodied and sensuous, and, in the process, perhaps, some of the spiritual aspects of self, too. But there are ways back from these disconnections, not least in a sustained reflexivity in our relationships at all levels: with others, the "natural" world, and our feelings.

In teacher education, at a more prosaic level, there is unease at the current influence of technical rationality and an associated ticking of competence boxes in highly routinised, even cynical, ways. There is anxiety at a relative neglect of creativity, judgement, of criticality, and of self and other awareness, or, at least, of space to give these matters sufficient attention. There is a tendency, certainly at a policy level, to think of teaching as a skill-set to be acquired simply through hands-on experience, working alongside those deemed to be competent practitioners. There has been intense debate on the role of theory, as against more practical competence, in creating professionalism, with the former often denigrated as unworldly and irrelevant. However, we would want to factor into the debate the whole dimension of learning from experience, which is often treated superficially. There is, reflected throughout this book and in other writing (Bainbridge, Chapter Nine; West, 2009), growing understanding that learning from experience is about deepening our understanding of our relationships at many levels: with students, colleagues, institutions, and the symbolic order, and often in contexts where the pain of the world—of racism, ethnic tension, violence, misunderstanding across difference, poverty, social fragmentation—can be pervasive, if we care to notice. Processing such experience, and its disturbances, and thinking systematically about it, really matters for professional wellbeing as well as competence. And we have a concern that schools, colleges, and even universities, in their busy-ness, over-regulation, and work intensification, might not offer the quality of space for student-teachers, or even experienced professionals, to process their responses, to build connections, and to engage in really sustained thinking. Many educators recognise this to be a moral and professional imperative, and know it needs much more serious and sustained attention.

It is important, for instance, as Claudine Blanchard-Laville and Philippe Chaussecourte have argued, in Chapter Four, to recognise the mental suffering derived from the apparently "simple" business of doing education. To be a teacher, experienced or trainee, day after day, means you are engaged, Blanchard-Laville reminds us, in what can be difficult relationships: with students, parents, colleagues, the hierarchy of the institution, and also the curriculum. Such work obliges a person to engage in intersubjective encounters of many kinds and to maintain these over time. Students or pupils might not like us, or are not what we hoped they would be, and, as educators, they might confront and confuse us. Teachers at all levels and in many places have to learn how to react and, to an extent, defend themselves appropriately without closing down to the other and her possible distress. We are caught, as educators, in a social role of enabling learners to enter into a relationship with learning, and/or to the knowledge we have "chosen" to teach, of which profession we are representatives. Such a process, and the connections this forges in our own psyche and development, might reveal what lies deeply inside us. This is Blanchard-Laville's territory of the *didactic transfer*: how each teacher projects her history of learning, and of being a student, into the classroom, or its equivalent, which creates a particular tone or atmosphere.

We also believe that there are many educators, and a number of researchers, who are sceptical about dominant forms of positivistic research, and accept that everything fundamental in good enough education is not directly observable or empirically verifiable, at least in traditional scientific ways. If we try to restrict our sense making in such a manner, we risk missing what is most fundamental. This might explain some of the scepticism that can exist among practitioners towards certain kinds of conventional research: they cannot see how it relates to them and their struggles. Yet, there are colleagues open to more pragmatic notions of truth and validity: that particular methodologies and insights really can and do illuminate the messiness of actual classrooms and relationships, even if we cannot directly observe, touch, or measure the phenomena involved. Indeed, who might recognise that seeking to measure causality, in linear ways, can do an injustice to the multi-dimensional, dynamic interaction of the factors involved; that a different quality of relationship, however difficult, might induce not only material changes in the brain, but also more vital experiences of selfhood for teachers and students alike. What is needed, in short, is a better sense of the complexity and dynamics of the whole rather than an obsession with easily measurable fragments. There might also be diverse educators, in the broadest sense, who, like us, become concerned at tendencies to over-generalise human behaviour, to the neglect, sometimes, of varied particulars. We require sensitivity to individuals and their unique histories while also remembering that rupture, loss, and also transformative possibilities, for example, are common experiences: psychosocial forms of understanding are, in fact, a major attempt to build better connections between the particular and the general, inner and outer, semantic and syntactical ways of knowing.

We have noted how, in the French clinical practice tradition, Balint-type groups can provide a much needed resource for educators, social workers, and others to connect their "professional" distress and muddle in careful, systematic observation, combined with intensive group enquiry and sustained reflexive writing. These groups can also be used for research. For many educators, however, certainly in the UK, no such resources exist, and supervision, which is ubiquitous and compulsory in analytic settings, whether of a group or one to one kind, is largely absent or, at best, unsatisfactory (West & Carlson, 2006). It is interesting, in this context, that biographical narrative research among diverse professionals (in programmes such as Sure Start, or among teachers working in difficult inner-city schools) can provide a space where difficult things can be said, processed, and better understood (West, 2001, 2009b, 2011). Research itself is filling some of the vacuum.

Next steps: building on good practice

We are planning to build on the work involved in this book: there will be future international conferences to develop the dialogue further, including among colleagues in our own institution. We want to establish more dialogue between research and practice, combining the intensive group processes of the French tradition among, for instance, students in Post-Graduate Certificate of Education and Education Studies programmes who have composed educational biographies. A number of our teacher education colleagues are enthusiastic about this. An interesting development, too, is the introduction of auto/biographical methods in teaching as well as in research. There are modules in doctoral and masters' programmes, which include people working as careers counsellors or in further and higher education. There has been a specific research and development project in using "narrative methods" and psychosocial frames of analysis among clients and counsellors in different parts of the South East of England, including in a very marginalised community (Reid & West, 2010, 2011). The theoretical framing of the work is psychosocial, in which the psychoanalytic has a central place, in a desire to connect lived experiences and the sensual with conceptual insight and theorising. We have witnessed, in the book, of course, how such methods are applied in creative writing, or other forms of artistic activity. And there are many other contemporary examples of using narrative methods, among, for example, children and teachers in London's richly multi-cultural communities ("where the pulse of the world can be felt" (Mehmedbegović, 2011)) to which psychoanalytic insights could be applied in illuminating difficult and traumatic processes of displacement and loss among migrant peoples. This is a potentially rich terrain for the application of psychoanalytic ideas by teachers.

We have mentioned the idea of combining more of the observational approach with biographical and auto/biographical methods. It is interesting, in thinking about this, that other groups of academics are pursuing similar eclectic objectives in research. An Economic and Social Research Council (ESRC) study in the UK, for instance, in the context of social work, focuses on identity changes involved when women become mothers for the first time (Hollway, 2008; Urwin, 2007). It is designed to explore the idea of an "intermediate area" lying "in between" reality and imagination. The theoretical frame combines the perspectives of Lorenzer and the German tradition (of using psychoanalysis alongside critical theory in interrogating everyday life) with Winnicott and the British school of object relations. Data have been gathered, in a manner derived from Esther Bick, but this is complemented by in-depth narrative interviews. There is a psychoanalytic epistemology in play, one that focuses not on discourse, but on what the researchers call embodied expressions. However, if there is something of a turn to such approaches, and to the use of biographical narrative studies more widely across some of the social sciences, including education, we need to remind ourselves that the turn remains marginal in an evidence-based world where positivist and quantitative forms of enquiry are more highly valued. This continues to apply in the psychological mainstream, although there is evidence that many social psychologists are more willing to engage with the worlds of meaning and inner states (Frosh, Phoenix, & Pattman, 2005; Merrill & West, 2009).

Despite the continuing marginal status of psychoanalytic ideas in educational practice and research, the work described in this book, and the crossing of conventional boundaries between psychoanalysis and education, is proving to be richly creative and meaningful. Yet,

thought has constantly to be given to boundary issues and to problems in this difficult, if crucial, territory. Josselson (1996), herself a
psychotherapist, has written of how working on others' lives, and our
own, can stir up a range of narcissistic tensions, not least in doing
research, and maybe in education, too. We need to be aware, for
instance, of engaging with others' lives for our own ends: "no matter
how gentle and sensitive our touch, we still entangle ourselves in
others' intricately woven narcissistic tapestries" (ibid., p. 70). We need
to take reflexive care, in this border country, of what we do and why.
Such terrain requires care-full, respect-full negotiation, including of
the defences as well as of the play of our own narcissism. Yet, the
ubiquity of unconscious processes and their power to undermine
learning and thinking underlines the fundamental importance of the
work encompassed in our book, and of its relevance to teachers and
learners of all kinds and at all stages.

References

Allman, P. (1985). Dialectical thinking: our logical potential. In: G. Conti
& R. Fellenz (Eds.), *Dialogue on Issues of Lifelong Learning in a Democratic
Society* (pp. 1–8). College Station, TX: A&M University/Kellogg
Foundation.

Britzman, D. P. (2009). *The Very Thought of Education: Psychoanalysis and
the Impossible Professions.* Albany, NY: State University of New York
Press.

Carroll, R. (2003). At the border between chaos and order: what psychotherapy and neuroscience have in common. In: J. Corrigall & H. Wil-
kinson (Eds.), *Revolutionary Connections, Psychotherapy and Neuroscience*
(pp. 175–189). London: Karnac.

Clarke, S., Hahn, H., & Hoggett, P. (2008). *Object Relations and Social
Relations: The Implications of the Relational Turn in Psychoanalysis.*
London: Karnac.

Ecclestone, K., & Hayes, D. (2009). *The Dangerous Rise of Therapeutic Education.* London: Routledge.

Fenwick, T. (2003). Reclaiming and re-embodying experiential learning
through complexity science. *Studies in the Education of Adults, 35*(2):
123–141.

Frosh, S. (1989). *Psychoanalysis and Psychology: Minding the Gap.* London:
Macmillan.

Frosh, S., Phoenix, A., & Pattman, R. (2005). Struggling towards manhood: narratives of homophobia and fathering. *British Journal of Psychotherapy*, 22(1): 37–56.

Hollway, W. (2008). The importance of relational thinking in the practice of psycho-social research: ontology, epistemology, methodology, and ethics. In: S. Clarke, H. Hahn, & P. Hoggett, (Eds.), *Object Relations and Social Relations: The Implications of the Relational Turn in Psychoanalysis* (pp. 137–162). London: Karnac.

Hollway, W., & Jefferson, T. (2000). *Doing Qualitative Research Differently*. London: Sage.

Honneth, A. (2009). *Pathologies of Reason: On the Legacy of Critical Theory*. New York: Columbia University Press.

Josselson, R. (1996). On writing other people's lives. *Narrative Study of Lives*, 4: 60–71.

Klein, M. (1975). *Love, Guilt and Reparation and Other Works, 1921–1945*. New York: Free Press.

Mehmedbegović, D. (2011). Developing intercultural competencies: classroom intervention in London schools. Paper presented to the ECER Conference, Berlin, September.

Merrill, B., & West, L. (2009). *Using Biographical Methods in Social Research*. London: Sage.

Mollon, P. (1993). *The Fragile Self*. London: Whurr.

Reid, H., & West, L. (2010). Telling tales: using narrative in careers guidance. *Journal of Vocational Behaviour*, 78: 174–183.

Reid, H., & West, L. (2011). Struggling for space: narrative methods and the crisis of professionalism in career guidance in England. *British Journal of Guidance and Counselling*, 39(5): 397–410.

Tennant, M. (1997). *Psychology and Adult Learning*. London: Routledge.

Urwin, C. (2007). Doing infant observation differently? Researching the formation of mothering identities in an inner London borough. *Infant Observation*, 10(3): 239–252.

West, L. (1996). *Beyond Fragments: Adults, Motivation and Higher Education, A Biographical Analysis*. London: Taylor & Francis.

West, L. (2001). *Doctors on the Edge: General Practitioners, Health and Learning in the Inner-city*. London: Free Association Books.

West, L. (2007). The radical challenges of families and their learning. In: L. West, P. Alheit, A. S. Anderson, & B. Merrill, B. (Eds.), *Using Biographical and Life History Approaches in the Study of Adult and Lifelong Learning: European Perspectives* (pp. 221–239). Hamburg: Peter Lang.

West, L. (2009a). Families and their learning. In: P. Jarvis (Ed.), *The Routledge International Handbook of Lifelong Learning* (pp. 67–79). London: Routledge.

West, L. (2009b). Really reflexive practice: auto/biographical research and struggles for a critical reflexivity. In: H. Bradbury, N. Frost, S. Kilminster, & M. Zucas (Eds.), *Beyond Reflective Practice* (pp. 66–80). London: Routledge.

West, L. (2010). Apprendre et le sujet apprenant: point de vue psychanalytique dans la recherche auto/biographique. *Cliopsy, Revue électronique, 4*: 21–36.

West, L. (2011). Family disputes: science, poetry and subjectivity in biographical narrative research. In: H. Herzberg & E. Kammler (Eds.), *Biographie und Gesellschaft* (pp. 415–434). Frankfurt: Campus.

West, L., & Carlson, A. (2006). Claiming and sustaining space? Sure Start and the auto/biographical imagination. *Auto/Biography, 14*(2): 359–380.

More away from screen

experiences → strengthen memory → particu
their lack,
absence?

Work discussion
- needs rules?
  ↳ confidentiality
  ↳ respect
  ↳ attendance
- no records

INDEX